STONEHENGE
—Revealed—

STONEHENGE
Revealed
DAVID SOUDEN

Facts On File, Inc.

For those who taught me to be a historian

Stonehenge Revealed

Facts On File, Inc.
11 Penn Plaza
New York NY 10001

C.I.P. data available on request from Facts On File

Facts On File books are available at special discounts
when purchased in bulk quantities for businesses,
associations, institutions or sales promotions. Please
call our Special Sales Department in New York at
(212) 967-8800 or (800) 322-8755.

You can find Facts On File on the World Wide Web at
http://www.factsonfile.com

Conceived, edited and designed by Collins & Brown Ltd
Editorial Director: Colin Ziegler
Editor: Robin Gurdon
Art Director: Roger Bristow
Art Director for English Heritage: John Hedgecoe
Senior Art Editor: Kevin Williams
Assistant Designer & Illustrator: Debbie Marshall

Printed in Great Britain

10 9 8 7 6 5 4 3 2 1

Contents

Foreword

WHEN I TOOK office at English Heritage in 1992, I made the firm promise that during my tenure real action would be taken at Stonehenge. Action to improve presentation and visitors' enjoyment of the site; action to present a full re-evaluation of the archaeological record for Stonehenge; and action to remove the menace of the heavy road traffic that thunders past and threatens this precious place. Stonehenge and its environs are deservedly a World Heritage Site, and the Stonehenge environment deserves a great deal more care than it has had for a long time.

This book is based upon the huge strides forward that have been made during the 1990s in the understanding of Stonehenge and its surroundings. We know now that the monument is even more ancient than we had previously imagined. So while the stones and the landscape still have many mysteries, Stonehenge is much less mysterious than it was. In the book's final section, David Souden describes the Millennium Park that English Heritage and the National Trust have jointly devised. These plans include the proposal for a new visitors' complex, with vehicle parking kept well away from the stones, managing the land so that much of it will be returned to grazed downland, and bringing together all the different monuments and parts of the broader landscape. One key element is the official recognition, finally won in 1996, that the road situation must be dealt with, by closure of the A344 alongside Stonehenge and construction of a tunnel to hide the traffic of the A303 where it is most visible and at its noisiest.

Achieving all this has been an astounding victory, of national and indeed international importance. For this is one of the nation's greatest treasures. When the plans for the Millennium Park have been realised, Stonehenge and 451 scheduled monuments within the World Heritage Site will be saved for the future. There will be free access for all. Visitors will be able to enjoy fully the isolation, the ancient atmosphere and the awesomeness of Stonehenge's prehistoric environment that this book describes and evokes.

SIR JOCELYN STEVENS
Chairman, English Heritage

Introduction

STONE HAS ALWAYS had a special cultural significance, from fireside collections gleaned from walks and on beaches to the vernacular buildings and grander architecture of the British Isles, which is largely a close reflection of their underlying geology. Stone feels secure – 'safe as houses', we say. Stone is monumental, adaptable, carvable. As with stone, so with Stonehenge.

Stonehenge is a unique structure and the world's most famous prehistoric monument. Over three or four centuries its allure has framed and focused the investigation of the ancient past in Britain. Spectators respond to it, travellers and Druids venerate it, people who live on the other side of the world and have never seen it know what it looks like, and often believe they know what it stands for.

When visitors come to Stonehenge – and they come in huge numbers, 750,000 per annum at the most recent count – they do not necessarily see what they expect. Some will come across the stone circle almost by chance, racing along the main road before breasting the rise, and Stonehenge comes into view at the bottom. It stands, almost at the roadside, as the traffic whizzes by. For those who stop to see, there is a collection of stones – some standing, some fallen, of differing sizes and shapes – that do not necessarily make a coherent entity until the arrangement is explained. Since access to the stones is denied, there is inevitably a certain distancing from the monument. 'It's so much smaller than I imagined' is a commonly heard exclamation.

Stonehenge is anything but small. Even today it is difficult for builders to shape and erect single pieces of stone that weigh up to forty tonnes and that tower the height of four men standing on each other's shoulders. We can only imagine how much more difficult it must have been when the only available technology used stone, wood, rope and human muscle-power. Stonehenge was a designed mass of stones, their shape and disposition emphasizing the enclosing circularity, the verticality and the monumentality that are the hallmarks of many great buildings, from the Pyramids to the Hong Kong & Shanghai Bank tower.

Moreover, Stonehenge does not stand alone. It is set within a downland landscape which is filled with the remains of many other structures built of earth, wood and stone: places of burial; other circular and linear religious monuments that range in date from well before Stonehenge's construction to well after. In fact there were three consecutive Stonehenges, their history stretching for nearly 1,500 years, and only in the third phase did stones form a part of the construction. At times Stonehenge was probably a junior partner among the complex of monuments that filled the surrounding area, but more often it was the dominant element. That dominance is still apparent today; from the surrounding slopes and downs, Stonehenge is rarely far from sight, the focus of attention from all around.

This most celebrated and most studied of all prehistoric monuments still holds many secrets. There are aspects of it and its surroundings that still await discovery, and things about it that can never be known. Only in the past few years has its age become more apparent, when a full-scale reappraisal of the available evidence revealed that the monument is even older than had been stated, stretching back in its earliest phases to nearly 3000 BC.

The archaeologist Jacquetta Hawkes famously said that 'Every age gets the Stonehenge it desires, or deserves.' Interpretation and reinterpretation of Stonehenge have fuelled archaeological investigation, astronomical enquiry, religious debate and a whole publishing industry. This present volume stands in a long tradition stretching back to the seventeenth century. *Stonehenge Revealed* presents a broader approach – as a monument, as a single element in a broader landscape, as an introduction to the people who built and used it, and as the monument that we desire, or deserve.

Midsummer sunrise at Stonehenge

While this photograph shows the sun rising over the Heel Stone, the correct alignment is to the left of the stone, directly along the Avenue to the centre of the monument.

UNDERSTANDING STONEHENGE

Engraving of Stonehenge from
Old England (1847).

STONEHENGE STANDS, SEEMINGLY alone, in the midst of a great tract of Salisbury Plain, the chalk upland in mid-Wiltshire. The city of Salisbury lies only 12 km/7½ miles to the south, and the town of Amesbury is closer still, but the bustle of the city and the green of the valley of the River Avon in which they both lie seem a world away from the more elevated, drier and depopulated setting of Stonehenge.

Stonehenge's origins lie in the Middle Neolithic Age of around 2900 BC, while the famous stones were erected and being used between 2550 and 1600 BC. Then – as now – Stonehenge was far from alone, for it stood at the centre of a huge complex of monuments, structures and settlements ranging in date from the Early Neolithic to the Iron Age, and even back to the Mesolithic of 10,000 years ago.

If attention is usually concentrated upon the stone circle itself, which was an incredible feat of engineering and design, at least equal attention should be paid to everything that surrounded it and how all these places fit together in the landscape. The stone circle at Stonehenge and its immediate setting are in the care of English Heritage, while the National Trust owns much of the surrounding land. The whole area (in conjunction with nearby Avebury) has been inscribed as a World Heritage Site for its huge archaeological and cultural importance. For Stonehenge and its vicinity have been a proving ground for archaeological enquiry and technique since the seventeenth century, and have excited speculation, wonder and not a little nonsense for longer still.

In the pages that follow, the stories of Stonehenge, its surroundings and the people who built these extraordinary monuments, unfold in different ways. This chapter places Stonehenge in its context, introducing the different eras of prehistory, the many people who have investigated Stonehenge, from the amateur antiquarians of the seventeenth and eighteenth centuries to modern archaeologists, and the techniques they have used to date and decipher the monument and its surroundings. There are descriptions of the various types of contemporary monument which highlight their complexity as well as the skills of their prehistoric creators. A timeline compares monuments across Britain with those from further afield in the ancient world, placing the area within the context of local, British and world prehistory – for Stonehenge is far older than many 'ancient' wonders of the Mediterranean or the Americas yet is itself junior to other major undertakings, such as the temples of the Minoan civilization and the stone alignments of Brittany.

Sir Richard Colt Hoare, the great excavator of the later Georgian era, wrote in his study of prehistoric Wiltshire that 'We speak from facts, not theories.' In reality, fact and theory can never be far apart where the Stonehenge region is concerned. There is so much that can only ever be surmised, and so many 'facts' have been reinterpreted in the light of experience. Seemingly every year something new emerges, either as a result of deliberate investigation or else by chance. Stonehenge and its setting have been among the most intensively studied archaeologically important regions in the world, yet there is still ample room for more digging, more theory, more facts.

A sarsen trilithon frames its opposite number
A horseshoe of five great trilithons, each capped by a massive lintel, forms the principal central setting around the Altar Stone. The trilithons are in turn surrounded by a sarsen circle, in which there were originally thirty upright stones, capped by a continuous ring of lintels.

Stonehenge in its Setting

Sitting in the centre of the map, Stonehenge is only one element in a huge landscape filled with the remains of monuments. Most of these relate to it, and are focused upon it; but some significant remains date from well before, further back into the Neolithic and even the Mesolithic eras, while others date from the Iron Age – a timespan of over 3,000 years.

The valleys of the River Avon, to the east, and the smaller River Till, which lies farther away to the west, frame the higher ground upon which Stonehenge and most of the other monuments were built, and where prehistoric people lived. Within this area, Stonehenge stands on a slight spur above a dry valley.

Sited across this landscape the principal monuments range from the earliest, Robin Hood's Ball (just off the northwestern corner of the map) to the latest, Vespasian's Camp in the southeast. Of the central monuments, the largest is the great linear earthwork of the Cursus, with its later neighbour, the Avenue, leading to Stonehenge from the River Avon. Durrington Walls on the eastern edge was one of the largest of the henge monuments with its much smaller, and shorter-lived neighbour, Woodhenge, below it. Almost every known type of burial mound, or barrow, is represented in this compact area of only 30 sq. km/12 sq. miles, which is one of the most pre-eminent burial areas known from prehistoric Britain. There are also remains of the places in which people lived, the fields they cultivated and some of the houses they inhabited.

Future proposals for the area include the closure and tunneling of the two major trunk roads which now enclose Stonehenge, together with the construction of visitor facilities and a low impact transport link into the Stonehenge landscape. In due course, when the landscape is restored to grass downland, something of the original feeling of Stonehenge may be recaptured.

Monuments within the Stonehenge landscape

The principal monuments – Stonehenge itself, the other henges, the cursuses and the like – are shown in red on the map and are described in greater detail in the pages that follow (see pp. 26–59), as are some of the concentrations of barrows. Additionally marked on the map in grey are the many other barrows, enclosures and monuments from the Neolithic to the Iron Age, numbered in their hundreds, that fill the Stonehenge region. The linear patterns concentrated to the west and north of Stonehenge indicate the boundaries of the early field systems – the so-called 'Celtic fields' that may still be discerned in the landscape.

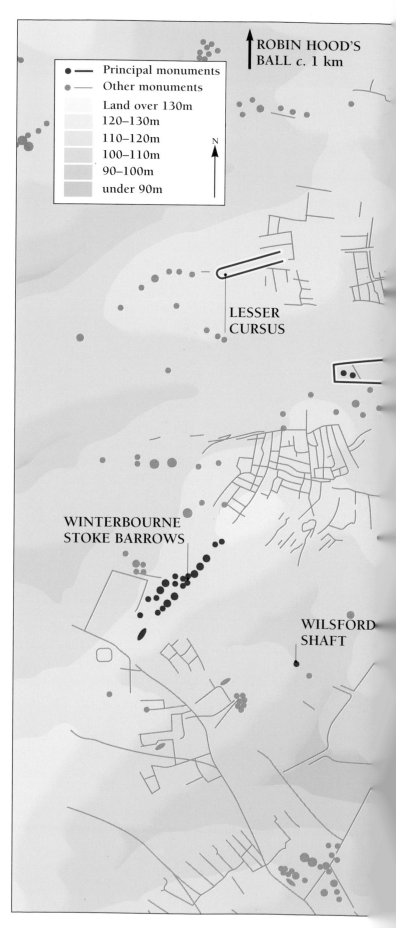

● — Principal monuments
● — Other monuments
  Land over 130m
  120–130m
  110–120m
  100–110m
  90–100m
  under 90m

N

ROBIN HOOD'S BALL *c.* 1 km

LESSER CURSUS

WINTERBOURNE STOKE BARROWS

WILSFORD SHAFT

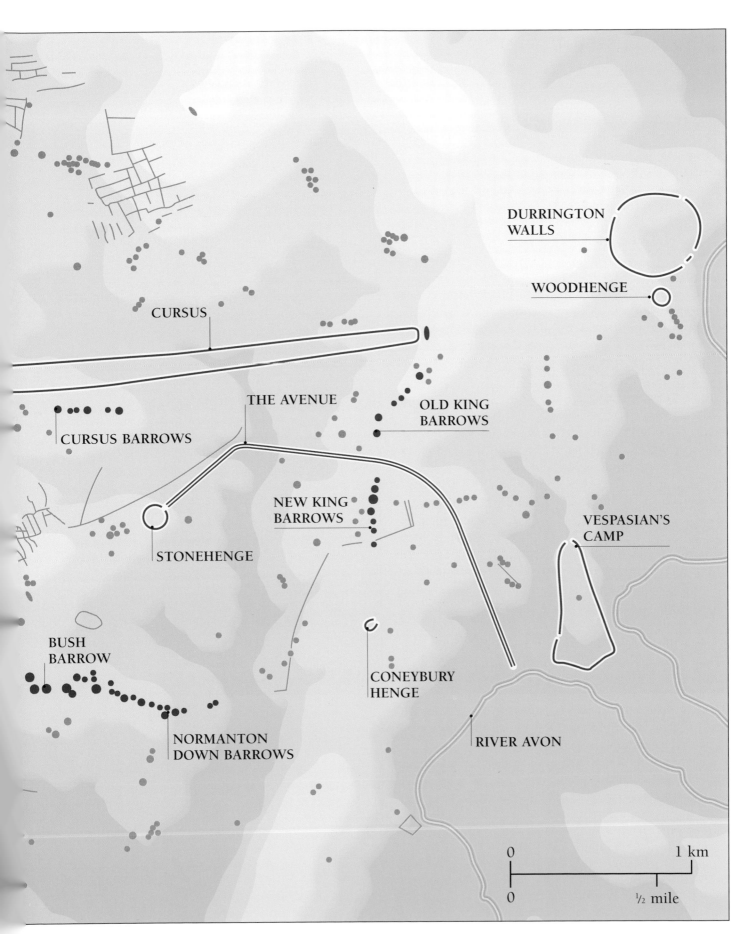

DURRINGTON
WALLS

WOODHENGE

CURSUS

THE AVENUE

OLD KING
BARROWS

CURSUS BARROWS

NEW KING
BARROWS

VESPASIAN'S
CAMP

STONEHENGE

BUSH
BARROW

CONEYBURY
HENGE

NORMANTON
DOWN BARROWS

RIVER AVON

0   1 km

0   ½ mile

Time and Place

The perennial question is: how old is Stonehenge? The answer is usually expressed in terms of a period, an era of prehistoric time, rather than in calendar years.

In 1836 a Danish archaeologist, Christian Jurgensen Thomson, devised a three-phase system to describe the prehistoric past. He came from an era when thinkers were trying to codify the world and find laws by which it operated. By observation and deduction, Thomson worked out that an age in which iron was extensively used was preceded by an age when people used bronze as their principal metal, which in turn was preceded by a time when tools were made of stone. With modifications, the system he devised has remained in use ever since. The principal alteration has been the further division of the age of stone into the Palaeolithic, or Old Stone Age, the Mesolithic (Middle Stone Age), and the Neolithic (New Stone Age).

Excavation and investigation have refined our understanding. The Bronze Age, for example, came relatively late to the British Isles compared to other parts of continental Europe, where there was a comparatively short-lived Copper Age, in which men in their first experiments with metal used copper, before turning to the harder alloy of bronze (copper with tin). Archaeological techniques have produced bracketing dates for all these periods – yet meanwhile archaeologists have begun to question their usefulness. For the sake of consistency, the conventional names (Neolithic, Bronze Age, etc.) are used in this book. Some authors, however, have begun to search for other names for these periods, names that have a wider application and meaning.

Name of an Age?

The conventional names describe the tools and materials that people used. It is as if the modern era were to be known as the Computer Age, or the Plastic Age. But does the term Computer Age say anything about the way in which our society is organized? About how we create wealth and sustain ourselves? Such terms describe things – indeed, objects and materials that are crucial parts of the fabric of our lives – that are still only one aspect of our existence. Might

we not prefer to think of the twentieth century as, say, the Age of Popular Democracy, or the Age of Cities? But, as soon as we do that, we begin to think of exceptions, of events and movements that do not fit the scheme.

So, however convenient the traditional names given to the prehistoric eras, they are limited and flawed. The age known as the Mesolithic, for example, stretched from around 8000 to 4000 BC. People used stone tools: axes, arrowheads, knives. They were also, on the available evidence, hunters and gatherers, rather than living in settlements and farming the land. Considerable areas of Britain were still covered with the post-glacial wildwood, which provided a happy hunting ground for animals and a place to gather wild foods. Settled food-producing economies were developing in western Europe from perhaps 7000 BC, but, as with many aspects of early life, they came much later to Britain.

The Neolithic period is now commonly divided into three, stretching from around 4000 to 2300 BC, with the Early Neolithic lasting for perhaps 800 years, the Middle and Late each for some 400–500 years. The New Stone Age people's tools were more highly developed than those of their predecessors; it is from this era that the first built structures of any scale survive, at least in the British Isles.

The shift from Mesolithic to Neolithic was marked by the introduction of more settled farming, with crops grown in demarcated fields and the domestication and husbandry of animals for food, and also for pulling power. On the evidence of their surviving buildings, this has also been called the 'Age of ancestors', because the built structures that we know about were pre-eminently designed to house the dead. Large tombs in a variety of forms – both for communal burial and, less commonly, for individuals – are characteristic of this period, as well as sites that were used for communal purposes, including exposure of the dead to the elements before burial, and feasting that was probably associated with commemoration of the dead.

Sacred landscapes

The first megaliths – large standing stones that were deliberately erected as monuments and markers – date from around 4000 BC in various parts of Europe, and the use of great stones for ceremonial purposes continued

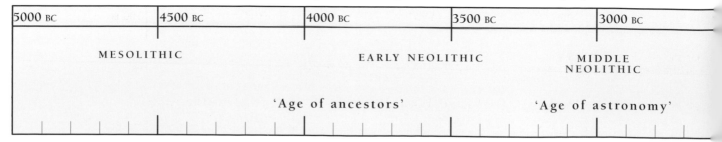

5000 BC	4500 BC	4000 BC	3500 BC	3000 BC

MESOLITHIC　　　　　　　　　　EARLY NEOLITHIC　　　　　MIDDLE NEOLITHIC

'Age of ancestors'　　　　　　　'Age of astronomy'

to the dawn of written history, and indeed beyond, for significant stones were later used as markers, coronation seats and wayside crosses. Although we tend to associate the Stone Age with stone monuments, especially given the example of such major structures as Stonehenge and nearby Avebury, many more monuments were constructed of earth: banks and ditches, enclosures, processional ways, mounds and so on. By the end of the fourth millennium BC, as settled farming became more fully established, a new tradition arose of monuments that were (at least in part) intimately concerned with the heavens, with the 'movements' of the sun, and also of the moon. In Britain there is ample evidence for the widespread building of 'henges' (see p. 22) – a word that derives from Stonehenge itself – which were circular enclosures that had a ritual purpose associated with the burial of the dead, and with the celebration or observation of the skies.

By the Late Neolithic this had developed into a seeming obsession with so-called sacred landscapes, in which great complexes of monuments were built – some new, some based on old monuments, and interrelating in a manner that is only now becoming apparent. The developments of both the Stonehenge and the Avebury landscapes are just two, albeit remarkably preserved, examples. This tradition continued into what is conventionally known as the Early Bronze Age, when metal tools first came into general use. The break between stone and metal was far from absolute; bronze items have been found as rare objects in a clear Neolithic context, and stone tools continued to be used well into the ages of metal, but the shift to metal-working was one of the most momentous transitions in history.

The scale of the construction undertaken during this era, of which Stonehenge is the supreme example, as well as the evidence of increasingly individual burials associated with 'grave goods' (items, especially pottery 'beakers', deposited alongside a burial or cremation), suggest a far greater degree of stratified social organization. If this was an age of metal and sacred landscapes, it was also an age of chiefs and important families.

Changing ways of life
In the two thousand years before the beginning of the Christian era, there is considerably greater evidence for more settled living: permanent houses, field divisions, more extensive agriculture, including a greater use of arable cultivation. Moreover, the concentration on the dead, at least as witnessed by the number and variety of surviving monuments, had by now come to an end. It was in this period that Stonehenge, having reached the final stage of its building history, together with much of its surrounding landscape, finally went out of use as a ceremonial site. People clearly continued to live there, but equally clearly they did not follow the ways of their ancestors in building great monumental structures, investing their resources in houses and the land.

The transition from the Late Bronze Age into an era when iron was widely in use for tool-making also saw the influx of Celtic peoples and the cults associated with water and woodland – and eventually of the Druids, who are often erroneously associated with the then-abandoned Stonehenge. The need for defence, at least as shown by the construction of forts from 1200 BC, also suggests that the political and military climate had changed radically.

By trying to provide a chronological framework, and by giving names to particular divisions of time, we are usually making inferences from what little has managed to survive from the past. Stone tools and metal objects do decay, but very slowly, compared to textiles and wood, which survive only rarely. Wood, for example, may have been just as important as any of the other materials, but, with the exception of post-holes, its presence barely survives in the archaeological record and so is commonly discounted. Hunter-gatherers doubtless coexisted with settled farmers for much longer than conventional divisions of time might suggest. The ready assumption that each phase of change was associated with the influx of a new type of people – the invasion of the so-called Beaker Folk, for instance – denies the possibility, or likelihood, of internal change within a society and the fusion of different traditions.

What is perhaps remarkable about the prehistory of the British Isles is how sophisticated its set of societies seems to have been. The structures that remain, both above and below the ground, are among the earliest surviving man-made structures in the world. Those at Stonehenge are not necessarily the oldest, but they are ancient indeed and a constant source of wonder.

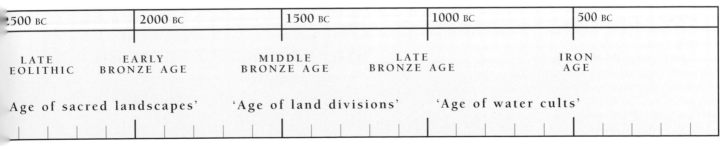

2500 BC	2000 BC	1500 BC	1000 BC	500 BC
LATE EOLITHIC	EARLY BRONZE AGE	MIDDLE BRONZE AGE	LATE BRONZE AGE	IRON AGE
'Age of sacred landscapes'		'Age of land divisions'	'Age of water cults'	

Dating the Landscape

For the historian, finding an object's date is usually a straightforward task. The date may be written on a document, or calculated from a related event. We usually know what happened in what order in the recorded past; we can, for example, compare a document with others of known date. For the archaeologist dealing with the prehistoric, difficulties are frequent, especially with a complicated set of monuments such as Stonehenge and its neighbours. Dating is all-important; but dating may be the most difficult thing of all.

In the historic past, all is relatively fixed; and, although there is much that may be argued over, such as, for instance, the exact date of the receipt of coded wartime messages, nobody fears that the dates in dispute may be decades, even centuries, apart. But without signposts, archaeologists have a much more difficult task and may well have margins of error of many hundreds of years. Many of the dates advanced for parts of Stonehenge, for example, bracket a period of four or five centuries, and some even a thousand years. Archaeology uses a wealth of means of dating, constantly seeking ways of improving them.

Digging

At least in the view of most outside observers, digging is the one thing that archaeology seems to be all about. Most objects from the distant past are buried, whether by design or by the action of time, and so they need to be uncovered. The activity of digging, with the patient uncovering layer by layer, the sieving of soil, the labelling, photographing, logging and describing of every find, however small, is indeed an important aspect of the archaeologists' stock-in-trade. They place great emphasis on the physical location of the objects they uncover: the deeper down, the older, generally speaking. If one set of remains in the ground has been cut through by another, then the first must be older than the second. Stratigraphy – the study of these archaeological layers – and establishing a sequence of finds is one of the most basic of practical archaeological activities.

At one time, the comparative method was paramount. If we know the date of one item with a fair degree of exactness, then by comparing object with object, place with place, things may be put into a general order and assigned dates accordingly. We know through experience that one type of flint-working predates another, that one style of pottery was commonplace in one era, and another type later

on. Home-grown comparisons have not always been thought sufficient explanation. A little more than a generation ago, comparisons of Stonehenge were made with Mediterranean cultures of known date; and since it was assumed that Western civilization diffused from that southern cradle, it followed that buildings like Stonehenge came later than, and were palely influenced by, cultures in the Ancient World – Malta, Egypt and Greece.

Radiocarbon dating

More scientific forms of enquiry have since been developed that provide more precise dates, and which have overthrown such pet theories of the past. The principal development has been radiocarbon dating. The basic principle is quite straightforward, but soon it all becomes complicated. All living things contain carbon, one of the essential building-blocks of life. Once death occurs, decay sets in; a radioactive isotope or atom, known as 'Carbon 14' (C^{14}), which is absorbed by all living things, also decays in a long, and measurable, way. The technique of radiocarbon dating therefore measures the amount of C^{14} within an object; the smaller the amount, the older the object, and dates may thus be assigned with a fair degree of accuracy.

When the method was first developed in the 1940s, it was assumed that the carbon isotope decayed at a constant rate. In reality it appears that the difference between 'true' dates and uncorrected radiocarbon dates may be considerable, even as much as a thousand years' discrepancy in the Mesolithic. The anomalies were discovered when objects of known date were

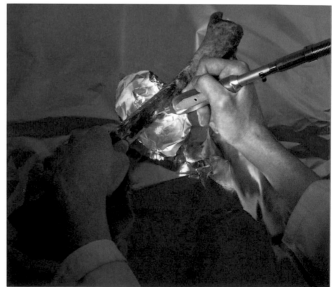

Radiocarbon dating
An antler is tested for levels of the radioactive atom C^{14}. The amount present indicates the likely age – the lesser, the older.

tested and the findings shown to be woefully inaccurate; rather than rejecting the methods, archaeologists set out to find ways of refining them.

One obvious way is by recalibrating dates according to another, known constant. Such was the bristlecone pine, the oldest living tree on earth, specimens of which may be 6,000 years old. Since trees grow at different rates each year, depending on climate and other factors, by counting their annual rings of growth it is possible to count back to arrive at specific dates (as well as to learn something of past climatic conditions and variations in C^{14} in the atmosphere). Using these new skills of dendrochronology, cross-matching between tree ring series, such as the bristlecone pine, or bog oaks in Ireland and Germany, has provided a means of recalibrating radiocarbon dates. In the absence of old, waterlogged timbers on the Stonehenge site, which would allow precise dates to be calculated directly – as in the Somerset Levels, for instance, where an ancient trackway may confidently be allocated to 3806 BC – radiocarbon dates suffice.

But in order to acquire something, another thing often has to be sacrificed. So it is with radiocarbon dating. Fragments of the object need to be destroyed in order to discover its date. Of the two types of dating employed on the collection of deer antlers, human and animal bones that came from Stonehenge, the newer, high-precision radiometric dating method destroys more material than the Accelerator Mass Spectrometry, but provides closer results. The archaeologist needs to be very careful and selective in what he or she chooses to have analysed, since all or part of it will be lost for

ever. Each process requires a complicated set of physical and chemical preparations: washing, rinsing and soaking in hydrochloric acid, the residue twice-filtered and twice-dried in the first process; extraction of the protein collagen and then purification by gelatinization and ion-exchange in the second; before combustion and the C^{14} counting.

The resulting date is never as precise as 3806 BC, but rather a probability, a span around a year: for instance, 3450 BP (Before Present), otherwise called 1500 BC, plus or minus 150 years, that is 1650–1350 BC. Comparing dates will therefore involve measuring how far the spread of dates coincides. How likely, for example, is 1500 BC±150 to be really the same date as 1700 BC±85? The answer is that there is a distinct possibility.

Radiocarbon dating has allowed archaeologists to undertake a considered reappraisal of Stonehenge, discovering it to be older than had previously been thought, and also determining that the post-holes found beneath the visitors' car park were for timbers approximately 10,000 years old, more ancient than anything else so far identified in the area (see p. 44).

Geophysical examination

The archaeologist's conventional tools of spade, trowel, brush and measuring rod have now been supplemented by extremely high-tech methods. Indeed, there are many archaeologists who do not dig in the conventional sense at all. The action of excavating the ground will disturb it for ever; subsequent generations with new questions, new methods and new interpretations will be denied their share of the primary record. Among the newest archaeological methods is geophysical examination (invaluable even when used at such a well-investigated site as Stonehenge). Methods such as magnetometry and resistivity are used to survey the land surface and produce maps of underlying structures. These methods do not themselves significantly aid the process of dating, but they are very useful adjuncts to it. At Stonehenge, for instance, magnetometry has established the line of the so-called Palisade Ditch, a Neolithic feature running to the northwest of the stones which was probably once a substantial wall of upright posts, as well as many new features within Durrington Walls (see p. 57); while resistivity has confirmed the existence of various holes that once held stones, which have long since disappeared from view.

Digging, surveying and dating techniques have been used at Stonehenge since the seventeenth century. Some, if not all, of the archaeologist's tools may have changed in the interim, but the object of enquiry remains the same.

Dendrochronology
Counting the rings of a tree is a known way to tell its age. Cross-matching ring series helps to calibrate carbon dates.

Timeline

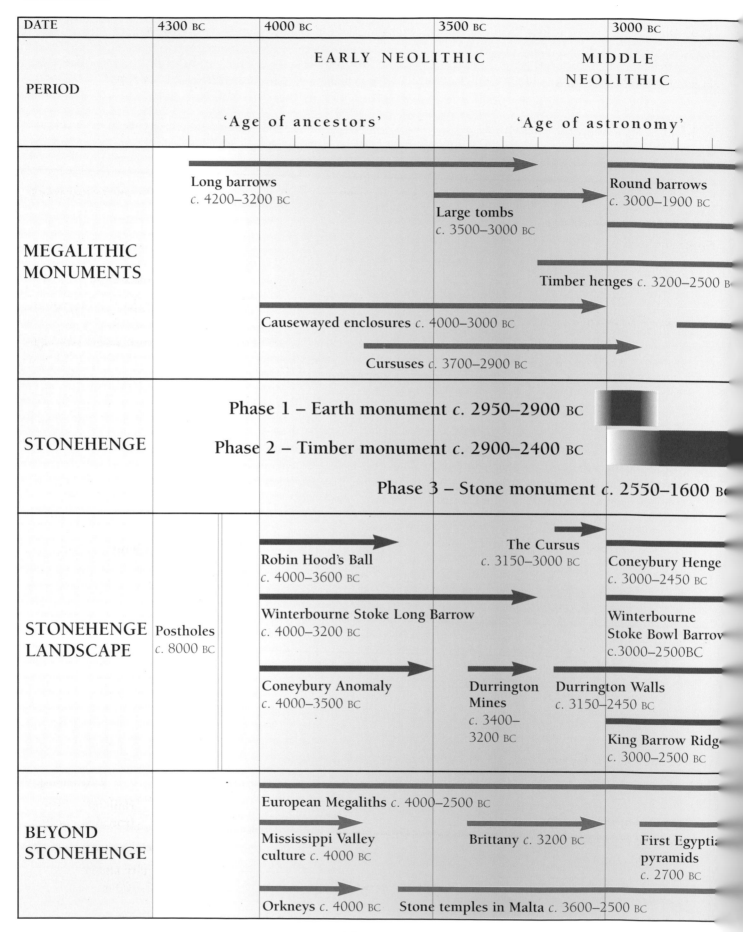

DATE	4300 BC	4000 BC	3500 BC	3000 BC

PERIOD

EARLY NEOLITHIC　　　MIDDLE NEOLITHIC

'Age of ancestors'　　　'Age of astronomy'

MEGALITHIC MONUMENTS

Long barrows *c.* 4200–3200 BC

Round barrows *c.* 3000–1900 BC

Large tombs *c.* 3500–3000 BC

Timber henges *c.* 3200–2500 B

Causewayed enclosures *c.* 4000–3000 BC

Cursuses *c.* 3700–2900 BC

STONEHENGE

Phase 1 – Earth monument *c.* 2950–2900 BC

Phase 2 – Timber monument *c.* 2900–2400 BC

Phase 3 – Stone monument *c.* 2550–1600 B

STONEHENGE LANDSCAPE

Postholes *c.* 8000 BC

The Cursus *c.* 3150–3000 BC

Robin Hood's Ball *c.* 4000–3600 BC

Coneybury Henge *c.* 3000–2450 BC

Winterbourne Stoke Long Barrow *c.* 4000–3200 BC

Winterbourne Stoke Bowl Barrow *c.* 3000–2500 BC

Coneybury Anomaly *c.* 4000–3500 BC

Durrington Mines *c.* 3400–3200 BC

Durrington Walls *c.* 3150–2450 BC

King Barrow Ridg *c.* 3000–2500 BC

BEYOND STONEHENGE

European Megaliths *c.* 4000–2500 BC

Mississippi Valley culture *c.* 4000 BC

Brittany *c.* 3200 BC

First Egyptia pyramids *c.* 2700 BC

Orkneys *c.* 4000 BC　Stone temples in Malta *c.* 3600–2500 BC

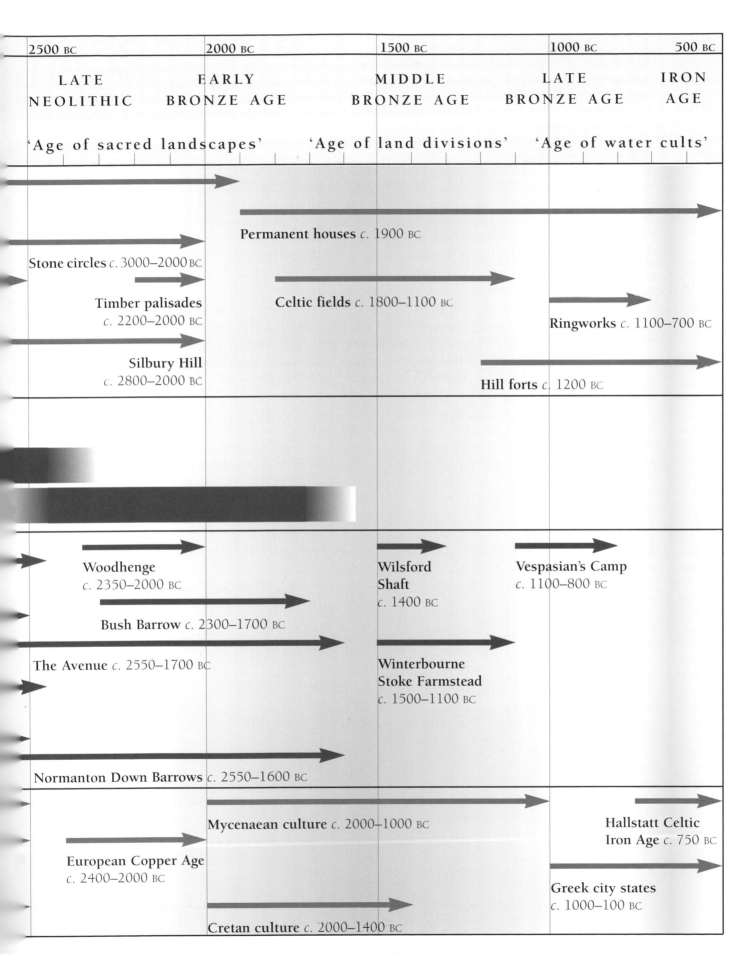

2500 BC	2000 BC	1500 BC	1000 BC	500 BC

LATE NEOLITHIC	EARLY BRONZE AGE	MIDDLE BRONZE AGE	LATE BRONZE AGE	IRON AGE

'Age of sacred landscapes' 'Age of land divisions' 'Age of water cults'

Permanent houses *c.* 1900 BC

Stone circles *c.* 3000–2000 BC

Timber palisades
c. 2200–2000 BC

Celtic fields *c.* 1800–1100 BC

Ringworks *c.* 1100–700 BC

Silbury Hill
c. 2800–2000 BC

Hill forts *c.* 1200 BC

Woodhenge
c. 2350–2000 BC

Wilsford
Shaft
c. 1400 BC

Vespasian's Camp
c. 1100–800 BC

Bush Barrow *c.* 2300–1700 BC

The Avenue *c.* 2550–1700 BC

Winterbourne
Stoke Farmstead
c. 1500–1100 BC

Normanton Down Barrows *c.* 2550–1600 BC

Mycenaean culture *c.* 2000–1000 BC

Hallstatt Celtic
Iron Age *c.* 750 BC

European Copper Age
c. 2400–2000 BC

Greek city states
c. 1000–100 BC

Cretan culture *c.* 2000–1400 BC

Causewayed Enclosures

These earthwork monuments, built in the first half of the fourth millennium BC and in use for perhaps as long as a thousand years, were the first of all the large-scale monuments. Causewayed enclosures consisted of open earth hilltop platforms surrounded by a circuit of ditches. These ditches were not continuous, but had land 'bridges' or causeways between their sections. The sites were closely associated with both the living and the dead. The living gathered at them, sometimes apparently dwelling for at least part of their seasonal round just outside the entrance; they feasted in a ritual fashion; and sometimes they fought or defended themselves there. The dead were probably exposed to the forces of nature before their skeletal remains were deposited in the ditches and pits, often along with other detritus of communal life.

About forty causewayed enclosures are known across southern and midland England. It seems that these camps helped give definition to particular tribal groupings. The camps at Windmill Hill close to Avebury, Robin Hood's Ball, Hambledon and Maiden Castle in Dorset are remarkably evenly spaced apart on the chalk uplands. Each may therefore have been the focal point of a locality or tribal territory.

What remains clear is that the causewayed enclosure stands in a direct line of descent leading to other, later structures: the cursuses and henges. They shared such features as earthwork ditch and bank construction, alignments on the sunrise, and an intertwined concern both with those who were alive and with those who had gone before them.

Cursuses

The Stonehenge region boasts two examples of a prehistoric monument whose original use remains (perhaps more than any other) controversial. A cursus is a lengthy linear earthwork: a narrowly-set pair of more or less parallel banks and ditches extending sometimes for many kilometres across the countryside. In date they belong after causewayed enclosures, but before many henges. Stonehenge's principal example was first noted by William Stukeley in the 1720s. He gave it the Latin name *cursus*, meaning racecourse, imagining it to have been the site of chariot racing by Ancient Britons. This use, though, is quite inappropriate; a cursus was almost certainly some form of processional way, commonly aligned on a celestial event, such as a solstice sunrise or sunset.

Cursuses have almost always been ploughed out; their course and size is known by crop marks and minor surface variations. The longest is the Dorset Cursus on Cranborne Chase which is over 10 km/ 6 miles long, but others have been studied in Dorchester-on-Thames, Oxfordshire and elsewhere. Although most known examples are in western areas, the existence of cursuses at Godmanchester and Maxey, both in Cambridgeshire, and Springfield, in Essex suggests that more may be found in eastern counties. Two have also been found recently in new areas, one on the north side of Milford Haven (close to the Preseli Mountains which were the original source of Stonehenge's bluestones), another in Galloway. As more are uncovered and examined, so their purpose and use may become better understood.

Robin Hood's Ball causewayed enclosure
One of the earliest monuments in the Stonehenge landscape, Robin Hood's Ball consists of two circular rings of discontinuous ditches, which are just visible from the air.

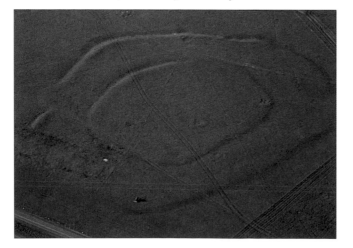

Stonehenge Cursus
To the north of Stonehenge lies the Stonehenge Cursus, named from the Latin word cursus, *meaning racecourse. It is a narrow enclosure bounded by ditches and nearly 3 km/1³/4 miles long.*

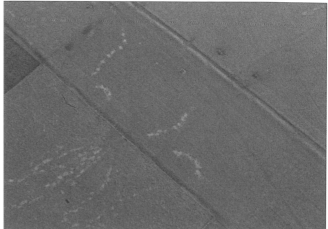

Long Barrows

Graves are among the very earliest man-made structures to have survived to the present day. In the context of Stonehenge, the earliest known funerary structures are the Neolithic causewayed enclosures and especially the long barrows. West Kennet in Wiltshire, further north from Stonehenge, is one of the best-known examples of a long barrow. It dates from the middle or later centuries of the fourth millennium BC and contained chambers in which bones from disarticulated skeletons were placed (that is, human remains that had first been left in the open so that the connecting tissues and sinews dissolved and the bones became separated); the burial of the dead in this type of barrow continued until approximately 2000 BC. West Kennet and its neighbouring East Kennet barrow are the longest examples in Britain, being 100 metres/110 yards in length.

Some long barrows incorporate stone chambers leading off a central spine and an earth covering, others a timber structure covered with earth, in a rectangular or trapezoid plan. West Kennet stands on a dividing line between these two types of Neolithic burial mound: the chambered tombs of the upland north and west, and the earth-built barrows of the lowlands. The latter is found more commonly at and near Stonehenge. Some at least of these tombs were aligned with the rising and setting sun, usually in an east–west direction, though many were also built along natural ridges. They were superseded by the round barrows that were particularly characteristic of the Bronze Age.

Belas Knapp long barrow

A classic stone chambered long barrow of the type distinctive to upland and western Britain, contrasting with the timber and earth-built barrows of lowland Britain.

Marker Monuments

If barrows and graves, whether constructed of earth or stone, are among the defining visible survivals of prehistoric society, they are joined in importance by stones deliberately erected as markers or signifiers. We often speak of these as being 'megalithic' societies: megaliths being 'big stones'. Stones may have been perceived as having particular properties and resonances – links to the past, to the ancestors, connecting the earth to the skies.

Great stones marked the continued occupation of a place, a highly visible symbol of a living community that also aligned itself with those who had died before. Single or small groups of stones were markers for particular sites, or pointers for observing celestial events. Occasionally they marked a grave site; they might represent the point at which the sun rose or set at a particular date; though often they remain enigmatic. In some places stones were used for the prosaic reason that they provided a ready source of building material; elsewhere, although timber and earth were in plentiful supply, stone was probably a preferred medium for the prestige it might confer, emphasized when the stone used was not the nearest available.

Above all, stones were permanent and long outlasted the people who erected them. Often they were brought some distance – perhaps as a symbol of power or territory. Stones were also part of other prehistoric cultures, and in some places continue to be so; but their importance, distribution and history have been most consistently studied in a European context, and particularly that of the British Isles.

The Piper Stone, Cornwall

An upright stone might be a single-element monument, a grave marker, or a horizon point used in celestial observation. The purpose of this single stone remains enigmatic.

Round Barrows

The whole of the area surrounding Stonehenge is filled with the remains and the memorials of the long-dead. On all the ridges that form the skylines – King Barrow Ridge to the east, Durrington Down to the north, and Normanton Down, to the south – and in many of the areas closer to the monument, there are numerous types of barrow – the earthen burial mounds that were constructed in various periods to receive the bodies or cremated remains of the dead. The barrow systems were clearly built to exploit the lines of sight, or were aligned with certain of the monuments. The Stonehenge landscape is an object lesson on barrows in their many forms.

Many barrow groups surround Stonehenge and monumental landscapes similar to it. The majority of them are made up of the round barrows characteristic of the latter part of the Neolithic Age, and especially of the Early to Mid Bronze Age. In addition to the common bell form there were many, usually later, variants (see p. 49). Sir Richard Colt Hoare and William Cunnington opened many hundreds of barrows during their excavations in the early 1800s.

Monuments like the cursuses, and other henges, similarly attracted barrow building. The Stonehenge Cursus has groups of barrows aligned on either side of it, while Woodhenge is located at the northern end of a line of barrows, now all ploughed out, of which it was itself originally believed to have been one. The goods that these graves contained (see p. 52) often provide an unrivalled glimpse into the world and wealth of the Bronze Age.

Henges

A henge is a circular earthwork that has an exterior bank and an internal ditch, punctuated by one or two entrances. It may have had some internal structure of timber or stone, for the performance of whatever rituals accompanied its use. These henge monuments are known from all over the British Isles, but the most famous examples are concentrated in Wessex, with a secondary large group in Orkney (see p. 68). The term 'henge' actually derives from Stonehenge, which is anomalous for two reasons: because Stonehenge stands separately from the main tradition, being early and having its ditch set *outside* the bank, and because the name Stonehenge itself probably refers to 'hanging stones', its unique post-and-lintel construction (there is a link to the word 'hinge'). Stonehenge was also much smaller in area than some of the other important earthwork monuments, such as its near neighbour Durrington Walls or, slightly further afield, Avebury.

Frequently a number of circles were erected in close proximity, as with the many smaller timber circles that have been recently discovered within the vast, encircling henge bank and ditch at Durrington Walls (see p. 56). Aerial photography in the dry summer of 1995 also revealed more circles and henges than had previously been known, both at Avebury and at the Dorset site of Knowlton. There was also a concentration of small henges, linked by a linear earthwork, in Northumberland's Milfield Basin, while in Orkney, where some authorities believe the tradition may have originated, henges and stone circles survive within view of each other.

Bowl barrow, Normanton Down
Bowl Barrows like this one on Normanton Down are simple bowl-shaped mounds, frequently surrounded by a ditch. The larger they are, the earlier in date they are likely to be.

Knowlton Henge, Dorset
Typical of henge monuments, in that it consists of a circular earthwork with an outer bank and inner ditch, Knowlton Henge was later taken over by a Christian church.

Stone Circles

A tradition that lasted for over a thousand years, the construction of stone circles was almost entirely confined to the British Isles. The Stones of Stenness, in Orkney, was probably one of the first circles to be built, perhaps around 3000 BC; hundreds of others followed in the next thousand years.

Stone circles tended to be built in the upland regions of Britain and Ireland (with honourable exceptions, such as the Rollright Stones in Oxfordshire). Sometimes they stood alone and proud; but frequently a number of circles were erected in close proximity. They were related to henges; but a henge need not have stones, a stone circle need not be a henge. Many stone circles probably predate the majority of henges anyway.

Many legends have attached themselves to these circles of standing stones over the centuries. The Merry Maidens were said to have been turned to stone for dancing on a Sunday, and their often evocative names – Nine Ladies, Long Meg and her Daughters – underline the awe with which they were often viewed.

What were stone circles actually for? Ritual observance, study of the passage of the seasons, years, and phases of moon and sun, burial and cremation ceremonials all seem to have played a part in their history. Since many of these monuments were in continuous, or certainly continued, use for almost a millennium, the particular purposes to which they were all put may well have changed over time. Stone circles remain an enigma; but little by little their secrets are being opened up.

Castlerigg Stone Circle, Cumbria

This almost complete circle of 38 stones is one of the most beautiful in Britain. Nearly 30 metres/100 feet across, its entrance is marked by two fine portal stones.

Celtic Fields

Less prominent than many monuments, and perhaps even more vulnerable to agricultural destruction, have been the field divisions and earthwork boundaries that were put up throughout much of the British Isles, including the Stonehenge area, in the later part of the Bronze Age. Usually, if erroneously, called Celtic fields, these divisions may be traced in many parts of western England, including the western part of the Stonehenge region (see map pp. 12–13). Scatters of pottery and flint fragments on the surface are often associated with these areas. The best-preserved of all the field divisions that have survived from the Bronze Age are to be seen on Dartmoor (see p. 66), largely because of the depopulation of an increasingly marginal landscape. In the west of Ireland the retreat of the peat in some areas has revealed sophisticated field systems that date even further back, into the Neolithic era. Meanwhile, continuing investigations on a systematic basis are uncovering extensive early field systems (akin to those at and near Stonehenge) in many areas of Wessex. Some field boundaries that still survive in certain parishes may be very ancient indeed.

The field patterns were but one aspect of the switch to mixed farming, with clearly bounded arable fields within the integrated agricultural system that marked these regions in the period when Stonehenge was going out of use. The foundations of the houses uncovered at Winterbourne Stoke (see pp. 49 and 106), focus of one important farming area, provide a further glimpse into the agricultural economy that sustained the Bronze Age people of the region.

Celtic fields, Bishopstone, Wiltshire

Systems of interlocking 'reaves' or low drystone walls and earth boundaries enclosing the moorland slopes were laid out during the early part of the second millennium BC.

Since Prehistory

The excavation of Stonehenge is, in a sense, a secondary history. From its halcyon days of the second millennium BC until its Iron Age and Roman abandonment, civilization left its mark on the site, from iron belt buckles to coins and a Romano-British hairpin.

Considerable amounts of stone were taken from the monument over time – either robbed, as from a convenient quarry, or perhaps removed for religious reasons, dismantling what to a Christian society was obviously a pagan temple. The first pieces of literary and pictorial evidence for Stonehenge come only in the early medieval era.

John Aubrey, the Wiltshire gentleman-scholar best known for his humorous and acidic pen portraits, *Brief Lives*, was the first antiquarian to bring attention to Avebury. At Stonehenge, Aubrey followed in the footsteps of the Duke of Buckingham's 1620 investigations and Inigo Jones, Charles I's court architect, who conducted the first detailed survey and judged it to be a Roman temple. Aubrey's surveys of the site revealed a set of depressions in a circle (inside the bank and ditch), which were rediscovered in the twentieth century and named after him. These 'Aubrey Holes' were among the earliest features of Stonehenge; the great stones upon which everybody lavished so much attention were actually among the latest.

Perhaps the greatest single early investigator of Stonehenge, and especially of its region, was William Stukeley. In his illustrated study of 1740, Stukeley considered the landscape in its entirety and identified such important features as the Avenue and the Cursus. He systematically examined many barrow burial mounds, recognized the solar alignment and was the first to try to calculate it accurately, and – most importantly perhaps, for a later use of the monument – he believed the builders to have been the Druids of Celtic Britain and that Stonehenge was their temple.

Sir Richard Colt Hoare, from the great Wiltshire seat of Stourhead, instigated many excavations and expeditions in this part of Wiltshire and throughout the county. He and his collaborator, the cloth merchant-turned-archaeologist William Cunnington (whose doctor had advised him to find a suitable outdoor activity for the sake of his health), excavated many hundreds of barrows. In the process they discovered some of the finest artefacts of Bronze Age culture ever unearthed. Their principal excavations were undertaken in 1802; and thereafter a growing band of surveyors, excavators and especially visitors came to measure, dig and wonder. In the mid-nineteenth century the Ordnance Survey carried out a detailed measured and photographic survey, while distinguished figures such as Sir Flinders Petrie and General Pitt-Rivers continued the tradition of excavation and surmise as to the monument's date and origins. As the discipline of archaeology became more established in the later nineteenth century, so Stonehenge came to be prized as a significant monument – despite its physical deterioration. The successive excavations of this era provided a deeper understanding of the stone circle and its surroundings.

Twentieth-century pioneers

The first modern investigator was Sir William Gowland, whose dig in 1901 was associated with the straightening of a dangerously leaning stone, amid

John Aubrey
One of the first investigators, Aubrey's 1666 report noted cavities that were later named 'Aubrey Holes'.

William Stukeley
Stukeley identified key elements of the site during the 1730s, suggesting Celtic and Druidic origins for Stonehenge.

William Cunnington
During excavations between 1801–1810, in which he collaborated with Colt Hoare, over 300 round barrows were excavated.

public concern over the monument's state. Although he excavated only a limited area around a single stone, his scientific approach and meticulous working methods gave archaeologists critical information about the monument's construction and possible age.

In the Great War, the Air Ministry even wanted Stonehenge demolished as a danger to low-flying aircraft: wiser counsels prevailed. Stonehenge was given to the State in 1918 by its then owner Sir Cecil Chubb; its management passed through successive government ministries before being vested in its present owners, English Heritage. The Society of Antiquaries long exercised a watching archaeological brief, and it was under its auspices that Lt-Col William Hawley conducted excavations for many seasons between 1919 and 1926. He discovered and recognized many features and began the refinement of dating and phasing that continues to the present day. Although he has been widely criticized for his excavation methods, he has now been shown to have been a much more rigorous investigator than previously credited.

Two of the great figures in post-war British archaeology were Professor Stuart Piggott, the first to identify a specific 'Wessex culture' during the Bronze Age, and Professor Richard Atkinson, who popularized the monument's archaeology. Their research at Stonehenge began with a re-examination of Hawley's field notes, which necessitated new excavations. Piggott and Atkinson continued the process of detailed investigation between 1950 and 1964; their findings were published in 1960. Atkinson's phases of construction remain the basis for describing its history, although the 'radiocarbon revolution' (see p. 16) has resulted in major revisions to the assigned dates. At each of these stages there was some limited attempt to consolidate the monument's structural condition, which included straightening some of the stones, the last repair being the re-righting of one of the leaning trilithons in 1964.

In more recent years there have been many, often limited, additional excavations at the site (some the result of seemingly mundane events such as the laying of new electricity cables). Meanwhile, perhaps even greater attention has been paid to studying the surrounding landscape, with a more systematic approach to identifying burial mounds and their contents, the close examination of photographs taken from the air, field-walking as a means of combing a large area with limited excavation, and the application of new 'high-tech' methods, such as measuring electromagnetic responses in the ground and a range of geophysical investigating techniques (see p. 17).

Luck, as much as judgement, has played a considerable part in discovering new features in the landscape, from shafts and pits to new henges. Just as the volume of criticism about the way in which Stonehenge has been presented to the public was rising in the 1980s, so the need for a proper re-evaluation of the academic work for such an important monument was being felt equally keenly. The task was entrusted to Wessex Archaeology. In 1995 an English Heritage publication marked a first attempt to assemble a coherent and consistent archive of all the material from the twentieth-century excavations of Stonehenge, together with the new datings that they had prompted. More than ten years after the public access controversy *Stonehenge in its Landscape* excited popular and academic attention, opening a new chapter in the appreciation of Stonehenge and its place in prehistory.

Sir William Gowland
Gowland's 1901 scientific excavations revealed construction methods and the first estimated date of 1800 BC.

Lt-Col William Hawley
Between 1919 and 1926 Hawley, an amateur archaeologist, made a series of major excavations and discoveries.

Professor Richard Atkinson
The most distinguished post-war authority on Stonehenge, Atkinson's findings are now being refined by radiocarbon dating.

THE STONEHENGE
LANDSCAPE

Bush Barrow in the 1720s.

THE ENDURING FOCUS of attention upon Stonehenge itself has tended to exclude from consideration – both in the minds of general observers and even some academics – the wider area in which the great monument stands. It is, however, an area that is filled with monuments: some of the same age as Stonehenge in its various incarnations; some newer; others older still. The Stonehenge car park even contains evidence of some of the oldest man-made structures known in England. Pride of place clearly goes to Stonehenge itself, but, as will readily become apparent, it was never isolated on Salisbury Plain.

The area defined as 'the Stonehenge region' is bounded by the River Avon to the east and the smaller River Till to the west. Although there are no such obvious natural features to north and south, the area encompasses the land south of the Packway, the ancient trackway that runs through modern Larkhill, and south to Wilsford Down. The whole area is a square with sides about 6 km/3¾ miles long. Of all the monuments and features discussed here, the only one just outside this envelope is the ancient causewayed enclosure of Robin Hood's Ball. To the north, much of the land is in the care of the Ministry of Defence, since Salisbury Plain is an important military training area. Elsewhere, land remains in private hands, so access to all parts of the Stonehenge area is not always possible without prior permission.

Stonehenge itself stands on a slight spur on the southward-dipping chalk plateau of this portion of Salisbury Plain, beside the dry valley of Stonehenge Bottom. Slight ridges provide a near boundary to Stonehenge, on which many burial barrows were built, as they also were on the further horizon beyond.

Historically, this has been an area of extensive grassland and grazing, although in the twentieth century considerably more use has been made of the land for arable farming. Many ancient features have therefore been ploughed out, although the protection now given to the monuments should prevent further destruction.

The range of monuments is impressive, and almost without equal in its diversity and complexity. Apart from Stonehenge itself, with its great approach avenue, there are other examples of henge monuments at Durrington Walls, Woodhenge and Coneybury (and another still has recently been found at Winterbourne Stoke). There are huge numbers of barrows, exemplifying every stage of mortuary construction in the Neolithic and Bronze Ages, and two examples of the long, enclosed processional monuments known as cursuses. Pits, rubbish deposits, occasional houses, field systems and an Iron Age camp are also included in the inventory. It is a visually and archaeologically rich landscape, and the construction of many of these monuments required prodigious amounts of labour. This is not the only prehistoric region to have an impressive variety and combination of monuments, but it remains one of the most important and, because of the Stonehenge stones, the most evocative.

Stonehenge in winter (right)
A light covering of snow highlights some of the features at Stonehenge and enables the bank and ditch, and particularly the approach of the Avenue, to be identified more easily.

The stone circle today (overleaf)
An aerial view of the monument gives the best overall impression of the stone circle as it survives today.

Phase 1: The Earthwork Monument

The first phase of Stonehenge bore very little resemblance to the monumental remains that stand there now. For one thing, there were no stones, and very few of the surrounding monuments had yet been built. Yet underlying the standing stones and turf of today are still-visible remnants of this first phase.

The banks and outer ditch of the circle were begun around 2950 to 2900 BC, about the same time as the great length of the Cursus to the north was being constructed. These two monuments occupy an in-between period of the Middle Neolithic – too late for the main phase of causewayed enclosures (monuments such as Windmill Hill, further to the north in Wiltshire, and Dorset's Hambledon Hill), but too early for the main body of henge monuments to which this particular place eventually gave a name.

Stonehenge began as an encircling ditch, dug in a similar manner to the causewayed enclosures as a series of segments. It sat between two earth banks that were constructed mainly from the ditch material: a high internal bank, and a much slighter exterior counterscarp. There were at least two entrances through the ditch and banks, a principal one to the northeast – which was to remain the entrance point throughout the monument's long and varied life – and a much less significant entry-point to the south. Recent investigation of the excavation record and geophysical sensing has suggested that there was also a third entrance to the southeast, although the evidence has not convinced all commentators.

Ritual objects

Animal bones were placed on the bottom of the ditch at certain points, most notably at the entrances. The bone deposits included the jawbones of cattle, at least one ox skull and other smaller bones and objects, including pieces of deer antler that had been used to dig the ditch, and spherical or perforated pieces of worked chalk. The newly constructed ditch was not

deliberately kept clear and soon began to fill in with a dark organic layer, the residue of burnt animal flesh and bone, and silt.

At first sight it might be assumed that sacrifices or feasting had taken place at the inauguration of the new monument, and that the bones were simply remnants of those occasions. One of the most remarkable features of the first Stonehenge is that it can be shown that (even though ceremonial activities may well have taken place) at least some of the bones – notably the jawbones on either side of the southern entrance – were considerably older than the monument itself, perhaps by some 300 years. They had been kept deliberately. Possibly these were ritual objects with great spiritual significance for the builders and users of the monument; perhaps they were the sacred remains – whether actual or token – of ancestors of the cattle kept by the farming communities that built Stonehenge.

Ritual offering
A cattle jawbone and antler picks were carefully placed to define key points in the circular ditch.

Inside the encircling bank, the builders then dug a series of fifty-six holes, now called the Aubrey Holes after John Aubrey, the seventeenth-century antiquarian and wit who first recorded them. Set in a circle nearly 5 metres/16½ feet from the inner bank, they were all approximately circular, but differed greatly in their depth and size. (The evidence that the Aubrey Holes were part of the first phase of Stonehenge comes mainly from inference: their circle has the same centre as the outer ditch and bank, whereas the later stone settings were erected in a circle based on a slightly different central point.) Although there was little filling in of the holes, the bottoms were usually composed of compacted chalk, while dark deposits suggested that the holes had held timber posts, down which the remains of cremations dribbled. It is even possible, although far from certain, that at some point the timbers were deliberately burnt, rather than being allowed to decay and eventually rot away, as is usually supposed; or – more plausibly – that these upright posts were physically removed at a later date.

Comparisons

Certainly the wave of circular monuments constructed in the wake of the first Stonehenge – close at hand, the

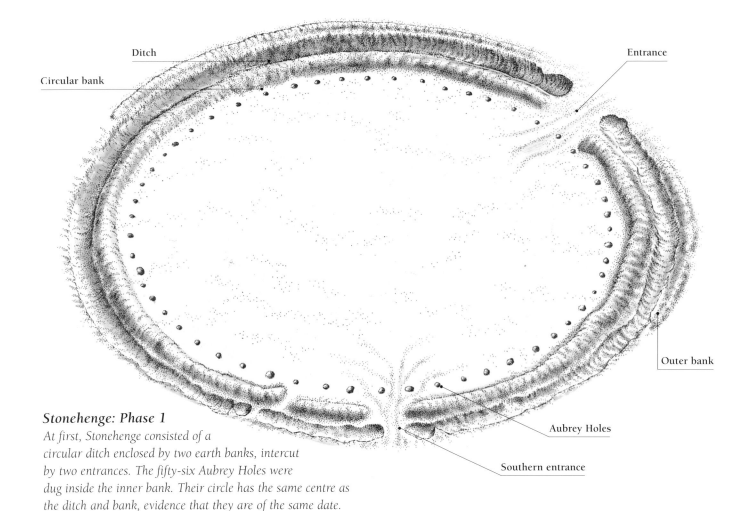

Ditch

Circular bank

Entrance

Outer bank

Aubrey Holes

Southern entrance

Stonehenge: Phase 1

At first, Stonehenge consisted of a circular ditch enclosed by two earth banks, intercut by two entrances. The fifty-six Aubrey Holes were dug inside the inner bank. Their circle has the same centre as the ditch and bank, evidence that they are of the same date.

South Circle at Durrington Walls and the arrangement at Woodhenge, or further afield such sites as Mount Pleasant, Dorset or Arminghall, Norfolk – all had settings of standing timber posts.

We cannot say what stood at Stonehenge before this first monument. It is just possible that the enigmatic Aubrey Holes were part of an even earlier monument, but the general consensus is that Stonehenge 1 was indeed the very first monument on this particular site. As with most aspects of its later history, Stonehenge stands very much on its own: too early as a structure to compare with the other henge monuments and, unlike them, having its main bank inside the ditch. The only example that is directly comparable lies just outside modern Dorchester, Dorset's county town: the so-called Flagstones enclosure was similar in its size, layout, date and the amount and type of archaeological finds. That monument too was used as a ritual site for a considerable period after its first construction. This discovery raises the possibility that other structures of similar type and date may yet be discovered. Yet it appears that no other place was to develop into anything like the extraordinary edifice that Stonehenge subsequently became.

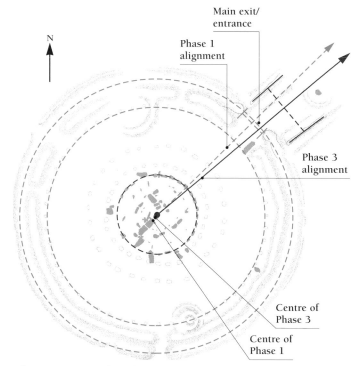

Main exit/ entrance

Phase 1 alignment

Phase 3 alignment

Centre of Phase 3

Centre of Phase 1

Alignments on the rising sun

With its principal entrance facing northeast, Stonehenge was most probably intended to align with the midsummer sunrise The stone monument in Phase 3 refined the alignment.

Phase 2: The Timber Monument

In the archaeological record it is still unclear how long the first Stonehenge was in existence before being altered significantly, with the introduction of more complicated timber structures, both inside it and beyond. There may have been little time difference; on the best available evidence, the second phase of Stonehenge was in use between approximately 2900 and 2550–2400 BC, the dates usually given to the later phases of the Neolithic era.

The first feature of the new Stonehenge was that the encircling ditch was in parts deliberately filled in with fresh chalk, and in others allowed to silt up. Small cuts into the infilled ditch and into the Aubrey Holes, which had also been partially filled in, had animal bones or the remains of human cremations placed in them. More obviously, above ground a complex setting of upright timber posts was put in place.

A wooden structure?

The post-holes identified by archaeologists seem, on first seeing a plan of their location, to be scattered at random. However, various clusters quickly emerge: a roughly circular group in the centre, although the many gaps in the archaeological record (since not all the floor area of the monument may be dug, and some contains stones) mean that they do not form easily recognizable circles, as do the holes at, say, nearby Woodhenge; an extension in a sort of corridor towards the southern entrance; and close settings of posts within and beyond the northeastern entrance.

The centre settings are the hardest to interpret. There were certainly post structures in the middle, and it is tempting to join up the dots to make circles, but the actual arrangement of the post-holes defies that. The ground has been so disturbed in many places, and there may have been so many sequences of timber posts erected during this phase of the monument's life, that it is possible now only to speculate that there may well have been internal, and probably circular, timber settings of a type found in other 'henge' monuments of this general date, not least nearby Woodhenge and Durrington Walls (see pp. 54 and 56). Certainly, it has always been assumed that the later phases of Stonehenge were versions in stone of wooden structures that had once existed there.

Rather easier to identify are the post-hole arrangements at the main northeastern entrance. These suggest a series of wooden walls that made a narrow triple entrance into the monument, through which the rising sun would have shone directly on midsummer morning (see p. 124). (Of course, since we only have the plan of the holes that once held upright posts, there may have been a parallel series of wooden barriers, rather than passageways, obstructing access into the monument, but that seems less likely.) This sense of narrowness and access is also evident at the southern entrance: again the post-holes suggest parallel walls, or rows of posts, which channelled those entering or leaving into a corridor, with a line of posts running across this passageway as a further barrier. That is an architectural device that has been used to telling effect over the centuries, taking people through a confined space before allowing them into a larger, and often holier, space within.

These were not the only post-hole arrangements, for in recent years archaeologists have identified the remains of a palisade that ran to the west and north of Stonehenge, with close-set wooden uprights in a ditch; some objects, such as an engraved chalk plaque, were deliberately deposited in the trench. These palisade fences, which may have stood very high, have been found in other places of a similar Late Neolithic date. There were substantial lengths at West Kennet in Wiltshire, close to Avebury, and a palisaded enclosure at Mount Pleasant in Dorset. Interpretations vary as to whether these were for defensive purposes or to form sacred enclosures. The latter seems a much more likely explanation at Stonehenge since the palisade was linear: it divided space, rather than enclosing it.

Cremation burials

At this stage of its development, and probably into the next stage, Stonehenge was almost certainly being used as a cremation cemetery. The Aubrey Holes, having been filled in both by natural silting and by deliberate action, were now being used as a place for cremation burials. It is interesting to note, given the solar orientation, that more were found on the eastern side than on the western, although this may be caused by a skewed archaeological sample. In a few cases, the cremations were accompanied by skewer pins made of bone, which had held together the bag in which the ashes had originally been kept. These pins are almost always of Late Neolithic/Early Bronze Age date. Cremation burials have also been found cut into the infilled ditch and in the monument's interior, all suggesting a fairly intensive use of Stonehenge as a burial site at this time. The emphasis of the monument had changed; but it was to change even more dramatically in the course of the next thousand years.

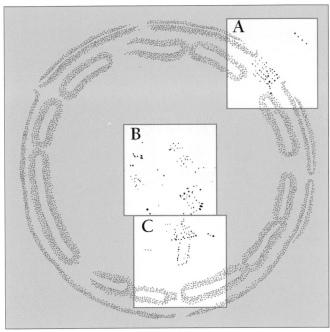

The excavated post-holes

Although the post-holes providing evidence of a timber monument appear at first sight to have a random arrangement, closer inspection reveals three distinct groups: one by the principal northeast entrance (A), a second in the centre of the monument (B) and a third near the southern entrance (C).

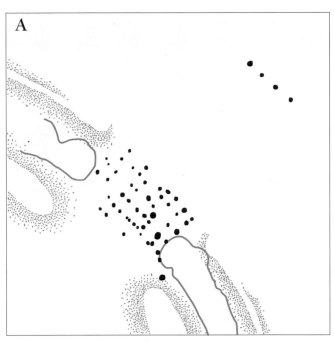

The northeastern entrance

This is the most ordered of the post-hole groups and its inner arrangement suggests a triple entrance to the monument, comprising a series of wooden walls, forming a solar corridor through which the rising sun would have shone at midsummer. Alternatively, it may have restricted access to the interior.

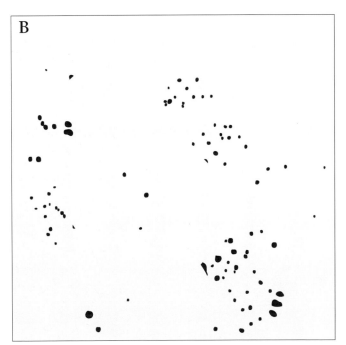

The confused central patterns

There may have been circular timber structures here of the kind found at Woodhenge and Durrington Walls, but the post-hole arrangement is so irregular and has been so disturbed by subsequent activity and excavation that it is possible only to speculate on its significance.

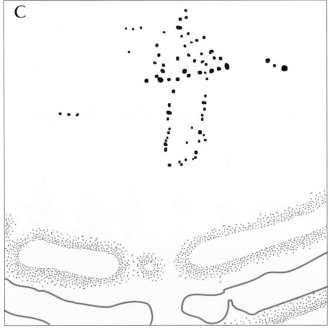

The southern entrance

As at the northeastern entrance, the arrangement here suggests a corridor of wooden walls or rows of posts, possibly designed to funnel people through a confined space before entering the sacred area within. A line of posts confronting those entering would have acted as a barrier to further restrict their movement.

Phase 3: The Stone Monument

The third phase of Stonehenge's existence was also its longest, and witnessed an even greater, and more radical, re-ordering than had been undertaken in the two previous phases. The late Professor Richard Atkinson, the principal investigator of Stonehenge in the 1950s and 1960s, drew up the original three-phase scheme, indicating the different stages of the monument's construction. No fewer than six sub-phases of Phase 3 have now been identified in the newest assessment, with the erection, dismantling and re-setting of a variety of stones within the basic circular monument that had already been a focus of activity and attention for centuries.

The stone phase at Stonehenge extended from 2550 BC (or perhaps a century later) to 1600 BC, a period greater than that of almost any British structure of the modern historic era. Today the Tower of London, for example, is still more than a century younger than Stonehenge was at the end of its third period of construction and development.

Phase 3i: arrival of the bluestones

The first stones to be erected at Stonehenge were the so-called bluestones, the smallest of the stones in the existing setting. They are not particularly blue in colour, more a blotchy grey through to red, and are not all the same type of stone, although they are related forms of igneous rock. They do, however, share a common origin, all coming from a small area of south-west Wales in the Preseli Mountains. They were brought – almost certainly by human agency – many hundreds of kilometres by water and land to this chalk upland, and they featured many times in the arrangement and rearrangements at Stonehenge.

The bluestones were originally set in pairs in the dumbbell-shaped Q and R Holes to form two concentric settings. Whether these made a perfect circle is very much open to doubt; excavation has shown more evidence of stone-holes on the northern and eastern sides than on the western, and the first bluestone settings may well have formed an arc, or even a squarer setting with rounded corners, which sheltered some internal activity. Although it is generally assumed that these were simply upright standing stones, some 2–2.5 metres/6½–8 feet in height, two of the bluestones, reused in later phases, have a tongue and a groove in their sides, meaning that they may have fitted snugly together; others show evidence of the 'mortice-and-tenon' fixing used for the later, sarsen stones with lintels on top.

This suggests that there may have been a more complicated arrangement that prefigured the final structure – or that the first setting of the largest stones incorporated new bluestone arrangements, now lost; but the evidence is still slight as to where, if at all, this use of the bluestones fitted into the building sequence.

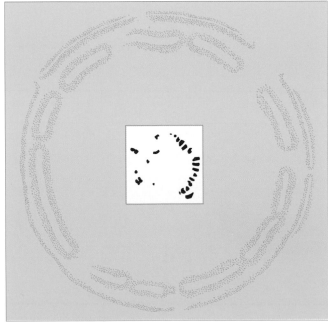

Earliest bluestone setting
The first bluestone arrangement was concentrated in the centre of the site. There appears to have been more bluestones on the northern and eastern sides, rather than a complete circle.

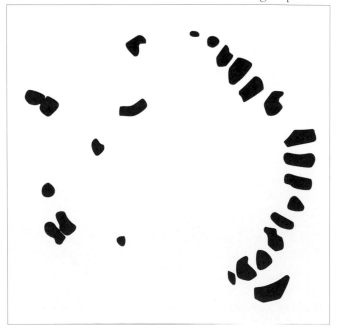

Q and R Holes
Dumbbell shaped holes, known as Q and R Holes, formed the excavated sockets into which the bluestones were originally set in pairs, as is evident particularly on the left of the setting.

Bluestone joints

Some bluestones were originally joined using both tongue-and-groove (top) and mortice-and-tenon (above) techniques.

Two bluestones from the outer circle

Transported from the Preseli Mountains of southwest Wales, the bluestones stood in various configurations before being finally placed as inner circle and horseshoe. The stones may have been quarried in Wales, or taken from an existing Welsh henge.

There was also almost certainly a separate and larger stone standing in the western portion, in a focal point that faces the north-eastern entrance; the evidence for its continued use comes from the difficult manoeuvring that seems to have been required to erect the later sarsen stones. The great likelihood is that this was what has since become known as the Altar Stone – a piece of Cosheston Beds sandstone (see p. 82) that is larger than the other bluestones – and quite different from them in composition, although it too came from south-west Wales. It seems most likely that the Altar Stone stood upright, as do all the other stones, rather than being set flat as a place for sacrifice as legend and romance usually assume.

Phase 3ii: arrival of the sarsen stones

Within perhaps only a hundred years (although the dating is still unclear), all this was to be dismantled. In the process something very close to Stonehenge's final form emerged. Enormous blocks of sarsen stone – a super-hard form of sandstone found particularly on the Marlborough Downs some 30 km/18½ miles to the north – were brought to the site to form a circle of

The outer ring of sarsens
Today, only part of the outer ring survives intact. Directly to the left of the four stones with lintels still in position, is one of the massive sarsen trilithons that make up the horseshoe inside the outer ring.

standing stones, shaped to size and each about 4 metres/13 feet in height, crowned by a continuous lintel of stone blocks adding another 1 metre/3¼ feet to the circle's height. These were fitted together with techniques more commonly found in woodworking: mortice-and-tenon and tongue-and-groove joints. The interlocking stones added great strength and stability, like a ring beam in a modern building. The lintels were themselves shaped, with curved faces forming a circle. Remarkably, the top of this circle was almost perfectly horizontal, although Stonehenge lies on a slightly sloping site. Within that circle, an even larger set of stones was erected, five pairs of 'trilithon' sarsens with a lintel stone on top of each pair, graduated in height from the outer to the innermost (which were above 7 metres/23 feet), and set in a horseshoe open to the north-eastern entrance.

This stone circle was aligned on a slightly different axis from the earlier monument of Phases 1 and 2, a few degrees further east than before, with the changed axis also becoming the central line of the Avenue that was built to approach the monument from Stonehenge Bottom and ultimately the River Avon.

In the later stages of the monument's existence, Stonehenge's builders and users made further adaptations and additions to the stone arrangements over the course of perhaps 500 years, but without altering the overall basic arrangement, with its dominating sarsen circle and horseshoe of trilithons.

Phase 3iii: an inner bluestone arrangement?

The most recent scholars to analyse the stone arrangements have put forward the hypothesis that there was a short-lived bluestone arrangement, Phase 3iii, using dressed and shaped stones somewhere in the interior of the monument, probably re-employing old stone holes from both the original bluestone setting and Phase 3ii. The hypothesis, though, has not attracted universal support for what was in essence a continuation of Phase 3ii, while a new form emerged in the succeeding sub-phase.

Phase 3iv: bluestones and sarsens

The bluestones, which had been the first set of stones to be erected at Stonehenge, were frequently changed around in settings that complemented the larger stones. Inside the horseshoe of the great trilithons, more than twenty of the original bluestones were carefully shaped and dressed, then erected in an oval, probably around 2000 BC. The Altar Stone, also probably a survivor from the first stone phase, would undoubtedly have been installed in its present position at the same time. Other bluestones, less carefully selected and dressed, were

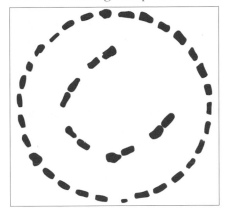

Phase 3ii: arrival of the sarsen stones

At this point the sarsens were positioned in an unbroken circle of standing stones, with the great trilithons forming a horseshoe within.

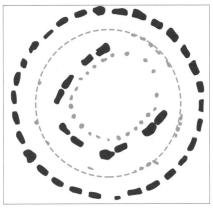

Phase 3iv: bluestones and sarsens

Dressed bluestones were set in an oval within the sarsen horseshoe, and a circle of largely undressed bluestones within the outer sarsen circle.

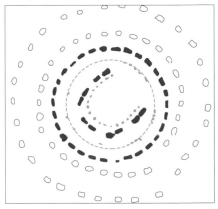

Phases 3v and 3vi: bluestone horseshoe and the Y and Z Holes

Finally, the inner bluestones were rearranged as a horseshoe, while two external circles of Y and Z Holes were dug, possibly to take another stone setting.

installed in a circle within the outer sarsen circle, possibly placed in a virtually continuous trench rather than in individual holes. Since these bluestones, being smaller and more readily transportable, have survived less well than their larger neighbours, it is now virtually impossible to be precise about how many there originally were.

It is of course always possible that extra supplies of bluestone had to be brought in to make up the numbers; it is difficult to imagine a centuries-old store of stones being kept 'just in case' they were needed at a later date, although there may have been other settings of bluestones elsewhere, but closer at hand than southwest Wales, which were dismantled to provide the necessary material for the extensions to the Stonehenge setting.

Phase 3v: two circles and two horseshoes

By around 1900 or 1800 BC the settings of Stonehenge were almost complete; the oval of bluestones from the previous phase was either rearranged or its northern part taken away, to form a second, smaller horseshoe within the horseshoe of the great trilithons. Thus there were ultimately two circles, of sarsen and bluestone, and two horseshoes, again of sarsen and bluestone, with a single standing stone, the now-fallen Altar Stone, as the focal point.

Phase 3vi: the Y and Z Holes

The last stage of Stonehenge's construction may never even have been completed. Two concentric rings of pits, about 6 metres/20 feet apart, were dug around the outside of the stones. They were given the names Y and Z Holes by their excavator, Lt-Col Hawley, after he discovered them in 1923 (X Holes being the name he

The final setting

The sarsen and bluestone circles enclosing the great trilithon horseshoe form the centrepiece of the wider monument, which now includes the Station Stones (see overleaf), the North and South Barrows, the Slaughter Stone and the Avenue leading to the Heel Stone.

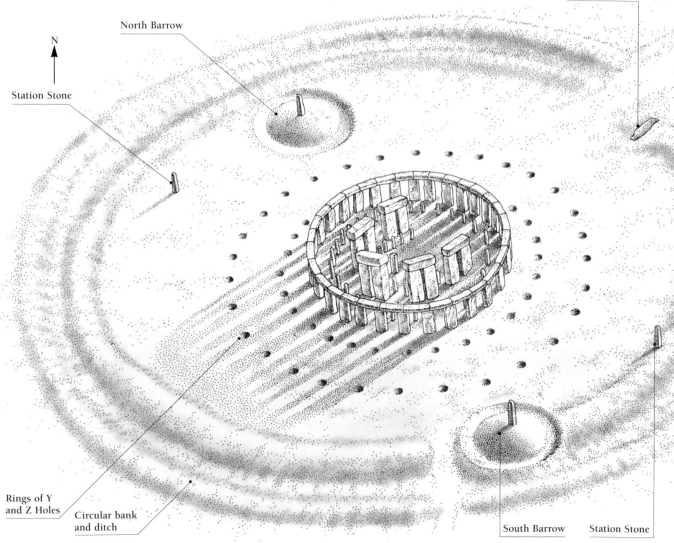

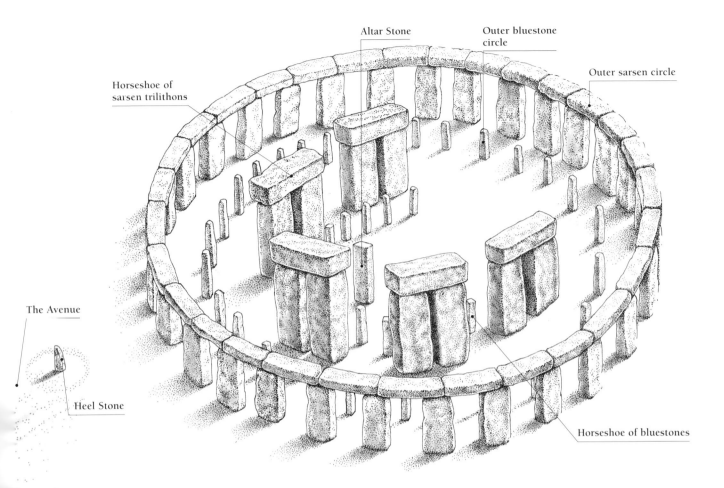

Altar Stone

Outer bluestone circle

Outer sarsen circle

Horseshoe of sarsen trilithons

The Avenue

Heel Stone

Horseshoe of bluestones

gave to the perimeter pits more usually known as the Aubrey Holes). The Y and Z Holes were roughly rectangular, rather than circular, in shape. The rings themselves, unlike the earlier settings, are not exactly circular. At one time they were believed to be much later than the rest of the monument, and Iron Age in date, but that assessment was later revised: material found in the holes, although of various dates up to the medieval period, also included Bronze Age items. Stag antlers that were deliberately placed at the bottom of one Y Hole have been carbon dated to around 1600 BC, right at the end of Stonehenge's life.

It is possible, even likely, that these holes were dug to take yet another setting of stones – possibly the bluestones, which had been moved so often in their thousand-year history on Salisbury Plain – but, for whatever reason, this phase was never carried out. The pits would have gradually filled in, finally being obliterated in the historic era, since some of the material found in them dates from the fourteenth century AD. Unlike the Aubrey Holes, there was no trace left for the first generations of enquiring archaeological observers to note.

Stone circle and horseshoe

The outer sarsen circle, complete with its continuous lintel of stone blocks, encloses the bluestone circle, the horseshoe of great trilithons and the bluestone horseshoe. The Altar Stone is positioned on the monument's axis, the focal point of the entire setting.

The sequences of the stone monument at Stonehenge are thus extremely complex, with their six sub-phases, and they have been subject to redefining and redating many times in the past half-century. As more evidence is uncovered, so the precision of phasing and dating the monument will undoubtedly increase.

The six outer stones at Stonehenge – the Heel, Slaughter and Station stones – have so far defied ready dating and periodization. Although of sarsen it is not apparent whether they are contemporary with any specific period of the main stone monument. They are described overleaf.

After 1600 BC, following more than a millennium and a half of activity and building at the site, Stonehenge was in effect abandoned, only to be rediscovered three thousand years later.

The Outlying Stones

In addition to the principal, central stones there are, or have been, a number of other stones that were set up at varying times on the edge of the monument.

The Heel Stone

The Heel Stone, standing within its own ditch at the north-east entrance from the Avenue, is the most prominent and most famous; near it, lying prone in the grass at the entrance through the bank, is the Slaughter Stone. These two stones are almost certainly survivors of a number of standing stones: a pair to the Heel Stone and at least one other stone alongside the (originally upright) Slaughter Stone, now removed. The fact that at the midsummer solstice the sun rises beside the Heel Stone almost certainly means that originally it was one of a pair of stones and that the first light would then have shone directly through them into the central enclosure. The Heel Stone and its companion would then have been a reinforcement of the power of the sun at the midsummer sunrise.

These outlying stones have perhaps more than any others at Stonehenge been the source of romantic legend. The Heel Stone, for example was once wrongly thought to be named after the Greek *helios*, or sun. It was originally christened 'Friar's Heel' after the indentation in the stone that was thought to represent a shoe mark – said to be the result of a friar's unsuccessful altercation with the devil. In earlier centuries, however, a different stone was identified as the one with the heel mark.

Although some have assumed that the Heel Stone was put up at an angle, it is more likely that it has settled away from an original upright position. Similarly, the Slaughter Stone may be flat not because maidens were sacrificed to vengeful gods upon it, but because it was in the way when in later times Stonehenge was used as a thoroughfare for wheeled traffic.

The Slaughter Stone

The large and heavy piece of sarsen stone, pitted with holes and marks, that lies by the Avenue entrance into Stonehenge, only came to be connected with the idea of sacrifice in the late eighteenth century. By then, the Slaughter Stone had probably been laying flat in the ground for a century or so – Inigo Jones had reported more than one upright stone outside the central circle when he measured Stonehenge in 1620. A trackway passed right through Stonehenge until the First World War, taking advantage of the firmer base that the monument's floor offered wheeled traffic. A line of what

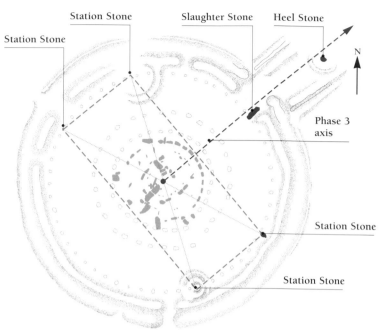

The Station Stones

Two of the four Station Stones (see below) survive. When lines are drawn linking the four Station Stones they form a rectangle whose centre pinpoints the centre of the monument. The short lines of the rectangle run parallel to the axis of Stonehenge, along the line of the midsummer sunrise and midwinter sunset. The long lines of the rectangle, possibly by coincidence, precisely indicate the northernmost and southernmost points of the rise and fall of the moon in its 18½ year cycle (see p. 120).

appears to be drill holes across one corner of the stone suggests that local people may have tried to break the stone up before deciding to topple it and leave it flat.

The Station Stones

The four so-called Station Stones were erected inside the bank, forming a rectangle, with its longest sides facing northeast and southwest; barrow mounds were built around the northern and southernmost stones. Only two of the four, those without the barrow mounds, even partially survive.

The function of the Station Stones remains unclear, although the rectangle they form has certain properties, lining up on the midsummer sunrise/midwinter sunset, and the extreme points of the long lunar cycle. These characteristics have led some observers to assume they played a key part in rituals associated with celestial observation (see p. 126). The fact that two of the stones stood on some sort of mound, while the

Heel Stone and Slaughter Stone
The Heel Stone (above) may have been one of a pair, while the Slaughter Stone (below) originally stood upright.

other two did not, contributes to the sense that there was some now-lost ritual function attached to them.

These outlying stones all seem to have been erected in the long third phase of Stonehenge's construction – as shown, for example, by a Station Stone cutting into an earlier Aubrey Hole. In the absence of other datable evidence or stratigraphic evidence, however, these outlying stones cannot confidently be tied into the sequence of sub-phases. Indeed, some commentators have suggested that the Heel Stone at least may have been erected in advance of other stones and been analogous to the stone 'guardian' of the otherwise timber structure at nearby Woodhenge.

Stonehenge's complicated building history is rendered even more complex by the questions attached to these outlying stones: what function did they serve? How many have been lost? When were they erected? As more effort is devoted to investigating them, so their place in the sequence may come to be better understood.

The Avenue

The ancient formal approach to the Stonehenge monument took quite a different route from the main roads that provide access today. As with many prehistoric stone circles and henges, a processional way provided access. The stones marking the West Kennet Avenue at Avebury, further to the north, are perhaps the best-known example. It has long been assumed that the Avenue reaching Stonehenge from the northeast was, or commemorated, the route along which the original bluestones were brought from the river up to their final standing place.

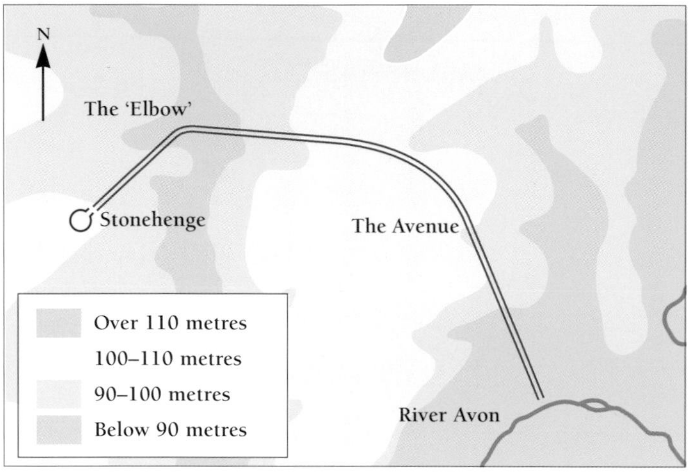

The processional route from the Avon

The Avenue was constructed to follow the gentlest contours from the River Avon before rising on its final direct approach to the stones.

From the River Avon, the Avenue follows a course for about 1 km/ 2/3 mile towards a prominent group of barrows. Passing through them, it then curves back towards Stonehenge on a line between the Old and New King Barrows (see p. 51), at which point Stonehenge becomes visible for the first time. Continuing its curve, the Avenue then makes a much sharper bend at the 'Elbow' in Stonehenge Bottom, once marked by an artificial mound, to run the last 500 metres/580 yards straight towards the northeastern entrance of Stonehenge. At this point the continuation of the Palisade Ditch, which was an important element in Stonehenge's timber phase, ran alongside the Avenue.

Visual effects

For much of its length the route exploits the gentlest slopes to gain the goal of the monument. In a visual trick that Edwin Lutyens and Herbert Baker were also to exploit in the processional Rajpath in New Delhi in the early twentieth century, Stonehenge itself is not visible for the almost-final section in the lowest stretch within Stonehenge Bottom for over 100 metres/ 330 feet, before it slowly and dramatically reappears.

The visual effects of the Avenue are heightened by the arrangement of the banks that flank it. Twin parallel banks, with a ditch on the outer side of each, mark the sides of the Avenue. These are set some 34 metres/110 feet apart in the early sections, but as the Avenue approaches the monument, the width gradually diminishes to 21.5 metres/70 feet, making the final approach even more dramatic.

The line of the Avenue has become clearer as it has been investigated during the twentieth century. As with so many features, it was first identified by Stukeley; his published researches in 1740 included the possibility of the existence of a northern extension to the Avenue from the Elbow, which was only finally disproved by geophysical surveys in 1990. The banks of the section running northeast from Stonehenge are still visible in the fields, but for much of its length the Avenue has been ploughed out and is apparent only as crop marks in aerial photographs. The final section, near the river, is extremely indistinct and it is still not absolutely clear just where its junction with the Avon lay, although there are vestiges of what may have been its banks running for 50 metres/ 165 feet from the river's edge.

Although in the past the Avenue was thought to have been built in two separate phases, it is now believed to have been constructed in a single operation. The Avenue was certainly a part of Phase 3 of Stonehenge; it is the longest approach route known, and is almost unique in being simply a pair of earthen banks, rather than a setting of timbers or stones. (Although some scholars believe there may have been stones set up along the Avenue, and the early investigators Inigo Jones and William Stukeley were both of the opinion that there had been stones there, no evidence for this has so far come to light from excavation or geophysical survey, other than some ambiguous possible stone settings near the Stonehenge entrance.) Stonehenge's Avenue, with its processional quality and regular banked sides, may have been a descendant of the Cursus, which it passes (see p. 46); like the Cursus, its purpose may have been to exclude some and include others, just as the monument itself was designed to do.

The Avenue

As it reaches Stonehenge, the Avenue is still readily discernible on the ground and is clearly visible from the air.

The Post-Holes

One of the most surprising and unexpected discoveries made at Stonehenge is marked by circles on the surface of the present-day visitors' car park. Three post-hole pits discovered in 1966, and another some 80 metres/260 feet away discovered in 1988, had once held huge, single timbers. These have been shown by radiocarbon dating to have been erected sometime between 7000 and 8000 BC, in the Mesolithic era. This was some 4,000 years or more before the first phase of the Stonehenge only a few hundred metres away and provides tantalizing evidence that Stonehenge Down was a significant site for a very long time indeed.

All these pits were large, up to 2 metres/6½ feet in diameter and over 1 metre/3¼ feet deep, and the timbers they held are likely to have been quite tall. Although they had all rotted where they stood, pieces of charcoal in the holes turned out to be pine and to date from the Mesolithic period. At that time this area still comprised ancient wildwood, of open hazel and pine. A clearing must have been made and the timber uprights, which, judging by their girth, represented seventy years' growth of tree, erected within it. Whether they were all put up at the same time, or one after the other as each decayed, is impossible to tell.

What were these posts? They were too far apart to have been joined together or to make a roofed structure, while the effort required to cut them down and erect them was considerable. The real possibility emerges that they were some form of totem pole, akin to that used by North American hunter-gatherer groups living in just this kind of 'boreal' landscape. There is some, if limited, evidence from flints found on the land surface of the existence of Mesolithic groups in the Stonehenge area. The earliest post holes may have had an even longer-term significance: areas of cleared wildwood would have grown back again in a different way from the surrounding vegetation. Even thousands of years later, the once-cleared area would have had less dense tree cover and so may have been an attractive location on which to build a new monumental structure – even acquiring some mystical significance because of that.

Robin Hood's Ball

Possibly the earliest of all the Stonehenge landscape's principal monuments, with the obvious exception of the Mesolithic posts, is located in the northwestern-most corner of the region. It is a causewayed enclosure (see p. 20), one of a class of Neolithic monuments found in various parts of Wessex that were precursors of the henge monuments. Situated within what is presently the army training area and so usually out of bounds to visitors, Robin Hood's Ball – which, of course, has no known connection with either Robin Hood or with balls – is nevertheless an interesting example of its type, comprising two circular rings of discontinuous ditches.

It is always important to remember that there was a period of perhaps a thousand years in which the Stonehenge area was a site of some importance for ritual, for living and for the burial of the dead, but long before even the first Stonehenge had been built. Robin Hood's Ball is the largest local monument to survive from that era.

Living with the dead

The ditches of causewayed enclosures were filled with the debris of feasts – pottery and animal bones – and with human bones from disarticulated skeletons (see p. 110), and almost certainly one of the most important functions that these enclosures performed was as a place for laying out the dead. The bodies would have been picked clean by the birds, and the skeletal remains finally deposited in the ditches, along with all the other material left over from communing with the dead.

The living, as elsewhere and at other times in the Stonehenge landscape, seem to have spent at least part of their year in close proximity to the dead. Excavations undertaken in recent summers have suggested that the region's earliest

A possible modern parallel?
It may well be that the earliest post-holes near Stonehenge contained ceremonial or totem poles, similar in size and form to those used by North American hunter-gatherer groups to mark territory and commemorate ancestors, like this totem pole from British Columbia.

semi-settled farmers lived and feasted just outside this causewayed enclosure at certain seasons of the year: there was a hearth for cooking, considerable evidence of animal bones placed in layers in the ditches and pits specially dug into the chalk, together with discarded flint tools scattered around and simple round-bottomed pottery vessels placed with them in the pits.

Causewayed enclosures were often built at prominent locations, perhaps the most spectacular being those at the Dorset hilltop sites of Hambledon and Maiden Castle. Their spacing apart (and frequent proximity to places of later importance) suggests that these enclosures were the focus of a particular tribal group or affinity – we have no means of knowing, but the patterns are extremely suggestive. Moreover, at Hambledon Hill, the manner in which one man died suggests either a defensive or a further ritualistic dimension. The skeleton, when unearthed, was shown to have been hit in the back by an arrow; the man had been carrying a child, and had fallen forward upon it. Whether this was the result of hostile attack, personal animosity, or ritual sacrifice, cannot be known. Although no similarly emotive record survives in the archaeological record at Robin Hood's Ball, there is a strong case for regarding it as a similarly important structure.

Other enclosures

On Normanton Down, to the south of Stonehenge, there is also evidence of a rectangular area, again with discontinuous ditches, which was almost certainly a Neolithic mortuary enclosure. This too would have been an area in which the dead were exposed to the elements, but probably without the more complex form and ritual associated with the causewayed enclosures. When it was excavated, no human remains were found, although animal bones and pottery shards were unearthed. Similar enclosures are known in other areas, notably close to Avebury.

For all the abiding interest in the lives of the inhabitants of the Stone and Bronze Ages, it is important not to forget that these people were – at least on the evidence of the structures they left behind (and Stonehenge is no exception) – just as involved in dealing with and, we can assume, remembering and venerating the dead.

Coneybury Henge
This henge to the southeast of Stonehenge was found to contain rich deposits of pottery, arrowheads, flints and animal bones, possibly with a ritual significance.

Coneybury Henge

In an area containing a number of henge monuments (see p. 20), not least the great prototype itself, that at Coneybury, on the hill southeast of Stonehenge, might well be easily overlooked. It has been totally flattened by ploughing and is only visible from aerial photography. Yet its existence underlines the importance of the landscape surrounding Stonehenge as a very particular concentration of monuments and ritual places, and Coneybury adds to a general understanding of henge structures and of life in the Neolithic.

Like Stonehenge, the Coneybury henge was entered from the northeast, the direction of the rising midsummer sun; and, like some other henge monuments, Coneybury was oval or egg-shaped, rather than circular in plan. From the environmental evidence recovered at it, this bank and ditch monument had been built within a woodland clearing. Dates from radiocarbon analysis indicate the henge was constructed somewhere around 3000 BC, with possible earlier use still of the site, so it is on a par with the second phase of Stonehenge. This henge, however, quickly passed out of regular use, being abandoned by c. 2450 BC. Since it lies within what was one of the medieval open fields belonging to the parish of Amesbury, the henge was probably ploughed out entirely many centuries ago.

A curious anomaly

If Stonehenge is remarkably silent about the lives of the people who built it – in terms of survival of their belongings and materials – a curious pit discovered during further investigations in the 1980s on the hill at Coneybury, barely 1 km/2/3 mile away from it, has turned out to be much more revealing. Containing what was essentially a time capsule of earlier Neolithic life – pottery, arrowheads, flint axes, bones of domesticated cattle, emmer wheat grains, and other artefacts – the prosaically named Coneybury Anomaly presented a microcosm of the early fourth millennium BC. Similar deposits have been found elsewhere within the Stonehenge region. The pits at Robin Hood's Ball were roughly contemporary, while the Wilsford Shaft (see p. 58) provides a cross-section for a later age. These deposits had some part in rituals, but their significance has now been lost.

The Cursus and Lesser Cursus

Aligned roughly east–west, and lying 700 metres/765 yards to the north of the principal Stonehenge monument, is the Stonehenge Cursus. Nearly 3 km/1³/₄ miles long, but only 100–150 metres/110–165 yards wide, and consisting of a slightly raised earth platform between a roughly parallel pair of banks and ditches, with an almost squared-off terminal at each end, this is one of an enigmatic set of prehistoric monuments dating from the Late Neolithic era.

As with so many features in the Stonehenge landscape, William Stukeley was the first to recognize and describe this monument, and he suggested that it had once been used by the Romans or Ancient Britons for chariot racing. Hence he gave it the name *cursus*, from the Latin for racecourse, a term that has been applied to such monuments ever since (see p. 20). There is a second, much smaller example at Stonehenge, further west of the plantation that now covers the western end of the principal cursus, although it is now completely ploughed out. This so-called Lesser Cursus is some 400 metres/435 yards long and 60 metres/65 yards across; running from west-south-west to east-north-east, it is slightly differently aligned from its neighbour.

The most substantial example of a cursus monument, which extended for over 10 km/6 miles when it was complete, was the Dorset Cursus in the northeastern part of that neighbouring county; others are known at Dorchester-on-Thames (which is one of the most completely excavated examples), Maxey and Godmanchester in Cambridgeshire, and Rudston in North Humberside. Others have recently been discovered in Galloway and in southwest Wales, extending the spread of this type of monument through the length of Britain. Most of these monuments have been more or less ploughed out (like the Lesser Cursus itself, which was obliterated between 1934 and 1954), and are now visible only in aerial photographs. Some portions of the Stonehenge Cursus, however, are well enough preserved to be visible in the landscape, especially at the point where it is cut through by the trackway from the present-day Stonehenge visitor car park to Larkhill, thus presenting a cross-section to the walker. A great cutting has also been made through the wood that covered the western terminal, and the field and fence pattern has been arranged in recent years to emphasize the existence of the Cursus, which would otherwise go almost unnoticed by all but the most dedicated observer.

Celestial alignment

As with other cursuses, this one was terminated by a long barrow set a little way beyond it. A cursus may well have been built specifically to 'aim' at an existing monument that was perhaps regarded as being of particular importance; or else a new structure was built beyond the cursus to provide that focus. Certainly,

Stukeley's Cursus

William Stukeley's elegant engraving of the Stonehenge Cursus, which he first discovered and named in 1723, suggesting that it was used for chariot racing.

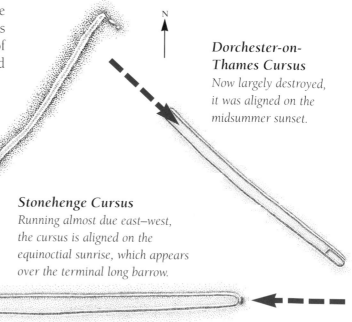

Dorchester-on-Thames Cursus

Now largely destroyed, it was aligned on the midsummer sunset.

Dorset Cursus

Constructed in phases, the central section, between the terminal and long barrow, of this 10 km/6 mile long cursus is aligned on the midwinter sunset.

Stonehenge Cursus

Running almost due east–west, the cursus is aligned on the equinoctial sunrise, which appears over the terminal long barrow.

cursuses were aligned like many other monuments to take regard of some particular celestial phenomenon. At Stonehenge, the Cursus faces the sunrise at the equinox, and also points in the direction of Woodhenge; more dramatically perhaps, the Dorset Cursus is aligned on the setting of the midwinter sun, and that at Dorchester-on-Thames on the midsummer sunset. At all of these sites, other burial barrows were later built in clusters or alignments nearby, with the dead 'sharing' somehow in the experience.

Why were cursuses built?

But what was that experience? What were the cursuses used for? They are far more ancient than Stukeley had supposed; the Stonehenge example is almost certainly contemporary or earlier than the first phase of the main monument, and so is some 5,000 years old.

However, in viewing them as some sort of track, Stukeley may not have been too far from the truth. The cursus was probably a type of enclosed processional route. The banks would have been sufficiently high when first raised not to allow those inside to see out, or those outside to see in – although they would have settled down relatively quickly towards their present height – and so the sights of those inside the cursus would have been concentrated on the activity within, and probably on the terminus or the celestial phenomenon beyond. In all these cases there were no formal entrances; but there was a bank running across the monument, dividing the western end from the rest – perhaps an assembly area, a smaller space for less important occasions, or a place reserved for important people. The Stonehenge Cursus was immensely long – longer than all England's cathedral churches laid end to end – and the Dorset example was longer still. We can still only speculate about their use.

A long line can also form a dividing line or a boundary. The Stonehenge Cursus separates two major groups of long barrows, each within an enclosure; it may even have separated two groups of people. This hypothesis is clearer in the case of the Dorset Cursus, which divides the area of streams and rivers flowing south to the coast and the chalk

The Cursus crossing the Stonehenge landscape
Although centuries of ploughing have obliterated the Cursus in many places, it may be discerned on the ground in a number of places and is still clearly visible from the air. The parallel line of round barrows and Stonehenge itself are clearly visible nearby.

uplands, which were then in the process of being colonized, from the hitherto more densely settled clay lands to the north. The Stonehenge Cursus has not been studied in as great detail as the Dorset Cursus, but it separates an area to the north of extensive chalkland from the south, which is more broken by river valleys.

Although the cursuses occupy a prominent part of the general Stonehenge landscape, they probably did not form elements in an inter-connected ritual space, since, given the lie of the land, the main Cursus and the Stonehenge circle are only occasionally visible from each other. The dating is still sufficiently unclear for us even to be sure whether these cursuses were still in full use by the time of Stonehenge's occupation. A likely descendant of this cursus was the Stonehenge Avenue, a linear embanked approach, there aligned on a monument of great significance. Often cursuses would not have been especially visible parts of the landscape, re-emphasizing the point that their greatest importance may always have been for those inside them. Here, as elsewhere, there is still much to learn.

Winterbourne Stoke Barrows

For motorists approaching from the west of Stonehenge, there is perhaps little opportunity to notice the collection of earthen barrows, partly obscured by trees, that cluster near the roundabout. This linear cemetery of barrows is one of the principal sets of burial monuments in the Stonehenge region and represents every type known, from both the Neolithic and Bronze Ages, in the whole of Wiltshire.

The primary monument was one of the long barrows built in the Stonehenge area, an earthwork some 75 metres/245 feet long and 21 metres/70 feet across. It is one of the best-preserved examples, with its characteristic side ditches (from which much of the earth and chalk would have been taken for its construction) largely intact. When it was excavated, it was found to contain as its primary, central burial a male skeleton together with a long flint implement, like a bludgeon according to the record of the dig.

In addition, there were six secondary burials inserted closer to the top of the 3-metre-/10-foot-high mound: a male, a female and four children buried in the characteristic Bronze Age style, crouched foetal position. Accompanying them was a plain urn-shaped pottery 'food vessel'.

Along the northeast–southwest alignment of this Neolithic long barrow and the low ridge crest on which it was built there is a string of later earthen monuments. There are nineteen bowl barrows, the most common type, in the Winterbourne Stoke group, with dozens more throughout the rest of the parish. In the crossroads group there were two bell barrows, two examples each of the disc and pond barrow (types that are easily ploughed out and so are rare), and two saucer barrows. In some cases, the sequence of construction is visible, since one barrow cuts into another; the disc barrows also stand away from the main line of barrows.

Funerary finds

Many of these barrows were excavated by Sir Richard Colt Hoare and William Cunnington some two centuries ago, and have in fact been little investigated since. Colt Hoare and his fellow-excavators were eccentric amateurs whose enthusiasm may have outweighed their skill, but they still uncovered a wealth of examples of funerary traditions, and of pottery and other artefacts. In some cases there were few items accompanying the human remains, but in others there were rich collections of goods. The grave in one barrow, for example, contained two cups, two whetstones, a bronze pin, fossils and pebbles, a piece of a stalactite and teeth from a beaver, together with other animal bones placed within the mound; in the neighbouring barrow, the skeleton lay in a boat-shaped wooden coffin, together with a necklace of amber and shale beads, a bronze dagger and an awl. The two burial traditions, of cremation

Winterbourne Stoke Barrows

The principal row of Bronze Age round barrows aligns on the Neolithic long barrow, built perhaps 1,000 years earlier.

(with the remains placed in a pottery vessel) and inhumation (burial of the body), are both amply represented at Winterbourne Stoke.

A Bronze Age farmstead and 'Celtic fields'

Recent roadworks at Winterbourne Stoke have also uncovered remains of a Late Bronze Age farmstead, dating from around 1300 BC. This is one of the very few direct examples of human settlement within the Stonehenge area. The remains of three circular houses, with their attendant animal and human refuse, were uncovered (see p. 106). In addition to the farmstead, a complex system of fields and enclosures extends to the west and south, forming examples of what are often termed 'Celtic fields' (although these usually long predate the Iron Age and its attendant Celtic culture). This particular set of boundaries runs for over 4 km/ 2½ miles. That it dates, at least in part, from a relatively early point in the Bronze Age is confirmed by the fact that some of the barrow earthworks in the area cut into these pre-existing boundary banks.

At Winterbourne Stoke, perhaps more than anywhere else in the Stonehenge landscape, the standing and the excavated remains of Neolithic and Bronze Age cultures demonstrate how the living and the dead coexisted.

Types of Barrow

Earthen burial mounds are among the quintessential survivals from the Neolithic and Bronze Ages. Following the Neolithic varieties of 'long barrow', the Bronze Age witnessed a development of increasingly complex 'round barrow' types. The standard type is a bell barrow; later varieties included more than one mound, or were flatter disk, saucer or pond forms. Some barrows, especially the later ones, stand apart from the more usual concentrations in 'cemeteries' that are such a prominent feature of Stonehenge's landscape.

LONG BARROW

DRUID BARROW

POND BARROW

CONE BARROW

DISC BARROW

BROAD BARROW

BELL BARROW WITH BANKS

SAUCER BARROW

TWIN BELL BARROW

LONG BARROW

BELL BARROW

BOWL BARROW

Bush Barrow

One of the most distinctive of the early Bronze Age barrows on Normanton Down, running to the south of Stonehenge, is known as Bush Barrow. It still has straggly undergrowth crowning the summit but, three centuries ago, had quite luxuriant bushes, as well as a pen on the top in which sheep were kept. This treatment may have indicated that some residual significance attached itself to this barrow right up to the recent past; beneath its exterior lay the vestiges of great and ancient wealth and power (see p. 52).

There is nothing quite as exciting in the investigation of the Stonehenge area as the excavation record for this particular barrow. Of the hundreds of barrows investigated by Sir Richard Colt Hoare and his companion, William Cunnington, Bush Barrow yielded the greatest treasure. Colt Hoare described the great finds in his narrative, *The Ancient History of Wiltshire*:

Our researches were renewed in September 1808, and we were amply repaid for our perseverance and former disappointment. On reaching the floor of the barrow, we discovered the skeleton of a stout and tall man lying from south to north: the extreme length of his thigh bone was 20 inches [50 cm]. About 18 inches [45 cm] south of the head, we found several brass [i.e. bronze] rivets intermixed with wood, and some thin bits of brass nearly decomposed. These articles covered a space of

Bush Barrow from the air

Bush Barrow drawn by William Stukeley

Although noted by Stukeley in the 1720s, it was left to Cunnington and Colt Hoare to excavate the magnificent artefacts in 1808.

12 inches [30 cm] or more; it is probable, therefore, that they were the mouldered remains of a shield... Near the right arm was a large dagger of brass, and a spearhead of the same material, full thirteen inches [33 cm] long, and the largest we have ever found...

Immediately over the breast of the skeleton was a large plate of gold, in the form of a lozenge, and measuring 7 inches by 6 [18 x 15 cm]... The even surface of this noble ornament is relieved by indented lines, checks, and zigzags, forming the shape of the outline, and forming lozenge within lozenge, diminishing gradually towards the centre. We next discovered, on the right side of the skeleton, a very curious perforated stone, some wrought articles of bone, many small rings of the same material, and another [lozenge] of gold... As this stone bears no marks of wear or attrition, I can hardly consider it to have been used as a domestic implement, and from the circumstances of its being composed of a mass of seaworms, or little serpents, I think we may not be too fanciful in considering it an article of consequence.

A powerful chieftain

Here in Bush Barrow were the remains of a personage of eminence, a man of stature with the trappings of power. The corpse was placed on the old land surface, not into a grave; the body was not flexed, as was the norm, but prone on its back and aligned to the north with Stonehenge at its feet. (Only two other known burials in Wiltshire had similar extended interments.) The grave goods placed with the body have been described as 'the image of a text written out around and on the corpse'. The value and magnificence of the artefacts make this burial quite unique. The stone object was some form of mace or sceptre, and the curious polished material of which it was made was of exactly the kind that was rare and highly prized.

To get at the grave goods, other bones were discarded. We may speculate that this skeleton, lying within sight, as it were, of the massive stone circle, belonged to one of the great chiefs who ruled this part of Wessex; perhaps even, given the prominent location so close to the monument, someone who had witnessed one of the great phases of Stonehenge's construction and power.

King Barrow Ridge

On the ridge to the east of Stonehenge, an impressive row of barrows punctuates the skyline. The Old and New King Barrows are another of the fine barrow cemeteries in Stonehenge landscape, and they are also among the most accessible. Most are standard Bronze Age bowl barrows, of broadly the same date as the third phase of Stonehenge. The ridge has also revealed many aspects of life and ritual from the era before Stonehenge and the barrows were built.

The route of the Stonehenge Avenue – which was still clearly visible in Stukeley's day, although already being eroded by agricultural activity – bisects the barrow group, dividing the 'Old' from the 'New', to north and south respectively. The great storm of October 1987, which uprooted a number of mid-nineteenth century beech trees, offered a rare modern opportunity to investigate the barrows. The surface upon which they were built, for example, was shown to have been short grassland, where animals had previously grazed for a very long time.

Links with the Cursus

The earliest element in the sequence, the long barrow, was either built at the same time as the Cursus, in order to provide a terminal for it, or was the point on which the Cursus was aligned (see p. 46) and so pre-dates that enigmatic monument. Certainly, other cursuses, such as the ones on Cranborne Chase, had a long barrow as their terminal feature. The sun rises at the equinox behind this long barrow, itself unusually aligned north–south. The barrow has been much

abused by time and agriculture; excavation failed to locate the initial 'primary' burial, although skeletons and part-skeletons of later burials were uncovered.

Neolithic survivals

These barrows have been subjected to more digging than most over the centuries. The Duke of Buckingham's investigations in the seventeenth century, for example, revealed 'a bugle-horn tipt with silver at both ends', and 'coales and pieces of Goates hornes and Stagges hornes'. Considerable numbers of artefacts have been found over the years on King Barrow Ridge, particularly in special deposits and pits. Stake-holes and pits were revealed by excavation in the 1980s, their contents proving to be largely Early Neolithic.

The King Barrow Ridge seems to have been a particular place of deposit in the era before Stonehenge was built and, as a cemetery, to have been an integral part of the Stonehenge landscape thereafter. The deposit in one of them was very similar to the Coneybury Anomaly (see p. 45), and dated to *c.* 3500 BC. A later Neolithic pit yielded up not only evidence of cremation burial, but also tubers of onion couch; their dry, dead stems were probably used as kindling for cremation fires. A site between the Old and New King Barrows that had been uncovered long before this proved to be a cache of flint implements – tools, axes, knives and the like. Perhaps most unusual of all, the Chalk Plaque Pit, located on the ridge, was named after inscribed pieces of chalk discovered within it, deeply cross-hatched with scratched markings including decorative chevrons, which had been deliberately placed there at some point between 2500 and 3000 BC. What the scratchings might have meant, history cannot yet tell.

New King Barrows from the air

Grave Goods

It is generally accepted that the development of single grave burial by the end of the third millennium BC represented a significant shift in social relations, displaying a previously undiscerned emphasis upon the status of the individual. The man buried beneath Bush Barrow, or more prosaically Wilsford barrow G5, had a very high status indeed judging by the range, rarity and beauty of the artefacts (now displayed in Devizes Museum) buried with him. He was almost certainly a person of considerable prestige. Although Bush Barrow was the most magnificent of Bronze Age burials, many other barrows have also revealed startling artefacts.

The Bush Barrow grave goods included the many items listed by Colt Hoare, arranged around the body: fragments of a shield; a flat bronze axe which bore the imprint of cloth on the blade; three flat bronze daggers, one with its haft set with the tiniest gold nails; a perforated mace head of fossil *tubularia*, and dentated bone fastenings for a wooden staff at the right side of the body; together with a golden lozenge-shaped plate and two smaller gold plates.

The larger gold lozenge has been made to bear a significance out of all proportion to its size. Its geometrical precision was interpreted by Archibald Thom, son of Alexander Thom who pursued the idea of megalithic science so vigorously (see p. 126), as

Mace head
This symbol of power was found beside the body in Bush Barrow.

Decorated staff
Although this and the mace head are shown together, opinion now suggests they may have been separate items.

Gold lozenges
The gold lozenges found at Bush Barrow are among the most magnificent items found in British Bronze Age burials and signify that the grave belonged to a man of high stature.

Belt buckle (above)
The dead man's prestige is emphasized by the fineness of his gold belt buckle.

Bronze axe
Unusually, a bronze axe was also found in Bush Barrow.

Copper and bronze daggers
Bush Barrow revealed dagger blades made of both copper and bronze.

some form of solar and lunar calendar for Stonehenge. The incised patterns appear to conform to rhomboid shapes defining segments of a circle, and some authors have seen this as a measuring or setting-out device. Others have interpreted it as an idealized map of the Stonehenge landscape or – because of the curvature of its profile – of the heavens.

Yet, for all its uniqueness, Bush Barrow shares many features with other burials. The place of burial was a place of approach and of departure of the living as well as a place of rest for the dead. Items that accompanied the dead may have been used by them when they were alive, but were placed there by the living. Daggers and necklaces are commonly found accompanying burials and cremations, in contexts far wider than these Wessex burials. In some cases these were objects that were already antique; necklaces, for example, may have been specially made up of elements that in some way represented the dead person and his or her life.

The magnificence of the gold and other artefacts that were taken from Bush Barrow, together with similar objects such as bronze tweezers and gold earrings excavated at other barrows in the region, provided the basis for Stuart Piggott's hypothesis of the existence of a particular 'Wessex culture' in the Early Bronze Age. Colt Hoare and Cunnington had removed all these wonderful objects – and all they left behind was a lead token bearing the date and their initials.

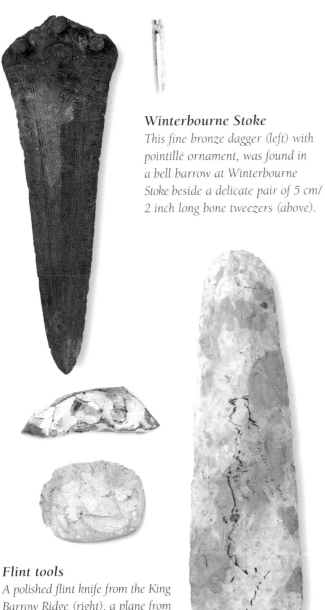

Winterbourne Stoke

This fine bronze dagger (left) with pointillé ornament, was found in a bell barrow at Winterbourne Stoke beside a delicate pair of 5 cm/ 2 inch long bone tweezers (above).

Flint tools

A polished flint knife from the King Barrow Ridge (right), a plane from Stonehenge itself (top) and a flaked axe from Manningford (above).

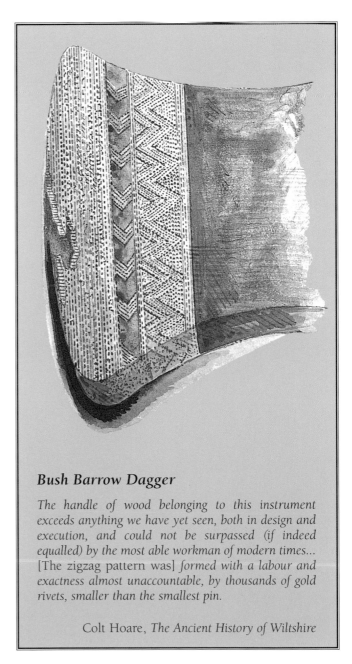

Bush Barrow Dagger

The handle of wood belonging to this instrument exceeds anything we have yet seen, both in design and execution, and could not be surpassed (if indeed equalled) by the most able workman of modern times... [The zigzag pattern was] formed with a labour and exactness almost unaccountable, by thousands of gold rivets, smaller than the smallest pin.

Colt Hoare, The Ancient History of Wiltshire

Woodhenge

Although tiny by comparison with its giant neighbour, Durrington Walls (see p. 56), the monument of Woodhenge is more readily interpreted and appreciated, both because of its size and due to the marking out above ground of the many features that have survived beneath. Named Woodhenge in punning reference to nearby Stonehenge (to which it was a marginally smaller partner), this was a circular henge monument that originally contained considerable numbers of standing posts arranged in concentric rings.

Woodhenge was built on a gentle slope about 200 metres/220 yards from the River Avon, although a steep cliff finally divides the two. Aerial photography in 1925 showed that what had hitherto been considered a ploughed-out barrow was a monument with concentric rings of holes. Subsequent excavation revealed a small circular henge monument, some 85 metres/280 feet across, with a bank and inner ditch punctuated by a single northeastern entrance and six rings of post-holes inside, arranged in a rough oval rather than circular formation. These are all marked today by short concrete posts. There were also holes in which two standing stones had been placed, between post settings in the second and third rings in the southern area of the henge. These were possibly slightly later than the rest of the monument, which radiocarbon dating has shown to have been constructed a little before 2000 BC. All the evidence points to Woodhenge having been built and used in one single sequence – unlike the timber phase at Stonehenge, it was never rebuilt, the original timbers instead being allowed to rot gently away.

The thatched building hypothesis

Great ingenuity has been used on various occasions to attempt to determine whether the posts at Woodhenge were originally the skeleton of a roofed building. Given their arrangement, any building would almost certainly have had an open aperture at its centre, forming some kind of thatched-ring doughnut. It is perhaps more likely, both here and at Durrington Walls, that the settings represented standing posts (whether or not they were linked by lintels, as Stonehenge's sarsens are) without a roof structure above.

Perhaps of greater significance to an understanding of the monument, although even less is visible now than the markers of the post-holes, is the evidence provided by the material and the burials excavated from the site, both in the 1920s and in more recent digs. First of all, there is evidence of activity on the site long before the henge was constructed: arrowheads and fragments of plain bowl pottery dating from the early Neolithic age, the fourth millennium BC. Then there are quite

Woodhenge
Discovered by aerial photography in 1925, Woodhenge contained six concentric rings of post-holes within a bank and inner ditch. Like its near-neighbour Stonehenge, its entrance (in this case the only one) faced the midsummer sunrise.

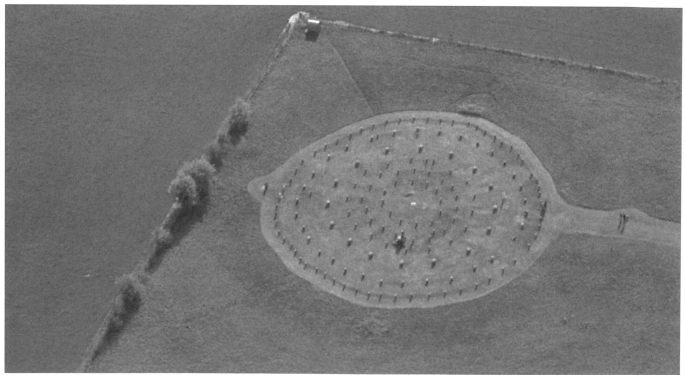

considerable amounts of broken pottery, of the later Grooved Ware type (but with decorative features not found elsewhere, see p. 114), that were found beneath the bank on the original land surface. These were deposited on purpose. They were almost certainly placed there immediately before the monument was built, since most were found in three pairs of pits, under the southern bank opposite the entrance and on either side of the entrance. The pits, which also contained flint implements and animal bones, had all been deliberately and swiftly filled in.

There have been even more finds associated with the monument and its construction: ceramic material from the eastern and western terminals of the outer ditch; antler picks from a central ring of post-holes and from a special deposit in the bottom of the eastern part of the ditch; arrowheads from the ditch terminals and from one of the outer post-hole rings, where there were also pieces of worked chalk.

A ritual sacrifice

Additionally there were many pieces of human bone, together with a number of complete human burials: a crouched male in the eastern section of the ditch; a cremation burial from one of the two northernmost post-holes; and, most emotively, the burial of a child aged three or four in the centre of the circle. The excavators claimed that the child's skull had been cleft in two and that this was perhaps evidence of some form of ritual sacrifice, but this can no longer be tested since

the skeleton was destroyed in bombing during the Second World War.

From all this evidence of deposited and buried material, there is reason to believe that Woodhenge was a special site long before the henge itself was built, and also that what was placed where in the pits and the post-holes had a particular significance. Special deposits are also to be found, of course, at Stonehenge, Durrington Walls and many other monuments.

There is a difference between the two halves of Woodhenge, divided along the northeast–southwest axis of the entrance: all the worked chalk objects and the main concentrations of bone and other artefacts are in the eastern portion. The largest post-holes, guarding access to the inner space, contained both human and animal bones, pottery, worked chalk and other items placed around their base. Given the degree of wear and breakage, it may even have been that the principal movement in the monument was on the eastern side and that the floor was covered in pottery, bone and other material. To us this might seem like mere rubbish, but to the builders and users of Woodhenge it may have had a ritual value and a link to the past about which we may now only guess.

Woodhenge reconstructed

The posts at Woodhenge may have formed the skeleton of a circular thatched-roof building, with an open lightwell at its centre. It is perhaps more likely that there was no roof structure – the posts instead being connected by lintels.

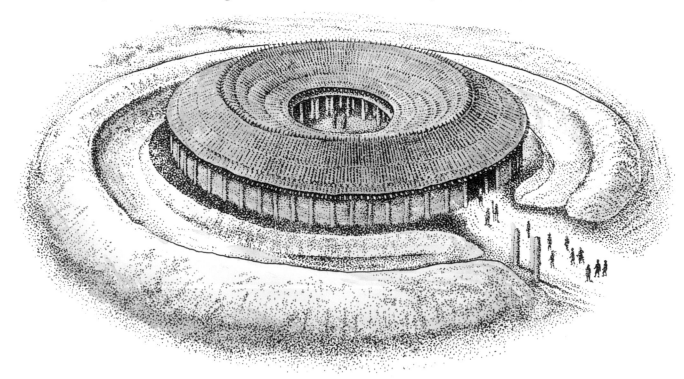

Durrington Walls

Passing along the main road at Durrington, on the easternmost flank of the Stonehenge area, it is not especially clear that one is traversing a very substantial Late Neolithic henge monument – so substantial, in fact, that it is one of the largest of which we have knowledge. Yet, at almost 0.5 km/¹/₃ mile in diameter, and with high banks in places, Durrington Walls dwarfs its near-neighbours and near-contemporaries, Woodhenge and Stonehenge. Only a portion of its huge area has ever been excavated, but even that has immensely increased our knowledge of the structure and meaning of these monuments.

Durrington Walls, which was so named because of the huge earth banks that surrounded it, is, of all the region's monuments, the one that is most intimately connected to the River Avon. It lies on a southeast-facing slope in a dry valley leading down to the river, and the southeast entrance is only some 60 metres/190 feet from the water's edge. The other entrance into the monument's enclosure is set diagonally opposite, on the northwest.

Although the action of ploughing, erosion and the encroachment of settlement have done much to diminish the monument, its surrounding bank survives on the east side as a huge feature – even today rising some 40 metres/130 feet across and 2.5 metres/8¹/₄ feet above the ditch. Excavations undertaken by Geoffrey Wainwright along a narrow strip in 1966–7 revealed a massive structure: the ditch was 5.5 metres/18 feet deep, some 7 metres/23 feet wide at its flat bottom and nearly 18 metres/60 feet wide at the top. The bank here had originally been 30 metres/100 feet wide.

Inside the enclosure, two circular timber settings, similar to those at Woodhenge, were uncovered by excavation. In recent seasons, geophysical testing has revealed the existence of other circles like these within Durrington Walls (and it is still possible that, as has happened in the dry summers of 1995 and 1996 at Knowlton in Dorset other such circles are yet to be discovered). The early aerial photographs suggested the existence of other enclosures and circles, some associated with the second, northwest entrance.

Another roofed structure?

The larger of the two excavated circles lay just inside the southeast entrance. Originally it had four concentric rings of wooden posts, from 2.3 metres/7¹/₂ feet to 30 metres/100 feet in diameter; there was also an entrance 'facade' of closely set posts to the southeast. As in the timber phase of Stonehenge, these settings may have been intended to help preserve the inner sanctity, to prepare the participant for the rituals within. In the monument's second phase there were six rings of posts, between 5.6 metres/18 feet and 38.5 metres/125 feet in diameter, many with ramps into the pits; in the outermost ring, two larger posts again marked a southeastern entranceway.

Although it has come to be accepted that this structure was roofed in some way, perhaps as a circular pyramidal building, that still remains just one interpretation of the evidence. As at Woodhenge, or indeed Stonehenge, the archaeological record is silent on the matter, while comparison with other monuments, whether of wood or of stone, suggests that it may well have been a setting of wooden uprights without a covering. Some interpretations have shown these as a timber version of Stonehenge's post and lintel form. Excavation of this site uncovered large quantities of flint, animal bones and pottery on a platform composed of chalk blocks and gravel outside the entrance, readily accessible from the river, and also inside a midden in a large hollow on the circle's northeastern side.

The second circle probably had two phases, but only evidence of the later structure survives in a way that can be interpreted. Four large ramped post-holes were arranged in a square, 5 metres/16¹/₂ feet apart, and surrounded by a ring of smaller post-holes 14.5 metres/47¹/₂ feet in diameter. From the south it was approached by an avenue of post settings in two parallel rows, crossed by a line of close-set posts that again formed a facade.

In 1996 a geophysical survey of a large area to the west of the old road confirmed the existence of a range of new enclosures, post holes and pits. A complex of Late Neolithic or Bronze Age monuments, including a large double ring-ditched enclosure 35 metres/115 feet in diameter, are located next to a later Iron Age settlement and field system. Magnetometry has allowed a large area to be explored without the need for extensive and time-consuming excavation.

Patterns of artefacts

Radiocarbon dating of finds at the monument place it around 2800–2200 BC, broadly similar in date to the timber settings at Stonehenge. As at Woodhenge, objects found beneath the bank – pottery, bone and worked flint – show that there was an Early Neolithic settlement beneath the later monument, as well as rapidly-exhausted flint workings.

The artefacts found from the era of the monument itself suggest a careful pattern of deposition of objects,

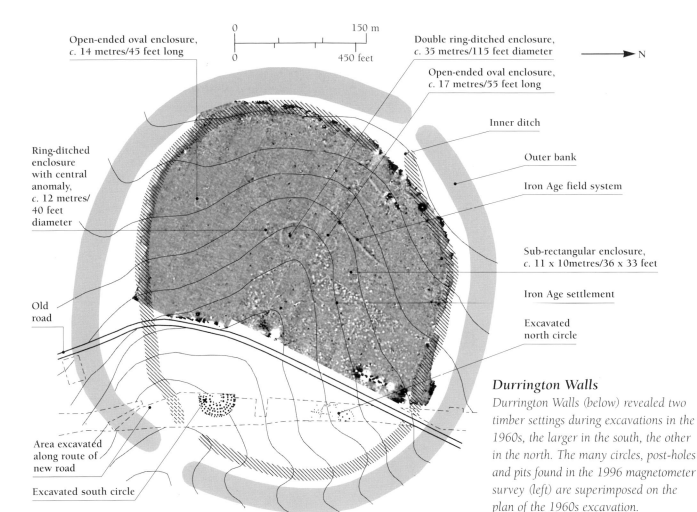

Open-ended oval enclosure, *c.* 14 metres/45 feet long

Double ring-ditched enclosure, *c.* 35 metres/115 feet diameter

Open-ended oval enclosure, *c.* 17 metres/55 feet long

Inner ditch

Outer bank

Iron Age field system

Ring-ditched enclosure with central anomaly, *c.* 12 metres/40 feet diameter

Sub-rectangular enclosure, *c.* 11 x 10metres/36 x 33 feet

Iron Age settlement

Excavated north circle

Old road

Area excavated along route of new road

Excavated south circle

Durrington Walls

Durrington Walls (below) revealed two timber settings during excavations in the 1960s, the larger in the south, the other in the north. The many circles, post-holes and pits found in the 1996 magnetometer survey (left) are superimposed on the plan of the 1960s excavation.

in the same manner as at Stonehenge and Woodhenge. Pottery was concentrated in particular areas of the southern circle, especially around and near the entrance. Scrapers made from animal bone, which were used for the treatment of hides, and flint arrow-heads were placed in the pits on either side of this entrance and at regular intervals around the circle's circumference. As at neighbouring Woodhenge, the bones of wild pigs and cattle were only ever, it appears, placed in the outer ditch, while the remains of domesticated pigs and cattle, although distributed throughout, were concentrated in particular areas: the post-holes, the midden, and the platform. Shards of elaborately decorated Grooved Ware pottery and of more carefully worked pieces of flint were found especially at this entrance platform. There would seem to have been careful segregation of spaces for feasting and different types of ritual and ceremony associated with the henge monument.

Much greater quantities of pottery were recovered from even the partial excavations at Durrington Walls than were found at Woodhenge, as well as many bone pins and awls, but no carved chalk or human bones. The evidence suggests that there were subtly differing

rituals and uses for these places, and probably that Durrington Walls, although broadly contemporary, was used on a much longer timescale. The construction of a special platform, deposits in a special midden, the placing of bones, pottery and other materials in a pattern that could not have occurred by chance, and proximity to water – the same river that had a specially built route to Stonehenge – all suggest a specific and a continuing ritual use of Durrington Walls over many centuries.

57

Wilsford Shaft

What had at first appeared to be a pond barrow on the northern edge of Wilsford parish, in the Stonehenge area just south of the A303, turned out on excavation in the 1950s to have been the upper portion of a curious and deep shaft, 30 metres/100 feet in depth and 2 metres/6½ feet across. This is supposed to have been originally a well dug down into the chalk, for parts of ropes, wooden tubs and barrels were found at the waterlogged bottom. But the shaft had subsequently been filled up with layers of material that were probably deliberately placed into it. It was just like a cross-section of life in the middle Bronze Age, a shaft of light into the past.

At the very bottom lay the organic material that is such a rare survivor of any prehistoric site, but was here preserved by the damp conditions. The dates for the wood were found by radiocarbon dating to be around 1380 BC, the earliest timber surviving in the Stonehenge area. Plant material and seeds found at the bottom suggested that the shaft when it was dug was situated in open turf downland, but that cultivated fields cannot have been located far away. Above that material were deliberately laid items such as bone needles, pins and amber beads, a ring made of shale and shards of pottery of two distinct types, separated by an ox skull. These items, together with plant remains, charred grains and other packing materials filled the bottom 15 metres/50 feet of the shaft. Since more than half of this was within depth of the fluctuating water level, the dampness had helped preserve the shaft's many secrets. The final 5 metres/16½ feet at the top of the shaft, in which much later artefacts were found – an Iron Age pot, and pottery from the Romano-British period – had opened out over time, on top of which the pond that misled the investigators had subsequently formed.

A ritual deposit?

Although some evidence points to the shaft having been a well, it is by no means conclusive. Why should there have been a well at this elevated position? The evidence from many of the other monuments within the Stonehenge region (from the stone circle itself to the Coneybury Anomaly) shows that ritual deposits, with carefully chosen material placed in the earth, were integral features. The Wilsford Shaft may have been a special version of this, and certainly the layering suggests a deliberate purpose and use. At least one other shaft like this of a similar date is known, and possibly others await their investigators. Like their Iron Age, Celtic successors, who dug deep shafts for their own religious observances, the Bronze Age peoples at Wilsford may have been trying to reach deep into Mother Earth.

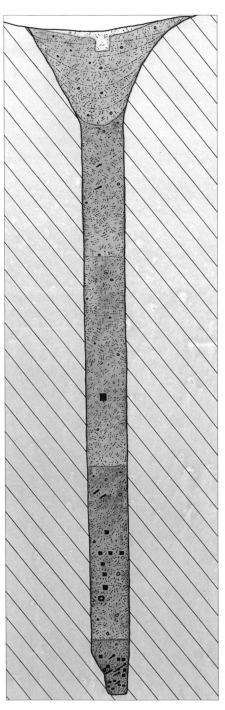

Cross-section of the shaft
The Wilsford Shaft turned out to be a time capsule of archaeological significance. The organic matter at the bottom, dating to 1380 BC, was covered with ritual deposits of jewellery, pottery, animal and plant remains, while the top layer contained later Iron Age and Romano-British artefacts.

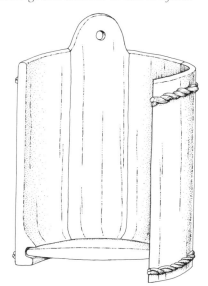

Reconstruction of a tub found at the bottom of the shaft
A wooden tub was reconstructed on the evidence of timber and rope found at the bottom of the damp shaft. The wet conditions had preserved materials that are normally rarely found.

Vespasian's Camp

Later in date than any of the other monuments within the Stonehenge landscape, Vespasian's Camp is an early Iron Age hill fort. By the time it was established probably all the other ritual monuments had long since passed out of use. The camp has a strongly defensive position at the end of a spur of land inside a long meander of the River Avon. Enclosing some 15 hectares/37 acres, the fort is one of many throughout Wessex and southern England, such as Battlesbury and Yarnbury Castle, which are both quite nearby, and Danebury and Maiden Castle, somewhat further afield. They were used for defence in what must have been considerable times of trouble in the last millennium BC, and also as a focus for local life, in the same way as many of the Stonehenge monuments had been used in earlier centuries.

This fort has natural slopes above the river at the south and east, and man-made banks elsewhere. The best-preserved part of the bank lies on the west, where it stands 6 metres/20 feet above the bottom of the ditch, and some 2 metres/6½ feet higher than the interior. Unlike later forts, with their complicated systems of banks and ditches with skewed entrances for extra defence, Vespasian's Camp has only one bank and ditch, and a straightforward entrance to the north, suggesting it was built during the early Iron Age.

Use and abuse

Because of its proximity to the town of Amesbury, this monument has had perhaps a more varied modern history of use and abuse than most of its prehistoric neighbours. The main road passes immediately beside the entrance-way, and road-widening in the 1960s obliterated the original level approach to that entrance. The construction of a road at the monument's southern end in the Middle Ages also probably destroyed a secondary entrance to the southwest, while many parts of the camp had by then been incorporated into Amesbury's open fields and were under the plough. In the eighteenth century the camp was fortuitously preserved when it was trans-formed into a prominent feature of the landscape garden of the Duke of Queensberry's house at Amesbury Abbey,

just across the river. The camp is still extensively covered in a dense planting of shrubs and trees. Although now considerably overgrown, it is arranged in belts and rides, much as it originally was in the 1770s, when a grotto, Gay's Cave, with ornamental paths to and from it and complete with hermit inhabitant, was dug into the camp's eastern river face.

The name Vespasian's Camp suggests a Roman history that the monument did not in fact have. It is rather a fanciful name given to the fort by William Camden, the Elizabethan antiquarian who was one of the first to tour Britain and describe its antiquities. The knowledge that there was a supposed *castrum* on this site was used by some seventeenth-century illustrators to give themselves artistic licence to show a fully fledged castle overlooking the Stonehenge stones, a device that was copied from view to view but which none of them can ever have seen.

Colt Hoare's plan of Vespasian's Camp

At the start of the nineteenth century, the ornamental planting and open rides on Vespasian's Camp were in their maturity, overlaying the earthworks and the natural slopes that commanded the approach from the river.

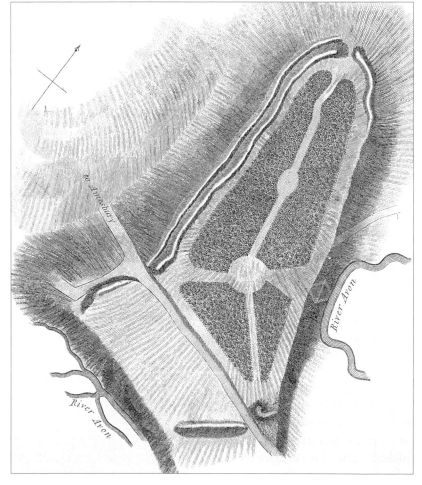

STONEHENGE AND PREHISTORY

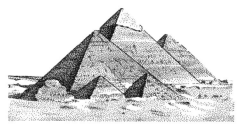

The Pyramids at Giza, Egypt.

OUR PERSONAL LINKS with the far-distant past are surprising and many. History is all about us, in two senses. Firstly it surrounds us: in the landscape, in the environment, and in buildings. Stonehenge is in many ways quite unique; yet it also stands squarely in an ancient tradition of monuments and settlements in the British Isles and beyond. Since some ancient remains have been discovered only recently, and often in unexpected contexts, it is likely that in the future many more prehistoric features will be found, or their true nature and age be recognized. Secondly, we ourselves are also the products of the past; the story of physical structures and places is also our human story. History may even be said to flow though our veins.

New approaches to prehistory

Every year, for example, at least one baby will be born in the maternity hospital at Salisbury who will need a complete blood transfusion because he or she has a father whose blood type is *rhesus positive* and a mother who is *rhesus negative*. It is hard to credit that there might be any connection between this fact of modern medical life and an assemblage of ancient stones on Salisbury Plain, yet there is one.

Very long-term trends in population movement over the past twelve thousand years or more have helped determine what we are. Many population geneticists now believe that the early human population of Europe was substantially *rhesus negative* in its blood type, but became gradually subsumed through the effects of migration and what is often known as 'genetic drift' into a predominantly *rhesus positive* population; those who are negative may therefore be descendants of an original core group of inhabitants. The discovery early in 1997 that a man – ironically, a history teacher – in present-day Cheddar, Somerset was the direct descendant of a prehistoric person

whose skeleton was preserved in a cave in Cheddar Gorge should alert us to the fact that we may be more deeply and intimately connected to the prehistoric past than we ever imagined. The Cheddar link was established by DNA matching (a technique which is only just being introduced into the archaeologist's repertoire but which opens up many exciting possibilities).

Archaeologists, geneticists and others are now studying language, trying to discover the underlying roots of linguistic behaviour and the prototypes of the languages we all speak. The fact, for example, that the word for mother in almost all languages across the globe incorporates 'ma' in some form may mean that that is the remnant of a once-universal base language from which all others derive. Research in this area is still in its infancy, but the day may yet come when – even in the absence of any sort of written record – we may have some idea of the language that the builders of Stonehenge spoke. If that appears far-fetched, so once did the possibility of finding a DNA match between Britain's prehistoric and modern population.

These are all examples of quite a different approach to prehistoric society and culture. Some of these aspects are explored in greater detail in later chapters, as are interpretations based upon finding shape and pattern in the landscape, or comparison and difference with other societies of past and present. Much of this chapter is concerned with placing Stonehenge in the context of other prehistoric societies and cultures – in the British Isles and elsewhere – and especially those that built great structures and monuments.

The Stones of Stenness

The celebrated Stones of Stenness on the Orkneys form part of a complex set of stone monuments on the islands and are closely linked to the nearby Neolithic settlement of Barnhouse. The twelve upright stones in their elliptical setting within a ditch and bank are similar to the henge monuments of Wessex.

Monuments and people

Stonehenge and its surroundings need to be thought about in a wider setting, and as part of a broader enquiry into the monuments and living spaces of prehistoric eras. Stonehenge is in many ways remarkably similar to monuments erected by entirely different and distant ancient cultures. Many civilizations have had traditions of building gargantuan structures. Stonehenge was being built when some developed cultures had already expired, while others were yet to rise to prominence and power.

The British Isles have a wealth of monuments that survive from the Neolithic and Bronze Ages: tombs, stones, mounds, alignments. These are structures that were made from eternal products won from the land: earth, turf, timber and stone. Some of these particular areas for monuments, notably Wessex (the region within which Stonehenge itself is situated), the uplands of the south-western peninsula, and the Boyne Valley in Ireland, are discussed in this chapter.

Yet the British Isles were far from alone as being a centre for prehistoric monumental structures. Across the world, many societies from prehistory have built huge structures, often of stone, for worship and corporate pride. A tradition of building massive edifices is to be found throughout prehistoric Europe, especially, but far from exclusively, on the Atlantic coastal fringe of the west and northwest of the continent. In many of these areas, such buildings long predate those at and near Stonehenge.

There are those archaeologists who believe that this monumentality – which was a novel feature of Neolithic cultures – was an essential element in the process of converting earlier, Mesolithic peoples to the new, more sedentary ways of life that marked Neolithic times. The change involved massive population growth – partly achieved by migration, partly by the greater opportunities and food availability that farming afforded – and the monuments may be but an echo of the underlying human condition.

Area of megalithic activity

0   1,000 km

0   500 miles

Megalithic Europe

The area over which megalithic structures were built in the Neolithic period covers a considerable portion of western and northern Europe. It takes in much of Spain, France and the northern Germanic and Baltic regions, as well as the British Isles. This was largely the coastal region on the Atlantic fringe of Europe, and it is quite likely that population densities were lower in the continent's interior than on the coastal margin.

The extent and the spread of megalithic building activity is in part an index of exchange of ideas between these different regions, although some areas, notably Iberia and northwestern France, had considerable activity well in advance of many others. Megalithic construction is also widely believed to have been one means by which a dominant (and perhaps incoming) farming culture imposed its presence and its will upon an earlier indigenous hunting society.

The western European experience

Diversity is one particular theme of the Neolithic and Bronze Ages in Europe that archaeologists have identified. The coming of settled agriculture from the fifth millennium BC (see p. 105) was slow and fitful, and in most regions the new way of life – farming – and the old ways of foraging and hunting co-existed for millennia. A patchwork of settled and unsettled living emerged. Yet in the midst of variety there were consistent features: the belt of great stone, megalithic monuments on the Atlantic coastal fringe, and round burial mounds, *tumuli*, in Eastern Europe and the steppe-lands.

Probably the most consistent of these features was the emphasis upon burial as a symbolic marker of the emerging new communities. From western France, and then spreading to southern Britain and to northern European coastal regions, a tradition arose of building mortuary houses of timber or stone, enclosed in an earthen mound. Each region developed its own tradition, but these were largely variations on a theme. Frequently these graves – especially where they were built using stone – were intended to be entered again and again. They were houses for the ancestors that were much more elaborate than anything in which the living ever dwelt.

Other, novel built forms were also developed: piles of stones perched (sometimes precariously) one upon another, or upright stones standing either singly or in groups. Between the later Neolithic and the early Bronze Ages the area containing these great stone, or megalithic, monuments expanded, from the Atlantic fringes of France, Spain and the British Isles, to encompass most of those countries and the northern Germanic regions. Megalith-building seems to have gone in waves, often as new populations moved into settled agriculture. The large numbers of upright stones or dolmens erected on the coastal lands and islands of the Baltic around 3000 BC, for example, has been linked to that region's adoption of farming, while stone (or timber) monumental graves were being built in most parts of western and northern Europe.

As the tradition of monument-building spread, so the monuments acquired a power, a sacredness and a permanence. That longevity did not necessarily mean that they remained untouched. Like Stonehenge, most great structures experienced renewal, rebuilding and redesign through often complicated lifetimes. They were being taken apart and re-assembled, often to make new types of monumental graves. In many ways, the British Isles rather stand apart from the rest of Europe, being slower to adopt many of these novelties and, when they did, developing their own indigenous varieties. Moreover, many new styles are found in Ireland, in the furthest west, before they appeared in the British mainland, while many of the earliest structures are to be found in the remote Orkney islands. The process of change was not smooth.

Further afield

Whilst northern and western Europe was building these great megalithic structures, the Mediterranean and Middle East were experiencing somewhat different patterns of change. Malta was perhaps the very oldest of all the gargantuan stone temple-building cultures of Europe. In the third and fourth millennia BC the eastern Mediterranean possessed sophisticated urban societies, based on those which had first developed in Asia Minor and the Middle East.

Meanwhile, the central Mediterranean of the Italian peninsula and the islands witnessed a flowering of societies that built stone settlements, defences and communal graves; the sites on Sardinia are among the least-known and best preserved. By the second millennium BC, this Mediterranean culture had developed into the palace civilizations of Minoan Crete and Mycenaean Greece – the first urban civilization on Europe's soil – in the age of Troy and the Minotaur, and into the great civilization of the Egypt of the pharaohs.

In all these cases, the most characteristic and powerful survivals or discoveries from those eras have been great stone structures that often employ a similar range of techniques and forms, reaching for the sky, and impressive in their massive bulk. Many also incorporated an understanding of, and reverence for, the heavens, whether through alignment on the celestial bodies of sun, moon or stars, or by embodying a strict and surprisingly exact sense of geometry. This was not unique to European and Mediterranean cultures. That is also a feature of many other so-called 'primitive' societies and early civilizations, ranging from Great Zimbabwe in Africa, the royal mounds and arches of Polynesian kingdoms and the stone statues of Easter Island in the remote Pacific, to the diverse cultures of northern, central and southern America.

A glance at the timeline on pp. 18–19 will show how the timetable of events in the Stonehenge region corresponds to wider developments in Europe and elsewhere. Fanning out from the region in which Stonehenge stands, the pages that follow develop many of these themes of structures of great size, and the similarities as well as the differences that mark the buildings put up by various early civilizations.

Wessex

Although the name Wessex strictly applies only to the Anglo-Saxon kingdom, its usefulness to describe the southwestern counties – broadly speaking, Wiltshire, Dorset and Somerset – has given it a much wider application. Thomas Hardy revived it for his novels, while Wessex is also the name frequently given to particular aspects of prehistoric culture.

Professor Stuart Piggott, one of the eminent figures of British twentieth-century archaeology, applied the name to the Bronze Age culture that he identified from the rich grave goods, including gold, amber and other unusual materials. These were taken from the round barrows in the Stonehenge region and elsewhere in the southwestern counties, which had a variety and rarity not identified else-where in Britain or Europe. Although the uniqueness of the Wessex culture has been questioned, the beauty and wealth of the artefacts cannot be denied.

Wessex is also a term used in identifying apparent territo-rial regions of the Middle and Late Neolithic periods. The distribution of monuments such as causewayed enclosures, henges, cursuses and the like suggests political or tribal divisions that were centred on specific sites within a broader Wessex framework. Major sites such as the causewayed enclosure of Hambledon Hill, Dorset, or the henge structures at Mount Pleasant, near modern Dorchester, undoubtedly filled such functions.

Avebury

Certainly, the area that we have come to call Wessex is endowed with some of the most important of ancient British sites, with Stonehenge the most significant of them all. But in some ways the Avebury stone circles and its neighbouring monuments have a claim to be quite as impressive as those at Stonehenge.

The henge monument at Avebury is of broadly similar date to the great structures of the Late Neolithic. Like them, and especially like Stonehenge, with which it shares the distinctive feature of the erection of standing stones (as well as the joint inscription as a World Heritage Site), it underwent a sequence of construction phases.

The dates and the sequence are still imperfectly under-stood. The best estimates at present put the first extant earthwork features at 3500–3400 BC (although there may have been an even earlier earthwork some 400 metres/ 435 yards across, similar to

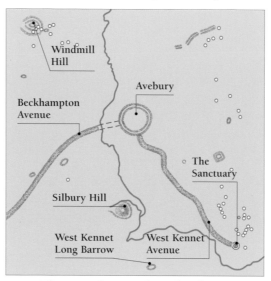

The complex Avebury landscape

The area around Avebury is rich in Neolithic monuments. The village (below) was built inside the giant henge. The standing stones originally numbered more than 180.

West Kennet Long Barrow
The long barrow at West Kennet, in which bones from disarticulated skeletons were placed, is, with its neighbouring East Kennet Barrow, the longest in Britain. Great sarsen stones guard the eastern entrance to the chambers.

that at the nearby causewayed enclosure of Windmill Hill). The sequence of building that culminated in the erection of the standing stones lasted for perhaps another thousand years. The end of this phase coincides with the likely dates for the start of the stone phase at Stonehenge.

In addition, an avenue lined by standing stones connected Avebury to nearby West Kennet, site of the famous long barrow (see p. 21) with its chambered graves (dated to around 3700–3500 BC, but continuing in use for over a thousand years), and a whole complex of timber circles and palisade fences that comprised a ritual area that is still being explored. The double concentric stone circle of the Sanctuary on Overton Hill close by (destroyed in the eighteenth century) was a further feature linked by the avenue. It has also been dated to around 2500 BC, as another element in

the same complex. Other evidence points to the existence of a second avenue, running from Avebury towards Beckhampton in the west. Most extraordinary of all, Silbury Hill – the largest man-made mound in Europe – was constructed at broadly the same time, perhaps as a pyramid structure straining towards the heavens, perhaps as a tomb, although no grave has ever been found despite strenuous efforts.

Links with Stonehenge

Avebury has, like Stonehenge, been the subject of sustained enquiry since the seventeenth century, and the names of Aubrey, Stukeley, Colt Hoare and Cunnington are important in the history of both places. The links between the two monuments are many, not least the sarsen stones – undressed, naturally shaped stones form the circles at Avebury, and sarsens were taken from the Avebury area to create the third phase of Stonehenge. Both sites, moreover, have acquired both mystical and archaeological significance. Theories abound and it is likely that Avebury was also a 'super-monument', outclassing other regional and territorial centres in a similar way as did Stonehenge.

The West Country

Many of us may be living in or on sites that people of the Neolithic and Bronze Ages inhabited, but only rarely can we tell, for the record has been wiped entirely clear by the actions of succeeding generations. In places where settlement has retreated, and the developments of later societies have impinged little upon the landscape, we expect to find more vestiges – and sometimes considerable remains – of prehistoric peoples. On Dartmoor, the bare upland plateau in Devon, instances of Bronze Age habitation are still preserved above ground.

The principal remains to be seen on Dartmoor are houses, field divisions and ceremonial rows of stones that march across the landscape. In a period when the climate was somewhat warmer than it is today, Dartmoor was a less inhospitable place and had substantial settlement and farming. A system of reaves, low drystone granite walls and other earth boundaries, was laid out early in the second millennium BC. These linear boundaries, which run for many kilometres over the lower moorland slopes – often continuing through such difficult natural features as steep-sided valleys – enclose ten major areas, each with territories of between 200 and 3,000 hectares/500 and 7,400 acres. They all interlock, which suggests that there was a high degree of communal co-operation, and are of broadly similar date, which suggests a powerful act of communal will to enclose this territory. On the high moor above 350 metres/1,150 feet there are no sub-divisions, indicating that this was left as common land.

Reaves and similar extensive boundary systems have been found elsewhere, such as in the East Anglian fen-edge, but not in such a well-preserved state as on Dartmoor. For in the years approaching 1000 BC, when the climate was becoming colder and wetter, the bog gradually encroached onto the field systems and they were progressively abandoned. The herds of cattle and flocks of sheep that had been kept on the upland fields were moved into the lower valleys.

Additionally, there are still many vestiges of earlier habitation and use. Well over a thousand burial barrows have been identified, as well as much earlier chambered tombs. Great rows of stones, which were arranged singly or in pairs, and even in threes, and which stretch for up to 3 km/2 miles, date from earlier in the Bronze Age, as do some of the circular, stone-built huts that can still be found on the moor. As many as 5,000 house sites are still visible: some stand singly, some in small groups, others occasionally in larger groups of up to ninety dwellings within an enclosure. Few people live on Dartmoor today, but three to four thousand years ago it was quite a different matter.

Fertility stones

Sexual symbolism is obvious in the Cornish Men-an-Tol stones which marked the entrance to a Neolithic grave.

Stone rows

Long rows of standing stones – set singly, in pairs or threes – traverse the Dartmoor plateau in enigmatic procession.

Prehistoric Britain

A surprising amount survives from the Neolithic and Bronze Ages in the British Isles. Some features are still above ground and therefore readily visible; others are barely discernible, except through aerial photography when the conditions are right, or discovered as a result of chance or enlightened guesswork. Excavation has uncovered the sequence and variety of building of other monuments in places as scattered as Montgomery (Powys), Dorchester-on-Thames (Oxfordshire), Rudston (North Humberside) and Godmanchester (Cambridgeshire).

A great concentration of prehistoric monuments, on the scale of the assembled groups in Wessex (see p. 64) and the Orkneys (see p. 68), is to be found in another part of Scotland, the Kilmartin area of Argyll. Chambered cairns, henges, stone circles and a particularly fine number of rock marks, on both these monuments and individual rocks, fill the whole area.

There are occasionally other, less ceremonial vestiges of people from earlier ages. At sites such as Grimes Graves in Norfolk, or the Great Orme near Llandudno, flints were mined in the Late Neolithic period for use as tools throughout Britain. The shafts dug at Grimes Graves are still visible and a number have been opened up; some 4,000 tonnes of flint were mined there. Elsewhere, particular sites such as Great Langdale in the Lake District were quarries for stone axes. Again, their products are to be found all over the country, while the vestiges of the quarrying and manufacture of axes remain on the upland surface.

Ridgeways and trails

In the low-lying Somerset Levels, the peat and marshes have preserved the remains of many timber trackways, some of which were built as early as c. 3800 BC. The dating of these features is more accurate than radiocarbon dating, since the timbers may be allocated to specific years through dendrochronology (see p. 17). Although the tracks probably linked communities in the wetlands with the nearby hills, the ritual deposit of objects that were seen as precious (such as an unused axe or a pot) suggests that their prosaic and religious uses were not far apart. It also links them to practices observed in the Stonehenge region and elsewhere at later dates. These structures were built with skill and care, suggesting a ready familiarity with the appropriate tools and techniques, and yet they are among the earliest to survive from the arrival of farming to Britain.

A network of ancient routes criss-crosses the country, some of which are still highly visible. For instance, the ancient Ridgeway track, leading north from Avebury past ancient Neolithic tombs, terminates in the great White Horse of Uffington, a stylized figure incised into the chalk. This too has recently been shown to be much earlier than was previously imagined, and Bronze Age in origin.

Often keeping to the drier high ground and chalk ridges, these routes were probably the trade routes of early times. Stonehenge stands not too far from the Ridgeway that still extends across England into East Anglia, and is connected by other chalk ridges to areas of both the southeast and the southwest; the Avon valley was undoubtedly an important corridor linking to the port at Hengistbury Head (see map p. 84). The importance of flint tools, that are associated with chalk lands and were often traded over considerable distances, underlines the effect. All these combined help explain Stonehenge's siting and evident importance.

Uffington White Horse

The stylized form of the horse cut into the chalk landscape above the ancient Ridgeway track has recently been shown to have its origins in the Bronze Age.

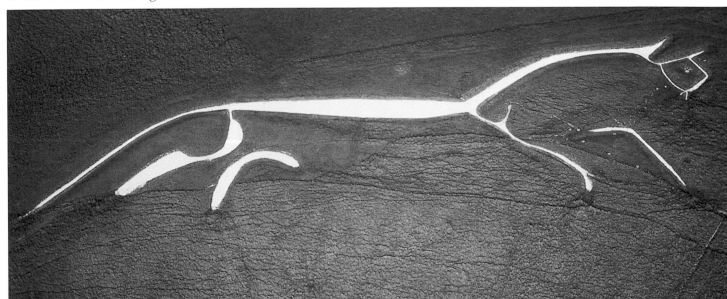

The Orkneys

Some of the finest and most extensive sets of ancient remains within the British Isles are to be found on the islands of Orkney, off the northeastern tip of the Scottish mainland. These islands have often been described as an archaeologist's paradise, since so much survives for the period 4000 BC, when they were perhaps first colonized, to 2000 BC, when the Orkneys began to fall behind as a major centre. Their survival is partly the result of good building stone – and the need to use it given the absence of sufficient ready stocks of timber – and partly the legacy of local pride in, and reverence for, the past. Some of the most evocative of all ancient structures in Britain survive on the Orkneys: houses, tombs, standing stones and circles among them.

Skara Brae

The most famous, and evocative, of the Orcadian sites is Skara Brae, the village lying beneath the turf, which was cocooned in its own midden. It is remarkable both for the completeness of its preservation and for its range of stone-built furnishings – it contains hearthes, furniture and drains. The consolidated rubbish that surrounded the people who lived there was a building and insulation material. Nine houses are visible today, with rooms up to 3 metres/10 feet in height, but these are the successors to even earlier dwellings lying underneath.

The Stones of Stenness

This is but one of a number of Neolithic settlements that have been uncovered on the islands; some, such as Barnhouse on the main island of Orkney, are closely allied to ceremonial monuments – in Barnhouse's case, the celebrated Stones of Stenness. Just as at Stonehenge, settlement and ceremony coexisted closely, and this monument was but one in a complex set of stone monuments that occupies the central point in the islands, the spur of land dividing the Lochs of Harray and Stenness. Investigations in the 1970s showed the Stones of Stenness to have been a henge monument similar to those in Wessex and elsewhere, with an encircling ditch and bank around the elliptical

Ring of Brogdar

The Ring of Brogdar is a henge monument like the Stones of Stenness. The setting originally comprised a circle numbering some sixty standing stones.

setting of twelve upright stones, and with a defined entrance to the northwest. Just across the water, the Ring of Brogdar was another henge monument incorporating a circle of sixty standing stones.

Maes Howe

Just as ceremony and everyday living coexisted, so they both stood alongside the dead. Orkney is also remarkable for its stone-built chambered tombs, often placed in prominent locations. These were elaborately constructed houses for the dead, their walls often carrying incised decoration. The finest of them, the tomb at Maes Howe, is aligned so that the setting midwinter sun shines directly into it, while others were organized so that they were lit by the rays of the rising midwinter sun.

The great difference between the ancient experience in the Orkneys and elsewhere in Britain was that the islands did not share in the changes brought by the Bronze Age. The beakers and burials familiar from the barrows around Stonehenge never became a part of Orcadian culture. Possibly climatic change played a part with the islands gradually becoming more remote, divorced from the mainstream in ways they had not previously been over two millennia.

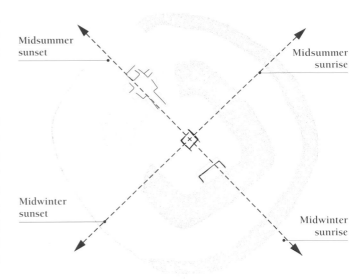

Barnhouse alignment

At Barnhouse, just as at other Orkney sites, the hearths were positioned in solar alignment – facing the rising and setting sun at the solstices.

Skara Brae settlement

The nine remaining circular stone houses at Skara Brae were built with their middens surrounding and insulating them, and they incorporate stone furnishings and hearths.

The Boyne Valley

More ancient still than the Stonehenge and Orkney monuments are the passage graves of the Boyne Valley in Ireland. Excavation of a string of monuments on the north side of the River Boyne has revealed sites of great antiquity and beauty at Knowth, Dowth and Newgrange and their satellite mounds, henges and cairns.

Solar alignment

In 1967 Professor M.J. O'Kelly, the excavator of many of these sites, witnessed Newgrange's most remarkable feature, the penetration of light at the midwinter sunrise. The sun's rays came through what had hitherto been an enigmatic 'roof box':

Newgrange

A cross-section (above) through the monument at Newgrange demonstrates how, at the midwinter sunrise, the solar alignment allows light to penetrate through a 'roof-box' and illuminate the entire chamber. The great stone (below) guarding the entrance to this passage grave is intricately carved with interlocking spirals.

> As [the shaft of light] *widened and swung across the chamber floor, the tomb was dramatically illuminated and various details of the side and end chambers as well as the corbelled roof could be seen in the light reflected from the door... At exactly 10.15 a.m. the direct beam was cut off.*

This remarkable solar alignment was achieved before 3300 BC, nearly a thousand years before the stone phase of Stonehenge began. At Knowth, by contrast, the grave chambers were found to be facing the rising and the setting sun at the equinoxes.

These passage graves have a central chamber built of stone that is set in the middle of an earth mound and approached by a long stone-lined passage. Variations on this theme are found throughout northwestern Europe.

There are many parallels between these Irish monuments and later features to be found at Stonehenge and other great monuments. They had solar alignments and were constructed from great stones, many of which were non-native and had to be brought in from outside.

The Boyne graves are among the earliest great stone structures to be found in the British Isles, but they too are quite young by comparison with some structures that have survived in other parts of the Atlantic fringe of Europe, notably in Brittany and in Spain.

Brittany

Some of the largest and most spectacular of all prehistoric megalithic structures are to be found in this northwestern area of France, which has long had strong associations with the islands to its north. 'Great Britain', after all, distinguishes the mainland of the British Isles from its lesser neighbour Brittany; the proximity is even more marked in their French names. But, however close the links, there are also many differences: the Breton style of megalithic monument is of greater antiquity. Some tombs, for example, date back to *c.* 5000 BC and the stone-building tradition lasted 3,000 years. The builders were more concerned with lines rather than circles, while some of the concentrations of Breton monuments are on a scale with which sites in the British Isles cannot begin to compete. The Ménec lines at Carnac incorporate over 1,100 stones extending over a kilometre.

The greatest groupings of megalithic structures are to be found on or near the Gulf of Morbihan in southern Brittany. The shores and islands of the gulf are filled with monumental structures, from the huge alignments of stones at Carnac and the enormous standing stones and Neolithic tombs at Locmariaquer, that were begun before 2000 BC, to considerably less well-known features. The huge rectangular arrangement of stones at Crucuno, for example, was possibly constructed to align with celestial phenomena. Cromlechs – large and grand U-shaped settings of stones that are found in Brittany – were perhaps the counterpart of stone settings of comparable and slightly later date, like the Stonehenge horseshoe and other similar arrangements in Britain and Ireland.

Cross-Channel parallels

The stone monument culture of Brittany was older than that of the British Isles. Observers who have sought parallels between the two have often failed to compare like date with like. Aubrey Burl's recent speculations that Stonehenge may have been built by the Bretons is perhaps only further confirmation that Neolithic cultures did not adhere to modern geo-political boundaries.

Axes, for example, are a major feature of Breton archaeology. And axes made in the region are frequently found in deposits and among burial goods in Britain, the southern coast of which was possibly only a few days' boat trip away. Perfect and unused axes have been recovered from mounds and the feet of standing stones in Brittany, while carvings of axes are frequently found on the upright stones that guarded the entrances to graves.

A common feature in Neolithic Brittany – but one which, with the much-disputed exception of a carving on the sarsens at Stonehenge, and a carved figure from Grimes Graves, has no counterpart in Britain – was a type of goddess or earth mother. Her form, sometimes realistic, sometimes almost abstract, is found carved at the entrances to Breton graves, often in the direction of the setting sun. Axe carvings, and deposits of axes and other weapons, are associated with her in the archaeological record.

The Le Ménec alignments, Carnac
The extensive alignments of hundreds of stones at Carnac are typical of Brittany's megalithic monuments, being arranged in lines rather than circles as in Britain.

Malta and Mycenae

The tiny islands of Malta and Gozo, set in the Mediterranean between Sicily and the north African coast, boast what are probably the oldest stone temples in the world. Stonehenge is at the very least 500 years younger than the temples of Ggantija, Tarxien and others, which were begun around 3600 BC. The Maltese tradition persisted for well over a millennium; and its early date means that, for reasons we do not, and may never, know, the culture was indigenous, rather than learned from some external source.

That the Maltese were capable of building sophisticated, beautiful and highly decorated buildings makes the somewhat later experience on Stonehenge Down all the more comprehensible. A chief-based Maltese society developed elaborate rituals, which were reflected in their religious buildings, constructed with many chambers to simulate the caverns where earlier ceremonies and burial rites had taken place. They carved mother-earth goddess figures, and incised complicated decorative motifs on their stone slabs. Some of the monolithic stone entrances bear an uncanny resemblance to the Stonehenge trilithons. Then, around 2500 BC, the culture trickled away, with bronze users moving in to supplant the stone users but not absorbing their culture. Whereas this ancient Maltese culture sank, to be rediscovered only in modern times, the legacy of other neighbouring cultures has shaped our view of the past and of ourselves.

Mycenae

As 'the cradle of Western civilization', the Mediterranean and its shores contained some of the most significant of ancient cultures, in terms of their continued influence upon the world that was to follow. Among the civilizations of Greece and Asia Minor, three stand out: Troy, Mycenae and Minoa.

The systematic archaeological record of Mycenae began in the later nineteenth century, with some spectacular discoveries. Mycenae's rulers had been buried in beehive-shaped tombs, and the ancient walls were so monumental that later Greeks believed they had been built by the Cyclops giants. These graves and walls have been dated to the centuries around 1600 BC; older still were the ruins excavated by Arthur Evans at Knossos on Crete, from the Minoan civilization. The palace there was originally built around 1900 BC.

Mycenae in particular, with the monumentality of its stone architecture and the intricacies of its graves, attracted considerable attention from those seeking the origins of the ancient buildings and societies of western Europe. At one time it was firmly believed that the eastern Mediterranean was the origin of civilization. The dating techniques that formed the 'radiocarbon revolution' (see p. 16) forced a major reappraisal in the 1960s: some of the prehistoric buildings and goods found around Stonehenge, Carnac and elsewhere considerably predated the archaic eras of Greece.

Lion Gate, Mycenae
The curved lintel and great uprights are reminiscent of the Stonehenge trilithons, which predate them.

North Temple at Ggantija, Gozo
Ggantija is among the oldest stone temples in the world, having been begun around 3600 BC. It is one of a number of sophisticated, beautifully carved stone monuments on the islands of Malta and Gozo.

Egypt

The pyramids and the tombs of the pharaohs of Ancient Egypt have long excited the imagination of Europeans. We are accustomed to thinking of Egypt as one of the most ancient and distant societies to which we have ready access, so it is salutary to remember that its great culture is younger than the megalithic cultures of western Europe (as well as the even more ancient civilizations of the Near and Middle East).

The dates of the Egyptian civilization are still subject to some re-evaluation, but the earliest known culture was that of the early dynastic period, on either side of 3000 BC. The Middle Kingdom was established a millennium later, the New Kingdom around 1500 BC. The monumental structures that we most associate with Egypt are the pyramids, and the great age of pyramid construction came relatively early, around 2500 BC. The pyramids of Cheops, Khephren and Menkaure at Giza are among the greatest monumental structures ever built, although the much less well-known, slightly earlier pyramid at Dahshur, built by the early pharaoh Sneferu, is only fractionally smaller in area, if not in height and complexity.

The Khephren pyramid, Giza
The tombs of the pharaohs, such as the pyramids at Giza, have many parallels with monuments in Neolithic Britain, being burial mounds and demonstrating that monumental structures could be built within the context of everyday life.

Aiming for the skies

In the traditional description of the building of these huge structures, with memories of Biblical stories of the treatment of the Israelites, huge gangs of slave labour were assumed; in reality, it now appears that most building was carried out by the ordinary population during the 'slack' season when the life-giving waters of the Nile flooded the fields and no work could be done in them.

The lessons of Egyptian culture for Stonehenge are many, and this last is not the least of them – that huge endeavours could be undertaken through a high degree of central organization within the context of the rhythm of everyday life. 'Practical archaeology', moreover, has demonstrated the range of building and setting-out techniques, especially in constructing great pyramids, which were well within the reach of civilizations lacking metal tools and highly sophisticated measuring devices.

The pyramids exhibit geometry, monumentality and relationships with the stars. Above all, there is a common language in monument building, of mounds and structures that are aiming for the skies. The pyramids of Egypt, and later those of Central and South America, incorporate many features also present in the monuments of Neolithic Britain and Europe: burial mounds, the pyramidal shape of Silbury Hill, as well as the stepping-up from the outer circle to the central horseshoe of Stonehenge, which gives some sense of it being a pyramid.

The Americas

When Europeans first encountered the peoples of the New World in the late fifteenth and sixteenth centuries, they discovered societies that used stone tools and built monumental structures, which in some cases eclipsed almost everything known in the Old World. The civilizations of ancient Mexico and Peru – the Aztecs and the Incas, and their predecessor cultures – built great cities, constructed walls whose masonry fitted together perfectly without mortar, and erected huge stepped pyramids. Upon these, sacrificial victims were slaughtered to appease the gods of the sun, the elements and war.

Even among the seemingly less 'developed' native peoples of the tribes of North American Indians, the newcomers saw huge earthworks, tribal circles and standing wooden poles and houses that, unbeknown to them, frequently recall structures from ancient periods within European cultures. Examples of rock art, with scenes depicting supernatural beings or human activities as well as more abstract forms, survive from Patagonia to northwestern Canada. In many cases, these art forms were not placed randomly but had an importance in the annual round: the midsummer sun might bisect a human figure, or the sun's rays at certain festivals strike a particular and distinctively-shaped figure. As archaeology has pushed back the boundaries of time, so some of these buildings and sites may now be seen to be quite as ancient as many similar features across the Atlantic.

The earliest known 'complex' society in Central America, the Olmec, flourished from *c.* 1150–400 BC, leaving as its principal legacy a tradition of carving grotesque giant stone heads. Rather better-known (not least because of the claims for extra-terrestrial influence and contact) is the Nazca culture of Peru. In addition to building mud-brick pyramids and platform mounds, they cut lines into the valley floor at various times between 2000 BC and 1500 AD. Some run straight as a die for many kilometres, others form the outline of animals – a monkey, a spider – or geometrical figures. Some lines point to celestial events, notably the midsummer solstice.

Pyramids and sun worship

Pyramidal structures were among the most prominent, and labour-intensive, of the monuments built by the civilisations of central and southern America – the Mayans, the Incas and the Aztecs. Rarely were these built as tombs, as the pyramids of Egypt were; rather, they usually embodied the complex mixture of worship of the sun and bloodthirsty warfare that characterized these peoples, seen to its fullest extent among the Aztecs, the first culture to be overrun by the Spanish conquerors. They served both as platforms for observing the sun – the central figure in the cosmology – and as places of sacrifice, rivers of blood running down the steps in some of the most gruesome episodes that have been documented. The sophisticated ways in which many of these cultures in the Americas observed and charted the heavens, was inspired by the need to fix celestial events, notably the sun at its turning points in winter and summer. In central America – as in

Pyramid of Kukulkan, Chichen Itza, Mexico
As the equinoctial sunset crosses the pyramid, the shadow creates the illusion of the feathered tail of the serpent god, Kukulkan.

China and Egypt at the same time – calendrical problems of the sun and moon were being wrestled with in the first millennium BC. By the time of the European invasion, the Aztecs had highly sophisticated calendar devices used in forecasting solar eclipses. The sun god, Huitzilopochtli, had to be satisfied with blood sacrifices. The Spanish conquerors in Peru found and eradicated most of the Inca religious centres. They failed, however, to find the remote site of Machu Picchu, with its central sun pillar and flanking stones to measure the solar solstices. Discovered only at the beginning of this century, it survives to amaze visitors to the present day. Calendrical observation and monument building were also characteristic of many early groups in North America.

North American burial traditions

In British and French North America there was a prevailing view in the eighteenth and even the nineteenth century that the natives were undeveloped and primitive. This was increasingly challenged, by the evidence of the burial mounds that certain tribes had built. Thomas Jefferson himself set out to find who had built the curious mounds that were scattered around his estate in Virginia, discovering within them several burial layers clearly of native American origin. Sixteenth-century explorers had seen similar sites in southeastern North America being used as 'temples and palaces', while in the southwest they had found remarkable cliff-face dwellings and rock art.

The antiquity of these places has aroused both wonder and passion. In places such as the Ohio valley, enormous ritual landscapes have recently come to light; great mounds with tail-like earthworks snaking away from them speak of the ingenuity and cultural cohesion of the native societies that had built them between eight hundred and fifteen hundred years ago. The Ohio and Mississippi valleys sustained cultures for some 6,000 years building monuments to rival Mexico or Egypt. The earliest earth mound structures – probably used as cremation platforms and sky observation posts – have been dated to 4500 BC. A thousand years later, this civilisation was building great circular and D-shaped mounds, such as that at Frenchman's Bend, Louisiana, while at the time of Stonehenge the huge earthbank enclosure of Poverty Point, Louisiana comprising six concentric half-circles and a central mound 24 metres/80 feet high, was under construction.

There is no connection between the buildings of the Americas and megalithic Europe or ancient Egypt, other than the desire and the ability of organized societies to express through monumental might and ingenuity their relationship with the earth and the sky, with their ancestors and their gods. It is in some ways remarkable that these structures, in widely differing places, frequently take such similar forms; yet the combination of materials both precious and ubiquitous, and the striving for geometrical perfection, height and breadth, are testimony to the ways in which people's minds work in common.

Hitching post of the sun, Machu Picchu

The centre of this Inca temple in Peru is dominated by an intihuatana, *a stone altar with possible sightlines to the sun.*

Red Canyon petroglyph

This petroglyph in Arizona was painted so that the sun cuts into its quadrants at daybreak on midsummer's day.

THE MAKING
OF THE MEGALITHS

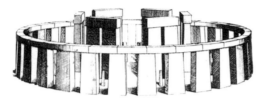

Inigo Jones's perspective of Stonehenge 'as built'
but with an extra trilithon.

THE LONGEST PERIOD of change and reconstruction in Stonehenge's history was the third and final phase, in which stones were set up inside the earth bank and ditch of the old monument to make one of the great wonders of the prehistoric world. Along with Newgrange in Ireland's Boyne Valley (see p. 70), and the Breton monuments of Carnac and Locmariaquer (see p. 71), which are far older than Stonehenge, the monument was one of the supreme achievements of Stone Age mankind. Unravelling the sequence of the stone settings, and the types of stone used in its construction, helps to explain the use to which Stonehenge was put and the type of organization of the society that produced it. Recent evaluation of all the available evidence both from the written archive and the programme of radiocarbon dating certainly suggests that Stonehenge is older than has generally been thought, with the principal dates of its construction lying well back in the Neolithic era.

As already described (see p. 36), there are concentric settings of stones at Stonehenge, with a small number of additional outlying and separate stones. The outermost circle of sarsen stones, and the taller sarsen stones in the horseshoe of trilithons that rear up in the centre, are what make an immediate visual impact upon those who come to visit Stonehenge. The smaller and rather less demonstrative 'bluestones', in their own circle and horseshoe settings inside those of their larger neighbours, contribute to the feeling of denseness, almost impenetrability, that Stonehenge must once have had. Some of that feeling remains when Stonehenge is approached or viewed from the east, since on that side more of the stones have remained upright, or retain their capping lintels.

There are so many stones to be identified that a consistent numbering system has been adopted, on the principles first devised by Sir Flinders Petrie over a century ago. The numbering begins with the outer sarsen circle, running clockwise from 1 to 30, starting at the stone on the right (looking from inside) of the Avenue approach. The lintels on top are numbered from 101, the last digits being the number of the right-hand supporting stone. Therefore, the lintels bridging stones 29, 30 and 1 are numbered 130 and 101. The sequence continues with the bluestone circle numbered from 31 (again starting at the same position) to 49. Then follow the trilithons set in their horseshoe, numbered from 51 to 60, and the inner bluestone horseshoe, numbered from 61 to 72. At the centre of the monument, the Altar Stone is conventionally numbered 80; outside, the remaining Station Stones are 91 and 93, the Slaughter Stone 95 and the Heel Stone 96. A similar numbering system has been devised for the Aubrey Holes (1–56), the Y Holes and the Z Holes (both 1–30).

The monument is far from being in the condition in which it was first erected and has suffered from the effects of time, wind, gravity and human intervention. Of the sarsen circle, only seventeen stones now stand, with five of their lintels still in place. Six of the bluestone circle stones are still standing, with another twelve fallen and nine as broken stumps. Three of the five trilithon pairs remain, with a single stone from

Sarsens at night
The massive sandstone sarsens, with their curved lintels, give Stonehenge its enormous visual impact from afar. Locals used to call them 'Saracen Stones' because of their strange appearance.

each of the others, making this the best-preserved part of the ensemble, while within that horseshoe six of the bluestone horseshoe settings remain, together with another six stumps. Finally, the innermost space has become a mass of fallen material, since Stone 55 from the central trilithon lies broken in two across the recumbent Altar Stone.

Where are the missing stones?

If it is still remarkable that so much survives of Stonehenge and its surroundings, it is also notable that from some aspects it appears surprisingly ruined. Stonehenge has been little used since its Bronze Age abandonment, and much abused. In the course of time, many of the stones and their settings have fallen, been taken away, or broken up.

Although Stonehenge and its enveloping landscape ceased to have a ritual function in the middle of the second millennium BC, or thereabouts, it was far from forgotten. The stones provided shelter for travellers and a convenient hard surface upon which to construct a roadway that, until the late eighteenth century, went right through the enclosure. The fall of the great trilithon in 1797, for example, was attributed at the time to the long-term activities of gypsies who used to shelter beside it and light fires for warmth and cooking in pits that they dug close to its base.

Constructing a road may have provided at least one reason why some of the stones no longer exist, since in some cases – notably in the entrance close to the Heel Stone – stones may have been an obstruction and therefore removed or, in the case of the Slaughter Stone, half-buried. Broken stones may also have provided some sort of hard standing, as well as a ready

The Stonehenge setting today

Today Stonehenge, while still retaining its ability to awe, is a shadow of its former self – time, erosion and robbery having had their effect. Within the wider setting, the two Station Stones, the Heel Stone and the Slaughter Stone (now fallen) remain, while the stone circle (shown in greater detail right) only contains a proportion of its original setting.

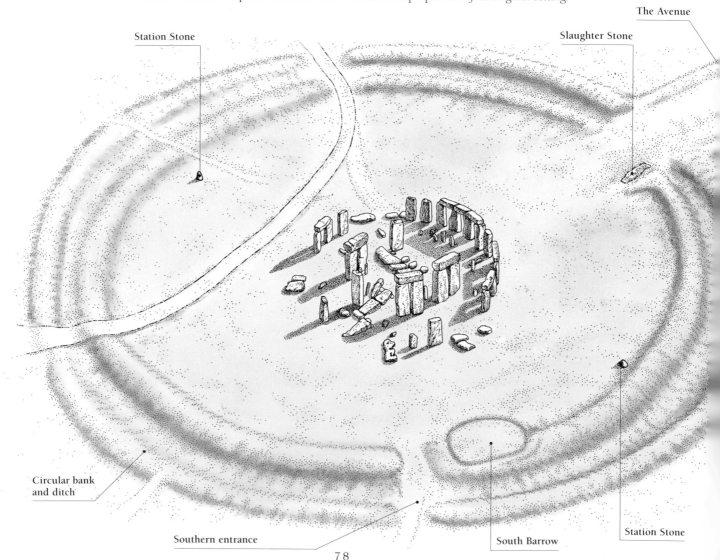

The Avenue

Station Stone

Slaughter Stone

Circular bank and ditch

Southern entrance

South Barrow

Station Stone

Horseshoe of sarsen trilithons

Altar Stone

Horseshoe of bluestones

Outer bluestone circle

Outer sarsen circle

Heel Stone

quarry for local farmers to build their houses and outbuildings, although it must be said that the extreme hardness of the sarsens may have made them less desirable. However, in an area largely devoid of good building stone, even sarsens might be acceptable, and certainly some older buildings on Salisbury Plain are partly constructed using this intractable material.

By comparison with the example of Avebury, it may be that superstition had a considerable part to play in the partial destruction of Stonehenge. When Stukeley came to inspect and record Avebury, he found local farmers were using methods of rapidly heating and cooling the great stones that stood in their fields – and obstructed their agricultural activities – to break them into smaller pieces that could more easily be taken away. However, some four or five centuries before, other stones were being taken down probably because they were regarded as pagan survivals.

Certainly by the sixteenth century, Stonehenge had largely reached the state in which it is seen today and systematic large-scale robbery was a thing of the past. Further weakening of the stone settings, which was

The stone circle today

The stone circle with its final placement of sarsens and bluestones, as it appears today. Only seventeen stones of the sarsen circle and three trilithon pairs remain upright, while many of the bluestones have fallen or remain as broken stumps and the Altar Stone lies recumbent.

fairly ominous by the opening of the present century, has been arrested by the programmes of propping and repair that have been associated with many of the investigations and programmes of excavation. Scattered throughout this part of Wiltshire, however, must be many pieces of the original Stonehenge that still go unrecognised.

Yet it is remarkable that any of these stones are still standing at all after the intervening millennia, while their erection and rearrangement were prodigious feats of procurement, engineering and organization. In the pages that follow, the questions about where the stones came from, how they reached their final destination at this particular point on Salisbury Plain and how they were put in place are addressed.

Bluestones

The bluestones were the first stones to arrive at Stonehenge. As they stand today, the outer circle consists of either undressed or roughly shaped blocks, while the inner horseshoe is composed of carefully shaped uprights; but probably – although we can never be sure – none of these stones was dressed when they first arrived on Salisbury Plain. The vexed question of how they got there in the first place has never been resolved, although a new consensus is emerging.

The igneous rock of the bluestones, which was formed from volcanic activity, is unlike any other stone found at or near Stonehenge. Since the geologist H.H. Thomas presented his original findings in 1923, it has been recognized that these stones had only one possible provenance: the Preseli Mountains in Pembrokeshire, in southwest Wales.

What special characteristics must the bluestones have had? Bluestone is perhaps a curious and imprecise description for this material: curious, because blue is not necessarily the colour that strikes the visitor, but rather a blotchy grey-brown; imprecise, because the stones are of different, if related, rock types: spotted dolerite, rhyolite, unspotted dolerite, altered volcanic ash, calcareous ash, tuff (rhyolitic ignimbrite), and a few pieces of sandstone with mica. The spotted dolerite is the most common type of rock among the surviving bluestones. The central Altar Stone also came from southwest Wales; it is usually identified as a greenish sandstone with mica, from the Cosheston Beds of the south coast, although other possibilities have been advanced.

Changing settings

The bluestones were brought to the site and erected there around 2550 BC (see p. 82), and were subsequently moved into their present positions as the stone settings evolved. Originally set in pairs in the dumbbell-shaped Q and R holes, they formed two concentric settings, although whether in a circle or an arc is still debatable. Two bluestones, later reused, have a tongue and a groove in their sides, so that they may have fitted together, perhaps with other bluestones worked in the same way that have since been lost,

The Preseli Mountains

Recognized since the 1920s as the unique source of the bluestones at Stonehenge, these hills themselves have many ancient monuments and tombs. One such stone circle may even have been removed complete to form the centrepiece of the earliest stone setting at Stonehenge.

while others have the 'mortice-and-tenon' fixing that was later used for the lintels on the sarsen stones (see p. 89). So the final structure may have been preceded by an even more complicated arrangement, or the first setting of the largest stones· may have incorporated bluestone arrangements that later disappeared.

After the sarsen stones were erected and the stone monument's circular structure was definitively established, there was probably a short-lived bluestone arrangement, now called Phase 3iii, using dressed and shaped stones somewhere in the interior; but the bluestone settings were frequently changed thereafter. Inside the great trilithon horseshoe more than twenty bluestones were carefully shaped and dressed into pillars, and erected in an oval formation, some time around 2000 BC. Other bluestones, less carefully selected and dressed, were installed in a circle within the outer sarsen circle. By 1900 or 1800 BC the oval setting of bluestones was rearranged to form the horseshoe and the stone settings had reached their final form. If there was intended to be yet another rearrangement, somewhere around 1600 BC, as the X and Y Hole evidence might indicate, it was abandoned before it was ever undertaken.

Stones taller than a man

Although they are now dwarfed by the sarsens which surround them, the bluestones themselves are far from inconsiderable in size and weight, those in the outer circle, for example, which are probably in a similar state to that in which they arrived, are on average 1.25 metres/4 feet wide and 0.75 metres/2½ feet deep, reaching a height of 2 metres/ 6½ feet, and therefore taller than a man. The dressed horseshoe pillars, although smaller, are themselves 0.6 metres/2 feet square and over 1.8 metres/ almost 6 feet high. Each must

Undressed and dressed bluestones

The bluestones in the inner horseshoe setting were carefully shaped and dressed into smooth pillars (far right) after arriving on Salisbury Plain, while those in the bluestone circle were generally left undressed (right).

therefore have represented a considerable feat in transportation, manoeuvring and engineering to be placed in an upright position.

In the context of Salisbury Plain, and indeed of Wessex, these stones are unique. Although other monumental stones, such as those at Avebury and West Kennet, were brought from elsewhere, the very unusual qualities of the bluestones and their far-distant origins, give them an importance out of all proportion to their size. Their origins perplexed early investigators, since it can be shown that these stones could only have come from outcrops in the Preseli Mountains. So how did they come to be standing on this particular spot, hundreds of miles away? What special significance can they have had?

There has been active debate on the transportation of the bluestones for decades. Essentially, the argument divides between those who believe that they were brought to Salisbury Plain by concerted human endeavour, and those who hold that the stones arrived through natural action, the process of glaciation. Each school of thought requires a particular suspension of disbelief, and each has had its devoted adherents.

How Did the Bluestones Get to Salisbury Plain?

The pendulum of scholarly and popular opinion has long swung between two explanations – human and glacial action. In the first instance, we are expected to acknowledge that Neolithic people were not the primitive savages of popular imagination, but were sufficiently organized (and highly so) to be able to transport substantial blocks of a very particular set of stones from a far-off land some 240 km/150 miles to Stonehenge. In the second instance, we must imagine a landscape on which large boulders rested, transported by the glaciers of the last Ice Age and left behind when the ice-cap retreated. Which hypothesis is it better to believe?

Human transportation

If we follow the first assumption then, since the stones are of a variety of geological types, they may well have formed an earlier monument of standing stones, which was raided, or else transported in its entirety, from Wales. That in itself is not implausible, since there are at least twenty-seven known monuments in southwest Wales formed in part, or in whole, from the same 'bluestone' materials. Most have been dated to 2000 BC or earlier, putting them in the same time-bracket as Stonehenge. They range from the two standing stones of dolerite (spotted and unspotted) at Cwm-garw, which lies within sight of the main spotted dolerite outcrops of Carnmenyn in the Preseli Hills, to stone circles at Waun-Mawn and Dyffryn Syfynwy. All these places lie within 10 km/6 miles of each other, and many of the monuments are clustered near the River Cleddau, which flows into the sea at Milford Haven. Detailed analysis of their chemical components has established convincingly that the majority of Stonehenge's bluestones can only have come from the outcrops at Carnmenyn.

For the bluestones to have been brought by human agency, they would have had to be transported by water. Overland transportation would have been entirely out of the question, given the terrain and the many areas of water between Pembrokeshire and Wiltshire, not least the Severn estuary and the Bristol Channel. Experiments undertaken in the 1950s demonstrated that it would have been entirely possible for stones like these to have been carried on canoes lashed together and navigated up even quite small waterways; how such craft would have fared in open waters is a much more difficult question to answer.

In order to make maximum use of water transport, the stones would have travelled around the whole southwestern peninsula and along to the Dorset coast. It would have been a feasible undertaking to travel up

A bluestone monument in the Preseli Mountains
The bluestones are known to have originated in the Preseli Mountains of Wales, where other bluestone monuments have been discovered. The cromlech or burial chamber of Pentre Ifan is one such monument.

the Avon to Amesbury, almost within sight of Stonehenge. There was certainly a thriving prehistoric port at Hengistbury Head, near the mouth of the River Avon. The shorter alternative would have been to travel up the Bristol Avon and its tributaries and to haul the bluestones across the intervening countryside, but there are many steep inclines and other obstacles in the way.

Is there any direct evidence that this was indeed how the bluestones got to Salisbury Plain? There are certainly tantalizing clues: a small piece of spotted dolerite has recently been discovered on Steep Holm, an island in the Bristol Channel, which would have been an obvious staging post, and a number of divers are convinced that a piece of bluestone lies on the bottom of the sea at Milford Haven. Otherwise, all remains conjecture.

Glacial action

What, by contrast, are the arguments for natural glacial, and not human, agency bringing the bluestones to Salisbury Plain? The extent of the ice-sheet across southwestern England and south Wales is still the subject of discussion and conjecture, but most commentators are united in their belief that the ice never reached as far as these chalk uplands, given the absence of obvious post-glacial features. The stones themselves have no visible signs of the scouring usually associated with the action of ice. Glaciers and ice-sheets certainly have enormous powers to transport large, single pieces of rock – but why should these rocks, and no others, all of a broadly similar size and from very particular hillsides in Wales, have been transported? Smaller fragments certainly did not find their way in an ice sheet, since no river pebbles of such glacial origin, or comprising these materials, have ever been discovered anywhere in the Avon system.

The argument for glacial origin rests in part upon a single piece of

Possible bluestone routes to Stonehenge

Water transport – either by sea around the southwestern peninsula of England, or by river along the Bristol Avon and its tributaries – probably enabled the bluestones to reach Stonehenge.

bluestone displayed in the Salisbury museum. This is supposed to have been taken from an excavation at Bowls Barrow – a long barrow some 18 km/11 miles away, and certainly of an earlier date than any stone setting at Stonehenge – and then to have been placed in the garden of Heytesbury House nearby. This evidence is probably deeply flawed: a bluestone was noted in Cunnington's 1801 excavation report, but he may well have misidentified it (or not recognized it as a secondary, later deposit in the barrow); there is no direct evidence to link that piece to one found many years later in a nearby garden. Many pieces of bluestone have gone missing over the years, and some may well still be garden adornments elsewhere.

Re-evaluation

For a long time, the argument in favour of human transportation was barely questioned; in recent years the arguments in favour of glacial origin have been taken more seriously. Considered evaluation of the evidence, however, still points squarely at the bluestones having been conveyed deliberately by Late Neolithic people and set up at Stonehenge. That requires a belief that these people were capable of such feats of organization and thought. The evidence of Stonehenge, and of considerable trade networks, suggests that they were. Coming as they did from a landscape rich in standing stone monuments, the bluestones may already have been an existing setting moved wholesale to Wiltshire: a trophy of war, an expression of priestly power, a gift perhaps?

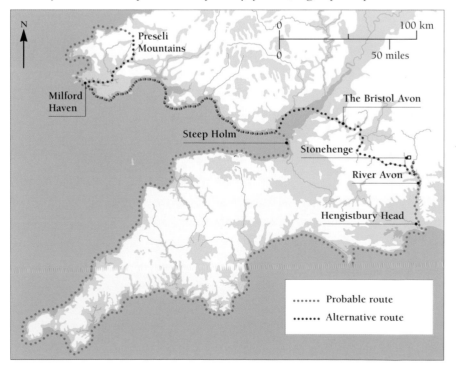

The Sarsen Stones

The larger stones that give Stonehenge its great visual impact are sarsen. These are natural blocks of a sandstone with a fine grain cemented together with a hard siliceous material. They formed up to 70 million years ago, in the geological Tertiary age when seabed chalk deposits were covered in sand. Where the sand was concreted into irregular blocks, then these sarsens would remain when the land was lifted up and the loose sand eroded. Sarsens are rare in Stonehenge's immediate neighbourhood; they too were imported into the Stonehenge area, although not from such a great distance as the bluestones, originating from the Marlborough Downs, some 30 km/18½ miles to the north. Local people used to call them 'greywethers', since they looked like recumbent sheep in their natural state, lying dotted around on the surface, or 'Saracen stones', as a comment on their strangeness – hence the name sarsen.

The great stone circle at Avebury, older and larger than Stonehenge's, was also made from sarsens, but they occurred locally to that site. Although sarsens are still visible on the Marlborough Downs today, especially in one section of Fyfield Down, none is remotely of the size of those transported to Salisbury Plain more than 4,000 years ago. Early observers at Stonehenge, in the seventeenth and eighteenth centuries, often convinced themselves that the sarsens could only in fact have been man-made, some form of sand-based composition that had been poured into moulds, such was their wonder at the hardness of the material and the regularity of the shaped stones.

Sarsen is a very hard stone – the survival of many parts of Stonehenge without serious erosion is itself testimony to that – which defeated most of the antiquarians' and early visitors' attempts to chip off large pieces or carve deeply into it (although some Georgian graffiti shows that there were those who triumphantly succeeded). Millstones in this region, for example, were frequently made of sarsen, until even more durable and appropriate stones were available from further afield; among the finds at Stonehenge was an early quern made of sarsen for grinding corn.

Yet these sarsen stones had almost universally been dressed: shaped into rectangular blocks, with integral projections and hollows as fixing features. In contrast to the bluestones, which were moved around a number of times, there is no evidence to suggest that there was ever anything but a single setting of the sarsens (although it is possible – if far from certain – that some of the outlying entrance stones, notably the Heel Stone, were installed earlier than the rest and may have been slightly relocated). The building of Stonehenge was therefore a very considerable architectural, as well as engineering, achievement.

The trilithon horseshoe

At the centre of the monument stands the horseshoe of trilithons (a name coined, as was so much at Stonehenge, by William Stukeley), five separate pairs of standing stones joined on top by horizontal lintels. They are graduated in height from the outer pairs to the central stones, from 6 metres/20 feet up to 7.3 metres/24 feet measured above the modern ground level. Their depth below ground varies from 1.2–2.4 metres/4–8 feet. So these are very substantial pieces of stone indeed, the heaviest weighing upwards of 40 tonnes. Of the largest central trilithon, the stone still standing had the deepest foundations – but its partner had some of the shallowest, and has long since fallen into the centre.

These trilithons must have been erected first, since they could not otherwise have been brought into the centre of the monument without disruption and rebuilding of the surrounding stones. The outer circle, about 30 metres/100 feet in diameter, originally consisted of thirty uprights spaced a little over 1 metre/3¼ feet apart. Each stone is, or was, 2 metres/6½ feet wide, and approximately half as thick, measured at ground level.

Dressing the sarsens

Although the great stones appear straight, that is in fact an optical illusion. The stones in the circle have a slightly convex taper in their 4-metre/13-foot height, which counteracts the foreshortening effect of looking

The sarsen trilithons (right)

The great trilithons are the overridingly dominant feature of the stone circle, the heaviest of them weighing upwards of forty tonnes. The lintels are fixed to the uprights by an ingenious mortice-and-tenon design.

The surfaces of the stones (overleaf)

Although the eroding forces of time and weather have had their effect on the stones, the tooling and the careful work which was used in the construction and dressing is visible everywhere. Some of the stones' faces were adorned with carved patterning, and some of the surface imperfections may be the residue of non-eroded decorative detail. It is also quite possible that some stones were particularly chosen for their surface detail, rough standing alongside smooth. The stones are also an object lesson for the study of lichen and other living material.

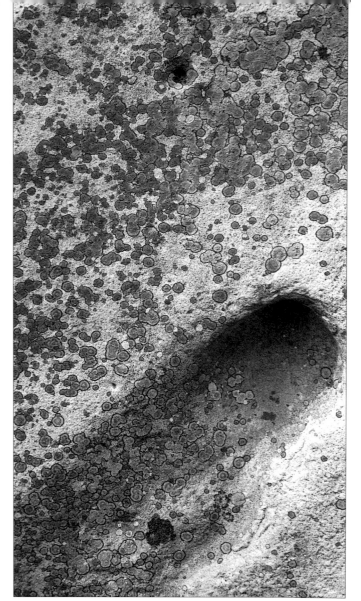

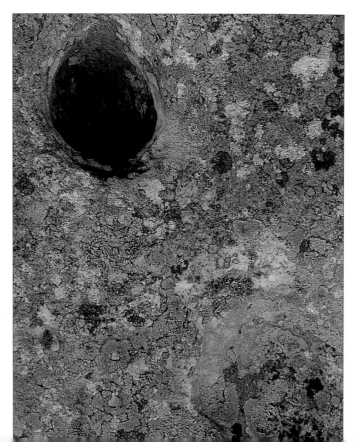

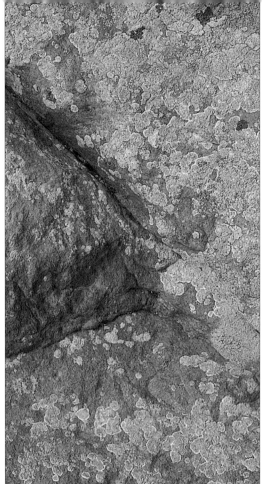

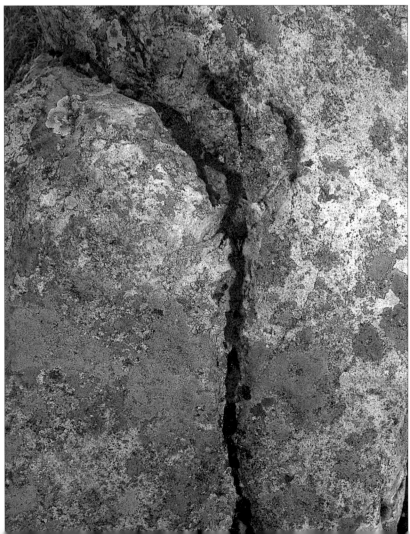

up at them from ground level – a version of the entasis (swelling outline) seen on the columns of classical temples, and another of the monument's architecturally sophisticated features. Although the uprights were not of equal widths (undoubtedly a reflection of the variability of the source material) they are all placed so that their centres are exactly the same distance apart, with the exception of two stones on the southeast that may have been set fractionally wider apart to form some kind of entranceway. The stone lintels on top were each shaped with a curve on their exposed edges, following the line of the circle. This was very much a designed structure.

The ways in which uprights and horizontals were fixed together were similarly ingenious. On the top of each upright, the stone was worked away to leave a projecting 'tenon', while in the corresponding place on the underside of the horizontal stones, material was hollowed out to form a 'mortice' into which the tenon could fit. The horizontal lintels were also linked together by a projecting 'tongue' on the side, which fitted into a 'groove' carved into its immediate neighbour. There is little room for error in this procedure, and it is remarkable how well all the standing elements still fit together.

There are many remarkable features to the sarsen ring. First, although the site is on a slight slope, the tops of the lintels are set almost exactly horizontal. This would be a great achievement for any building project in history. Second, the fixings acted not unlike a ring beam in a modern concrete structure, in that they held the circle together and gave it added strength. Getting, raising, and fixing these stones were among the consummate achievements of prehistoric peoples in Europe.

Modern attempts using cranes to replace some of the fallen stones, and experimental archaeology from building replicas, have shown how difficult the procedure of placing upright and lintel together actually is. One may only speculate what happened to the prehistoric work team that carved the hole in the wrong position...

Visual effects

The slight convex taper to the sarsens counteracts the foreshortening effect of looking up at them from the ground. This creates the optical illusion that the stones are straight.

The curve of the lintels

Seen from above, the outer curve on the exposed edge of the lintels, following the lines of the circle, becomes apparent. This was both a design and an engineering feature.

Commentators from the past

The great sarsen stones and the space they enclose have been a source of wonder for centuries – wonder that many commentators have recorded in memorable prose, and occasionally verse. The antiquity of the structure, and the ingenuity with which it was raised and made to fit together, excited earlier visitors just as much as their modern counterparts. These are just a few of the amazed and reverential descriptions that have survived from the past.

To this day there stand these mighty stones gathered together into circles – 'the old temples of the gods' they are called – and whoso sees them will assuredly marvel by what mechanical craft or by what bodily strength stones of such bulk have been collected to one spot.
Hector Boece, 1527

When you enter the building, whether on foot or on horseback, and cast your eyes around the yawning ruins, you are struck into an ecstatic reverie, which none can describe, and they only can be sensible of it that feel it... When we advance farther, the dark part of the ponderous imposts over our heads, the chasm of sky between the jambs of the cell, the odd construction of the whole, and the greatness of every part surprises.
William Stukeley, 1743

It is indeed remarkable that whoever has treated of this monument has bestowed on it whatever class of antiquity he was particularly fond.
Horace Walpole, 1786

The more we dig, the more the mystery appears to deepen.
Lt-Col William Hawley, 1927

The ignorant Rustic will with a vacant stare attribute it to the Giants, or the mighty Archfiend; and the Antiquary, equally misinformed as to its origins, will regret that its history is veiled in perpetual obscurity. The Artist, on viewing these enormous masses, will wonder that art could thus rival nature in magnificence and picturesque effect.
Sir Richard Colt Hoare, 1812

The retrieving of these forgotten things from oblivion in some sort resembles the art of a conjuror.
John Aubrey, 1665

Pile of Stonehenge! So proud to hint yet keep Thy secrets...
William Wordsworth

Mortice-and-tenon joints

A 'tenon' on the top of each upright was cleverly designed to interlock with a hollowed-out 'mortice' on the underside of the lintel (clearly visible above, and shown below in diagrammatic form). This may have recalled an earlier wooden form.

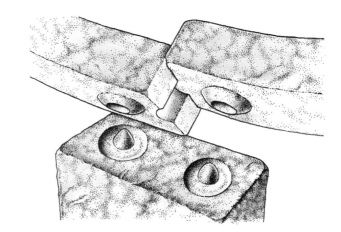

How Did the Sarsens Get to Salisbury Plain?

The boulders of sarsen stone lay some distance from Stonehenge across a broad valley, ensuring that their transportation to Stonehenge was an impressive feat of engineering in itself. The difficulties of moving huge stones across a landscape with at least one major hill to climb and others to descend, and limited technology and motive power available – principally human muscle – made a task which would be no trivial undertaking in a modern age of cranes and heavy lorries, a supreme physical and organizational effort. As archaeologists have begun to try practical experiments, at Stonehenge and other great ancient monuments in Egypt and elsewhere, so a variety of possible transportation techniques has emerged.

The only tools available to the builders were stone and natural organic material. These, however simple, were capable of achieving considerable results. Stone

Fyfield Down
Sarsen stones, although none the size of those that were taken to build Avebury and Stonehenge, still litter the north Wiltshire downland.

axes, for example, could be used to cut down trees, and the bark of the small-leafed lime tree supplied potential material for perfectly strong ropes. The inner bark of this tree, when soaked for a period of weeks, separates into ten or twelve layers, which are the strongest plant fibre native to England, and are capable of being twisted into ropes that could have been used to pull the stones and steady them on their journey. The trees, moreover, could also provide the wood on which the stones were transported.

The roller hypotheses

Most versions of how these stones were transported – whether at Stonehenge or the great pyramids of the pharaohs – suggest that they were moved on rollers, with a small army of men running with tree trunks from the rear of the stone to place them at the front, and so produce a conveyor-belt effect. There are various arguments against this as a likely method: such rollers would almost certainly have been crushed under the weight of the larger stones; forward motion is more easily achieved by a sliding action than by rolling; and practical experience suggests that it is inherently difficult to keep a heavy object on rollers moving in a straight line.

Recent investigations into the building of ancient Greek temples and the pyramids in Egypt have refined this argument. Experiments suggest that the great stones were surrounded by a protective casing which acted as a cradle – models of these cradles have recently been found inside the pyramids – allowing the stones to be rolled by a relatively small team towards their final position. When close by, they could have been slid into place simply on a dampened surface.

The sled hypothesis

A third, more likely hypothesis is that the stones were placed on some sort of sled, and pulled along a specially constructed wooden trackway – possibly greased with animal fat. Such a wooden route was well within the capabilities of prehistoric men: witness the skill shown in the construction and finish of Stonehenge, and the evidence of an extensive system of ancient trackways uncovered in the Somerset Levels. A specially prepared track also had the advantage of conserving the workforce's muscle power for the particular job in hand, rather than dissipating it following wayward stones and rollers. It would have been the task of a small, experienced team to construct a trackway in advance of the stone-pullers, possibly re-using each day the track that had already been passed over.

Even when climbing an incline, practical experiments undertaken on just such a trackway in 1995 showed that a group of a hundred people or so – many fewer than previous estimates of the numbers involved had suggested – was able to move a stone equivalent to one of the largest trilithons at something approaching walking speed, once the initial friction had been overcome. The volunteer labour force used only ropes, grease and a wooden trackway built from local timber. Whether, at Stonehenge itself, human muscle was the main motive power, or whether oxen and cattle were also used to help draw the heavy loads, is very much an open question.

The route

It is most likely that the smallest gradients were selected in advance to establish the route to Stonehenge. A line taken directly as the crow flies between the Marlborough Downs and Stonehenge would involve a substantial hill at one point (if not more), moving from the flatter River Kennet valley across the Vale of Pewsey up onto Salisbury Plain, and undulating land thereafter. Therefore the route taken with the stones was probably considerably further than the direct distance of 30 km/18 miles. It is impossible to estimate the numbers involved in the whole process at any one time, since there is no evidence as to whether the stones were brought a few at a time over many seasons or in larger numbers.

Such a process would have required both direction and considerable organization of manpower. We do not know over how long a period of time the construction of Stonehenge was being carried out – whether it took just a few years, or was a process lasting many centuries. The truth probably lies somewhere in between. If a trackway were involved, it would have been the work of a small group to prepare each section; the process of felling trees, making ropes, and making digging tools out of deer antlers may have involved many more, over a wider area. Given that animal husbandry seems to have been an important aspect of Late Neolithic agriculture, and that looking after animals produces slack as well as busy times of the day and of the year, the assembling of materials and the massing of the labour required to haul great blocks of sarsen stone may have been part-time, seasonal activities for the farming peoples who lived near and around Stonehenge.

Once they had succeeded in transporting these huge stones to their final destination, the builders of Stonehenge then had the equally daunting task of raising them into their final, erect positions.

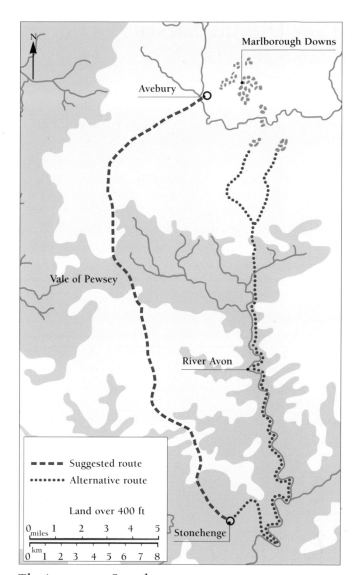

The journey to Stonehenge
It is likely that the smallest gradients, and not necessarily the most direct route, were chosen to convey the sarsens to Stonehenge. Two routes, one along the Avon valley, the other starting near Avebury before crossing the Vale of Pewsey, are suggested here.

Moving a 'sarsen'
Recent experiments have shown that even a stone equivalent to one of the largest sarsens could be moved using a wooden trackway and perhaps a hundred people.

Erecting the Stones

Once the stones were at Stonehenge, how did the builders put them up and fix them together? As has often been pointed out, the techniques used for fitting the stones together are wood-working rather than stone-working methods. That is one reason why archaeologists have speculated that there was a previous wooden version of the Stonehenge structure, which the stones replicated in some way. It has also been pointed out that the built solution is not only engineered, but over-engineered.

If the stone settings somehow derived from what had been there previously, they were certainly not a replica, since the post-holes show quite a different timber arrangement from the circles of stone. Techniques for the transportation, shaping and erection of large stones had already been developed in many parts of Neolithic Britain, so Stonehenge was not unique in that regard. It may be that, rather than not knowing the 'appropriate' engineering solutions and thus erring on the side of caution, the designers of Stonehenge consciously chose to employ techniques closer to working in wood for reasons of continuity, power or ritual that are now lost to us.

Raising the verticals

Excavation around the stones or in the pits in which stones once stood has shown that some pits, and certainly the largest ones, were cunningly dug with a sloping back edge. It would appear that the stone was then slid into the hole at an angle, before being pulled into an upright position. Even the deepest stone holes, for the great trilithons, might only have taken a couple of people three days to dig using antler picks (which have proved, when used by modern archaeologists, to be much more effective digging tools than they might appear). The easiest way to place the stone into its hole

Possible method of raising a vertical

First a foundation pit was dug, with a sloping back edge forming a ramp. The sarsen was then moved, base first, along rollers towards the ramp, until its centre of gravity lay just behind the leading roller. By levering, pulling and weighting the sarsen with

stones, it could then be moved to a standing position. It could be made fully vertical either with gangs of men hauling on ropes or with an A-frame providing leverage. Finally, packing material was used around the base to secure the sarsen in position.

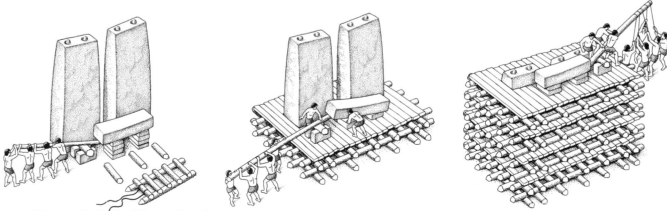

Possible method of adding a lintel

First the lintel was positioned on the ground, parallel with the vertical, then each end was alternatively lifted with levers and supported on timbers. Next a wooden deck supported by criss-crossed timbers was made and the upright transferred to rest on

this. The whole process was then repeated in stages until the lintel was level with the top of the vertical. It was then levered sideways to fit on the projecting tenon and the wooden support dismantled or reused.

would then have been to use a sort of seesaw action, changing the centre of gravity by pulling weights – probably other stones – along it, until the stone shifted from a prone position to stand in its hole at an angle of some 70 degrees from the ground.

Pulling the stone through the last 20 degrees to the vertical might well have proved one of the hardest tasks of all, requiring many hundreds of people, unless some lever system was in operation as well as ropes. A rudimentary A-frame, consisting of logs lashed together, would have provided sufficient leverage to require the services of considerably smaller numbers. Experiments in the summer of 1995 suggested that the difference between the two methods might have been a factor of four or five, from nearly 350 people pulling to just 75. Given the sophistication of design and construction methods used, it seems sensible to assume that the builders of Stonehenge were capable of devising these basic engineering skills, whether from first principles or on the basis of previous experience. Once the stone was fully upright, packing material in the form of smaller boulders, chalk, flints and stone fragments was used to secure it firmly in position. Just how firmly this was done is suggested by the numbers that remain standing to this day.

Adding the lintels

Even when the vertical stones had been raised, the task was far from over, since the horizontal lintels had to be put in place. Since even that piece of stone could weigh 9 tonnes and had to be placed way up high, other engineering and building principles were required. The conventional wisdom is that the lintels were raised gradually, using some sort of wooden crib: the lintel, standing on a platform of timbers beside the upright stone, would have been levered up so that more timbers could be placed underneath it, so it would be raised gradually to its final height, before being manoeuvred into position with other levers. However, excavation of the ground around the stones has suggested that, at least in some cases, an earth ramp was built beside the stones. Although that might have been used to slide a stone down and into its hole, it might equally have been used to drag a lintel up the slope and onto the top, using the materials to hand.

The sheer weight of the stones and the fragility of some of the materials – the ropes, the timbers – used in moving them would without doubt have led to the accidents and deaths that are rarely absent from any major construction site. The raising of the stones must have been a substantial investment in resources, manpower and lives.

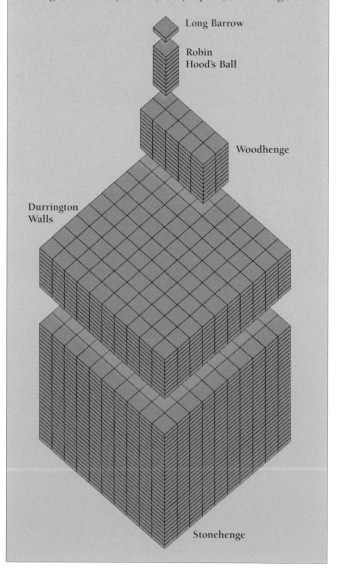

Megalithic Manpower

The sophistication and organization required to construct even the smallest of the monuments on Salisbury Plain – let alone something the size and complexity of Stonehenge – does not assist the belief that they were built by a primitive and barbarian people. The sequence of monuments seems to represent an ever-greater investment of time and labour. It has been estimated that it took 10,000 working hours to erect a long barrow and ten times as long – 100,000 manhours – to construct a causewayed camp. In the Late Neolithic, the time involved in building the larger structures was immense – a henge monument may have taken a million manhours. It has been estimated that Stonehenge, the largest of them all, had thirty million hours of work invested in it. Even though the figures are perhaps misleading in their exactness, they nevertheless represent orders of magnitude. To imagine that it took 3,000 times more effort to erect the great stone circle than the long barrow at Winterbourne Stoke is some index of the organizational power of the people of Stonehenge.

Long Barrow

Robin Hood's Ball

Woodhenge

Durrington Walls

Stonehenge

Tooling and Crafts

Manoeuvring the stones was not the only critical element. The sarsens (and also the inner bluestones) were all carefully dressed and shaped, with smoothed, convex, tapering faces, mortice-and-tenon and tongue-and-groove joints – and all this mainly in a stone remarkable for its hardness and resistance, and achieved with the most rudimentary of tools.

One of the most frequently found types of material in the many excavations of the Stonehenge site has been stone chippings – flakes and larger pieces of bluestone and sarsen that were removed in the process of dressing. Substantial portions of waste material must have been removed, especially to shape rounded boulders into squared-off stones, to cut down the top of an upright, leaving a single tenon standing up, and to gouge out a matching mortice in a lintel. Some of these fragments were used to pack the standing stones into their holes, while others were scattered over the monument floor or ended up, whether by accident or design, in many of the pits and holes dating from both earlier and later phases.

False start

The false starts on a mortice hole, upon what later became the upper surface of Stone 156, before the lintel was turned over and a mortice was made in the correct position on the other side (and similarly on the underside of Stone 122), are testimony to the care required when working the stone and the ease of making costly and time-consuming mistakes. During various excavations, certain areas (both inside the circle and outside) have been identified as 'sarsen floors' – working areas where the stones were honed into their final shape – given the volume of chippings and, in some cases, the remains of a hearth that would have kept the workers warm.

Stone mauls for dressing

Over two thousand pieces of worked sarsen have been catalogued from the Stonehenge site, the majority of which have been stone mauls, the very rudimentary tools used to shape the great stones. These were usually flattened spheres of sarsen (no other local stone being tough enough to work on this hard sandstone), and were used to pound the surface to work away the excess material. Many of them have been recovered from the packing material that helped support the standing stones that have now fallen: a case of either finding a way of getting rid of tools that had outlived their usefulness or, less prosaically, of deliberately placing with a stone the artefacts that had been used in its preparation. Careful examination of the condition of these mauls provides many clues to the manner in which they were used. Some of the mauls found were battered all over, others only around their 'waist'. Some had clearly been used for heavy pounding to cut away large volumes of waste stone, others had been smoothed by being used for final and more delicate work, employed with a rubbing or pecking type of action.

Sarsen hammerstones
Rudimentary sarsen 'mauls', ranging in size from a tennis ball to a soccer ball, were used to shape and dress the rough sarsen blocks.

94

Doubtless some smaller sarsen boulders were imported and broken up specifically for the purpose of providing tools, and there is evidence from the construction of many older local buildings that there were also some sarsen stones on Salisbury Plain (although not as large as those found to the north). Other tools would have been made from larger pieces that had broken off the worked stones, while occasionally other types of material were used, particularly quartzite pebbles. The average weight of these sarsen tools was just under 500 g/17½ oz, and most were in the range 200–1000 g/7–35 oz. By far the

largest maul weighed a massive 29 kg/63 lb, and it must have taken the concerted might of a small working team to wield it effectively.

Dressing the bluestones

Although there is considerable evidence for the dressing of the sarsens on-site, there is less to suggest quite where and how the bluestones were refined to their present shapes. Some of the worked tools that have been unearthed, including mauls, were made of bluestone. Fragments of bluestone are more scattered, and do not particularly cluster around the stones' settings, even in the inner horseshoe; nor are they particularly used as packing material. Whatever dressing went on within the circle would seem to have been only last-minute adjustments. There is also little evidence for the dressing and shaping of these stones away from the site, although a few signs of the stone-working of sarsens and bluestones have been uncovered beneath the present-day visitors' car park. Collections of fragments – from a variety of the blue-stone types – were recovered in both the 1940s and 1980s from close to the east end of the Cursus: whether these were from workings, or had been placed there for some other purpose, remains unclear.

Stone's value

Stone provided both the material for the monument and the tools for its construction. It also provided other tools that have been found at and around Stonehenge – principally axes, but also whetstones for sharpening, as well as some decorative objects. Some of these had been deliberately buried, possibly as votive objects or as part of a dedication ritual, others mislaid or discarded. One of the most exciting discoveries at Stonehenge in the course of the 1950s was the recognition that the surfaces of the sarsens had not only been smoothed, but also decorated. Incised patterns were noticed, cut into the hard surface with the same stone tools that had been used for dressing: first one pattern, representing a dagger, and then more were spotted, usually representing axeheads. Such tools had not only made Stonehenge, they were found represented upon it.

Fine tooling on a sarsen

The smooth surfaces of sarsens such as this one are testimony to the immense care and skill that went into dressing the stones. Despite the onslaught of time and erosion, they have survived remarkably intact for more than three millennia. Some sarsens were not only smoothed, but also decorated with incised patterns (see p. 96).

Decorating the Stones

Although it had long been suspected that deliberate carvings may have been made onto the surface of the sarsens at Stonehenge, and some had been tentatively identified in 1924, it was not until 1953 that a positive identification was first made. The date and time were precisely recorded, 5 p.m. on 10 July, by the discoverer of the first carving, Professor Richard Atkinson. Once one had been identified, new sightings came thick and fast, especially when people knew what they were looking for and peered at the stones in favourable lighting conditions in the late afternoon. The majority of the carvings represented axes, but the first had been a dagger, and other less distinct objects and shapes

The two most decorated sarsens

Stone 53 (left), one of the central trilithons, contains at least fourteen axe carvings, as well as more modern graffiti; Stone 4 (right), from the eastern side of the outer circle, has an abundance of carvings, although some of the more obscure ones may simply be surface imperfections.

have been seen. Most of the carvings were produced by creating a shallow, negative impression through pounding and rubbing away at the stone surface, although some also had a deeper edge incised to make the outline clearer.

Investigations and hypotheses

A series of investigations into the carvings has been carried out, ranging from taking rubbings on tissue paper and making plaster casts and latex moulds to stereometric photography, which gives a three-dimensional view of the surface of the stone. Twelve stones have been clearly identified as having carvings on them; and, perhaps significantly, they are fairly symmetrically disposed, both in the horseshoe of the great trilithons and on either side of the north-eastern entrance. The largest number counted on any single stone is twenty-six (on Stone 4 from the outer sarsen circle), although only about a dozen are distinctive enough to be positively identified and others may just be surface imperfections or erosions. Stone 53, one of the trilithon uprights, on which Atkinson first saw the dagger motif (which is some 30 cm/12 inches long), also bears at least fourteen axe carvings. By chance, it is also one of the most graffiti-decorated stones with carving from more modern times, including the initials ICD and WC and the legend ION: LUD: DE TERRE. Although various attempts have been made to identify the latter person, all have so far proved unsuccessful.

An Earth Goddess carving?

Additionally, but much more controversially, further figures have been identified, notably a shape on Stone 57 (another of the trilithon uprights and opposite Stone 53 in the horseshoe), which is said to represent an earth goddess. Professor Atkinson described this roughly rectangular outline 1 metre/3¹/₄ feet high, with a small projection in the centre of the top side, as 'not unlike the outline of an old-fashioned tea-cosy'. Although some observers have dismissed this carving in particular as just a surface anomaly, others are convinced — especially as it appears to be one of the symbols with a more deeply incised edge — that it does represent a conventionalized human shape, of a sort which is found in some monuments in Brittany but is otherwise unknown in Britain. Others still will note that this stone had fallen in 1797 and was re-erected in 1958, so that the carving may have been the work of a later wag — albeit one with considerable industry and purpose. Given the numbers of features that have now been identified, some of the circular markings also found on the stones may not be surface imperfections, as is usually assumed, but other carvings of the Neolithic cup-mark type that are commonly found throughout parts of northwestern Europe.

All of these carvings seem to be at or below eye level, although some others higher up on the stones may still await identification. This suggests, however, that the carvings were executed once the stones had been erected. The axeheads themselves are of a known type from the Early Bronze Age. Bronze-flanged axes of this type (and size) dated to around 1500 BC have been discovered in buried hoards across Wessex.

Before or after Mycenae?

These carvings have a very particular place in the history of the interpretation of Stonehenge. The distinctive dagger, the first carving to be seen, appeared to be Mycenaean. Here, then, was a powerful link to the known ancient world; Professor Atkinson developed an elaborate thesis linking Stonehenge with the eastern Mediterranean, and hoped to show that a Mycenaean prince was buried within Silbury Hill. Only a few years later, the radiocarbon dating revolution had overtaken the Mycenaean connection — Stonehenge, and these carvings, were far older, rather than deriving from this supposedly more sophisticated society. The identification of a distinctive Mycenaean shape may have been more the fulfilment of a hope overwhelming objective reality.

The carvings are, as far as may be discerned,

Axe and dagger carvings

The dagger carving on Stone 53 was the first to be identified and suggested parallels with the royal graves at Mycenae. The carved axes on either side of it were discovered soon afterwards.

another of Stonehenge's many very special features; this type of symbolism is not very common in British pre-history. The fact that the carvings, at least in their profusion, are so particular to Stonehenge has been used by some, notably Aubrey Burl, to argue that Stonehenge was probably built by people originating in Brittany. There, especially in the area around Morbihan, there are not only huge megalithic creations, but also many more examples of carvings such as these upon the stones. The 'earth goddess' in particular is much more of a Breton than British feature. There was undoubtedly considerable interchange over the millennia between the peoples living on the British and French coasts, which may account for some shared features; yet Stonehenge is unlike any comparable French structure — and is younger than many of the most important ones.

Additionally, there was some tradition of decoration in British monuments. Many examples in both Ireland and Brittany are of much earlier date or are abstract rather than naturalistic in form. There are, however, a few known examples of similar carvings, in Argyll and Kilmartin and, closer to home, in Dorset, which suggest that these axes and daggers, and perhaps even the so-called earth goddess, are not entirely unique and inexplicable. Most other carvings are associated with burial contexts — usually discoveries in barrows and other mounds — so if the Stonehenge evidence is taken to be a part of the same tradition, it may help give the monument a particular significance in a funerary context.

THE PEOPLE
OF STONEHENGE

Philip Crocker's engraving of the
"Shaman's necklace" found at Upton Lovell.

T HERE ARE STILL many things to discover about the people who built the monuments of the Stonehenge landscape. We want to know where and how they lived, how they died and how their remains were treated afterwards; what their surroundings were like, and how the landscape in which they lived changed; what influenced their ways of life; what they ate and how they caught or grew it; what tools and material goods they had, and how those were traded. Through these enquiries we may also be able to uncover more about the varied uses to which Stonehenge and the neighbouring landscape features were put. They provide the opportunity to learn more about the very forms of society in which the people of Stonehenge lived.

The essence of archaeology is deriving a picture of the past from the snapshots given by material remains and the residue that past occupation has left, together with the context of its time and place. Artefacts may come to the surface, while the landscape can contain visible clues as to how it was previously occupied. When a site is dug with care, what is found – including the 'ghosts' in the soil of structures and objects that had once been there – can be recorded. Surveying techniques reveal structures, sometimes otherwise unsuspected, beneath the land's surface. Chance finds, and objects discovered in earlier – and perhaps less careful – investigations, are then added to the picture. Objects may be beautiful, or they may seem mundane; sometimes they survive intact, more often they are broken and fragmentary. Some items that are collected may not even be objects in the generally accepted sense, but – like snails found in soil samples – provide equally vital clues to the past. Likewise, techniques from a great array of disciplines are now brought to bear in the course of archaeological investigation.

New genetic, demographic and linguistic approaches, although in their infancy, will undoubtedly open new possibilities for research, in the way that microscopic environmental data has done recently. Research into the coming of agriculture and its relationship with the domination of new cultures over old, as well as the questions of assimilation, adaptation or conquest in that process, all give further life to the societies of Stonehenge and its era.

Dating

When we think constructively about the past, we want to know what happened in what order. Thus dating is the other important aspect of archaeology alongside this series of snapshots. To achieve that, examining in sequence the layers beneath the surface in which objects are found, identifying artefacts from particular time periods, and the application of techniques such as dendrochronology and radiocarbon dating (see p. 16), are all vital forms of investigation.

Once assembled, all the clues from one site or from many places begin to build up an interpretation – a picture that may be influenced by the particular concerns of the individual archaeologist, but a view of the past all the same. The different elements combine to allow us to imagine how people farmed and traded, what sort of political organization they had and what their religious beliefs may have been. Imagination and inference are essential parts of the archaeologist's stock in trade, and we need a great deal of both in trying to discern the lives of the people of Stonehenge.

A Late Neolithic pot

Flat-bottomed for cooking, Grooved Ware pottery seems to have originated in Orkney. By 2800 BC it was widespread in eastern Britain but several examples have been found near Stonehenge.

A Changing Landscape

From intensive investigation at Stonehenge and its surrounding area we know a great deal about the people who, over the ages, have built on the land's surface and dug into the ground. Now, with recent advances in investigative techniques, we are discovering more about the landscape itself, both in the Stonehenge region and elsewhere; and from that we may begin to get a far better understanding of how the people who built these places actually lived and worked.

When we look at Stonehenge and its setting today, we see a classic southern English downland landscape: close-grazed grassland clothing the smooth contours of the chalkland on which the monuments were built. The shifts that have taken place in farming since the Second World War, with the advent of artificial fertilizers and

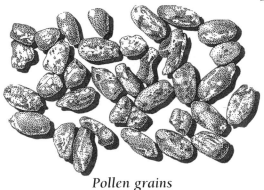

Pollen grains

Pollen grains found in different soil strata allow archaeologists to map changing vegetation patterns.

a greater emphasis on arable farming, have had a significant effect upon the Stonehenge landscape. More land has been put under the plough, which has had archaeological repercussions, since some prehistoric remains were being ploughed out until wider and stricter safeguards were put in place. Ploughing of these chalklands has certainly not been a new phenomenon, since at various times in the historic past – in the High Middle Ages, and during the Napoleonic Wars – crops were a significant element in the local farming economy, while for centuries farmers have been grubbing out ancient features that were getting in their way.

Nevertheless, for the most part this has been a pastoral, animal-raising region, with non-intensive agriculture the enduring keynote. The underlying archaeology has been less disturbed than would have been the case in many other places. One of the significant advances in investigative techniques in recent decades, alongside such new methods as radiocarbon dating and non-intrusive electromagnetic surveying, has been the exploitation of environmental data, which has benefited considerably from the relatively undisturbed land surface.

The Mesolithic landscape

Before 4500 BC, most of the landscape was covered in pine and hazel forest, with marshy floodplains running along the bottom of the river valleys. The earliest human settlements can be traced to the areas of cleared woodland within the forest.

Rough open savannah grassland

Willow, carr and sedge fenn

Birch, pine, hazel, oak and elm wood

N

Evidence in the soil

Archaeologists have tended to dig in order to discover objects, or their traces, in the soil. Now the soil itself has become a major feature of attention. Charred seeds, fragments of charcoaled wood and the remains of animals all help to reveal which plants were used by the people of the past (including, perhaps surprisingly, a grape pip at the causewayed enclosure of Hambledon Hill) and which animals provided their food. Since these forms of evidence have usually come from specific contexts, namely the pits in which material was deliberately deposited (as at Coneybury), or the ritual placing of items such as cattle jawbones (as in the Stonehenge ditch), the environmental evidence is limited in what it can say about the general pattern of life, as opposed to the deliberate actions of those feasting and taking part in ceremonial activities. Only

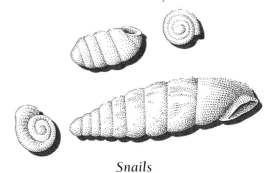

Snails

The habitats of different snail species are well-known. By dating their shells, changes in the landscape over the millennia can be deduced.

where – as in the packing around the houses on Orkney – refuse and general middens have survived is the detritus of everyday living preserved.

General ways of life and the physical environment may be better discovered by looking at microscopic evidence: at the land snails that are found in the various soil layers, and at pollen. On the chalkland, pollen sequences are unfortunately rare, although snail shells are readily found in the excavated soils; the flood-plain of the nearby River Avon has, however, yielded long-running sequences of pollen trapped in the soils, which extend back into the seventh millennium BC. Different concentrations of identifiable types of pollen, and the variety of species of snail depending on the vegetation that existed at the time, provide a remarkably detailed picture of what the environment was like at various points in the past.

The earliest and in some ways the most satisfyingly complete archaeological material has come from the post-holes that were discovered in the present-day car park at Stonehenge (see p. 44), which have turned out to be very ancient indeed. The eighth-millennium BC posts were taken from the wildwood landscape. They

The Early Neolithic landscape

By 3000 BC human activity had completely transformed the landscape. Much of the forest had disappeared, leaving open grassland interspersed with the arable plots of the first farmers. The earliest monuments have also appeared in the landscape.

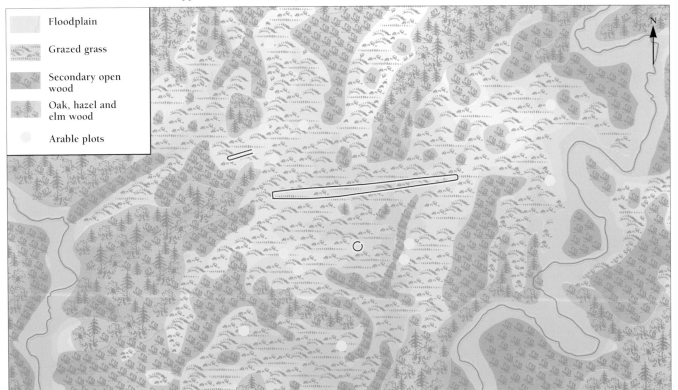

Floodplain

Grazed grass

Secondary open wood

Oak, hazel and elm wood

Arable plots

were the trunks of great pine trees, and what is now downland was then covered with open hazel and pine woodland. Settled farming had yet to arrive in the British Isles, and the population (which had migrated here by 10000 BC in the wake of the last Ice Age) lived by gathering and hunting among the tall trees of the woods and forests that covered most of Britain's land surface. Lime trees later came to be the dominant species in the mixed woods of the southern lowlands, as the climate became warmer and the pine woods that had previously covered huge areas retreated to colder and higher reaches.

Changing vegetation

The soil at Stonehenge was much deeper and richer than it is today, or even than it was in the Late Neolithic period. Perhaps 1 metre/3¹/₄ feet of soil has been washed or blown away since a group of Mesolithic people cut down four tall pine trees to make their totem poles. It is likely that a clearing was made in the forest to accommodate them (and whatever ceremonies or functions may have been associated with them), and it is even possible that the action had a

The Middle Neolithic landscape

By the time the timber monument at Stonehenge was being built the woodland was more open and varied, and there was more downland for cattle, sheep and deer grazing. As farming developed, emmer and other cereal crops were introduced.

long-term influence on the vegetation of the area. Although Stonehenge was probably not used, at least for ceremonial purposes or for settled living, for another 4,000 years, the woodland may not have grown back into its previous state, given the slowly warming general climatic conditions.

A varied landscape

The Early Neolithic Age, although not represented by any specific development at the Stonehenge site itself, was clearly the period when human activity within the surrounding area began, at Robin Hood's Ball (see p. 44) and the various long barrows. The soil underneath the later earth bank at Stonehenge contains pollen and snails that indicate that this was an area of open grassland, the wildwood having been substantially cleared in the neighbourhood. Similar findings have been recorded for the other important local henge monuments at Woodhenge and Durrington Walls (see pp. 54 and 56).

This was still not the open landscape familiar to us, since charcoal fragments indicate that there were elm, ash, oak, hazel and yew trees in the neighbourhood. The causewayed enclosures, for instance, were probably constructed in extensive clearings. Animal remains indicate not only the deliberate herding of domesticated cattle, sheep and pigs, but also that the people hunted deer, wild cattle, beaver and fish. A farming culture had reached Britain by 4500 BC or so, and

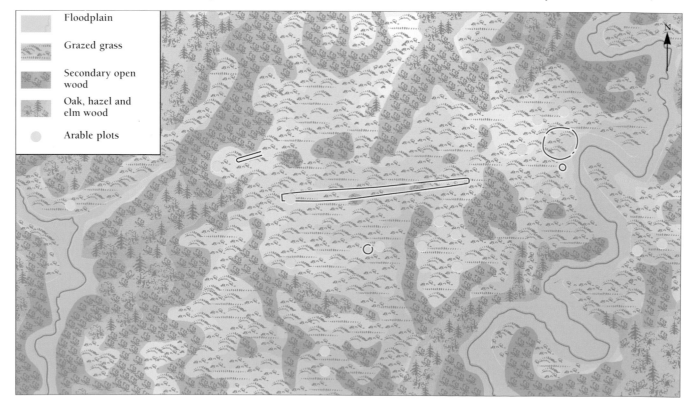

Floodplain

Grazed grass

Secondary open wood

Oak, hazel and elm wood

Arable plots

farmers coexisted with the hunter-gatherers for a long period thereafter. Stonehenge's was a very varied landscape in 4000–3500 BC: areas were locally clear-felled and subsequently allowed to regenerate. In the open areas of grass and shrub, the inhabitants kept animals and lived themselves, while they hunted in the surrounding wilder woodland and in the wooded river valleys. A few remains of cereal grains also suggest that crops were being grown in small patches.

Grazing and crops

By the Middle Neolithic era, when the monument at Stonehenge itself was first being built, the evidence points to there being a greater extent of open grazed downland in the vicinity, with more open woodland which had more varied species. A much more recognizable farming system was developing. Areas such as the King Barrow Ridge (see p. 51), which had previously been wooded, were now used as established grassland for grazing. Cattle, sheep and possibly deer grazed in these extensive clearings. Charred grains of emmer – a relatively poor wheat grain variety that was an important component of developing farming

The Late Neolithic landscape

During the Late Neolithic barrows were cut in the now well-established grassland, while the landscape began to be partitioned into arable plots where more cereal crops were grown. There may also have been some woodland regeneration.

systems – and other cereal crops that have been found in many locations, including the King Barrow Ridge and the nearby Cursus (see p. 46), also suggest that farmers were growing more in the way of arable crops in these open areas.

By using stone axes to cut down trees, or by ringing the bark and burning stumps, there had been substantial clearance of woodland throughout the British Isles. It might be expected that, without fertilizers, the crops grown in these cleared areas would soon exhaust the soils, but experiments undertaken in Denmark have suggested that soil fertility in these early fields may have held up surprisingly well.

Cultivation and soil erosion

Later in the Neolithic age, when Coneybury Henge (see p. 45) was being constructed and the stone monument was being built at Stonehenge, the environmental data becomes more extensive. The available information gives a much more rounded picture of what the area must have looked like. The barrows of the King Barrow Ridge and those nearer Amesbury were constructed in well-established grassland – the barrows on the ridge were in fact built from turf cut from a wide area of downland – while Stonehenge was also within an area of pasture. What woodland there was tended to be more open, with a great deal of scrub oak and hazel. More cereal crops were being grown, and over a wider area.

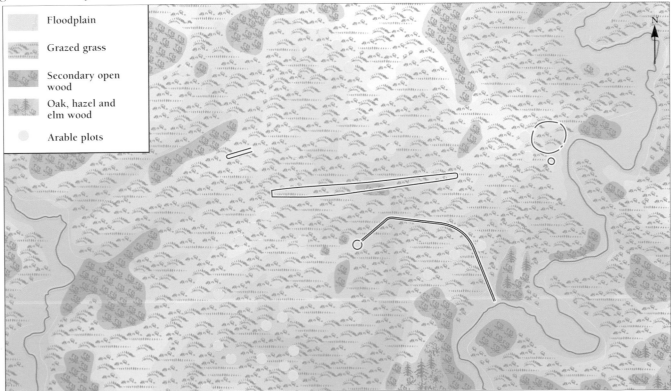

Floodplain

Grazed grass

Secondary open wood

Oak, hazel and elm wood

Arable plots

Some of the local evidence is contradictory, and until recently it was thought that Stonehenge itself had been abandoned for a while, before being reoccupied; current analysis now suggests that this belief is unfounded, although woodland regeneration did occur in at least some parts of the wider surrounding area. Settlement was certainly more dispersed than it had been, judging by the scatter of pottery and of tools, and more areas were being cultivated. To take one graphic example: the land beneath one of the Amesbury barrows, excavated in the early 1960s, had previously been ploughed, or, more accurately, ripped with an ard – a form of proto-plough that scored the land surface but did not turn the soil. More land cultivation inevitably led to some soil erosion, for the depth of the soil on the chalk upland was diminishing over time. It seems that it also entailed the necessity (as in the North Kite area south of Stonehenge) of partitioning the landscape in order to protect the arable areas from being eaten by the herds of animals.

Field systems

In later periods still – the Middle and Late Bronze Ages, when Stonehenge itself had gone out of active use – there were much larger and more extensive field systems in the region, while the woodland cover survived only in a few pockets. These fields are still evident in some places in the neighbourhood (such as the slope of the Till valley side). They are visible as 'lynchets', the characteristic terraces on slopes, which are the result of soil movements against the low stone walls that divided these early fields, and as the network of field boundaries that may still be traced in various parts of the Stonehenge region, and indeed in other parts of the Wiltshire chalk uplands. Some experts now believe that these field systems may even date from an earlier period. Farming populations were living locally, and clearly were long established there. The later Bronze Age settlement at Winterbourne Stoke is evidence of how and where people lived.

Agricultural tradition

From its origins in the Middle East and eastern Mediterranean, farming gradually spread westwards across Europe, reaching Britain by 4500 BC, or even earlier, and coexisting at first with the established hunter-gatherer lifestyle.

Hunter-Gatherers

The earliest inhabitants of the area around Stonehenge of whom we are aware were there some 10,000 years ago. The existence of land bridges between Britain and both Ireland and Europe meant that they would have had less difficulty in reaching Britain from Europe than later migrants. Yet there were few open areas that would have been particularly attractive to settled colonization. The forest cover was dense and extensive. Most early communities lived on the coastal fringe or the edges of the upland forests, where tree cover was thinner and the animals that they hunted were more readily spotted and trapped.

Deer, wild cattle, smaller mammals, fish and many other sources of food were available in the forests and rivers of southern Britain, including wild fruits, nuts and berries, and green plants. The only domesticated animal was the dog, which was kept for its usefulness in hunting, while the stone tools were those of a hunting culture using knives and scrapers. It was a transient life, following the seasons and the wildlife; groups tended to move from the uplands in summer to the warmer lowlands and coastal margins in winter. Population densities can only have been low; it has been calculated that a hunter-gatherer society needs 3–12 sq km/1–4½ sq miles of land per head of population. Little is known about the inhabitants' dwellings, which are likely to have been temporary assemblages of stout sticks and leaves.

An organized society

Yet there is the enigmatic existence of the exceedingly early pine post-holes at Stonehenge, which suggests not only that there were people in the region at the time, but also a greater degree of organization than this general picture of an endlessly shifting population might suggest. The posts may have had a practical purpose, in supporting nets or fences into which wild animals might be driven, but it is tempting to believe – especially given their size – that they had non-practical functions and were in fact totem-pole-like objects of veneration or monumental memorials.

No other artefacts of a Mesolithic date have been found in the Stonehenge landscape. But excavations in water-logged areas on continental Europe, for example

10000 BC	8000 BC	4500 BC	4000 BC
• Ice Age ends; hunter-gatherers cross land bridge to British Isles	• Land bridge to Continent severed	• First indications of farming in British Isles	• Farming communities established in British Isles

in Denmark, have demonstrated the great woodworking and boat-making skills that Mesolithic populations had – skills that are only exceptionally represented in the archaeological record.

The advent of farming

Hunter-gatherer activity continued for a very long period and well into the succeeding Neolithic age, but the advent of farming and a more settled form of existence became the norm, although there is still controversy over exactly when farming arrived in Britain.

At the same time as the earliest poles were being erected at Stonehenge, farming was already being developed in the lands of the Near East. Wild grass species and animals were progressively tamed and bred to improve ease of handling and yields. Sheep, cattle, goats and pigs – often smaller than their wild counterparts – were herded and kept in forms of enclosure, alongside the cultivation of larger and better cereal crops in fields. Certainly by the period 6000–5500 BC farming practices had reached central Europe and were expanding westwards over the light soils of north-western Europe into the Netherlands, France and the Scandinavian-German borderland.

From this springboard, domesticated animals and plants were introduced to the British Isles, by boat, since the land bridge had long gone. We cannot say whether the boats brought newcomers eager for new lands to colonize – or whether the native population changed to a farming way of life through contact with Europe and brought back the animals and crops that they encountered on their travels. The genetic make-up of Europe does suggest that there was greater migration than currently prevailing beliefs sometimes allow. Certainly, farming has usually been adopted as a response to increasing pressure of numbers on a fragile environment. Rather than necessarily choosing to settle down, the Mesolithic and Early Neolithic peoples may have had to do so in order to support an ever-growing population.

Field systems
The clearly defined boundaries of these Celtic fields, at Bishopstone in Wiltshire, were probably established in the earliest farming phases by those who wanted to place their own stamp on a piece of land.

Settled Agriculture

Farming probably arrived in the British Isles in the period 4500–4000 BC, although there is limited evidence to suggest that some farming communities may have been present in Ireland somewhat earlier, and parts of England were cleared of their forest cover before that date. Hunter-gatherers and farmers probably coexisted, since each needed different environments in which to live: coastal and upland areas, as distinct from land with light soils near rivers.

The environmental evidence, from charcoal, grain, pollen and snails, indicates the extent of the spread of agriculture throughout the period of Stonehenge's construction and use, as well as the variety of farming methods employed in the area. Although it is tempting to believe that new ways are usually the result of new people coming in, whether by force or peaceful immigration, older ways may have been adapted, either as a response to changing circumstances or by assimilating newcomers and their novel ideas. In the Stonehenge area, as elsewhere, the story seems to have

3000 BC	2500 BC	2000 BC	1500 BC
• Earliest fields in Ireland and Cornwall	• Textile production in British Isles	• Cereal-growing firmly established in British Isles	• Field systems in British Isles

been one of gradual and piecemeal change, winning new land from the forest and often employing a practice of shifting agriculture.

'Slash and burn' cultivation is a feature of many native societies, where land is relatively plentiful and the value of fertilizing the fields is not required or recognized. In these circumstances, where the clearance of land is a continuous process and crop-growing moves with the margin of clearance, areas that had been cleared and then deserted subsequently tended to revert to woodland and scrub. There is certainly some evidence for that at Stonehenge, although the main thrust seems to have been towards greater clearance and an ever-larger amount of land being devoted to both crops and animals, a feature appropriate to its evident status and importance. The areas around the monumental centres on the chalklands of the south and west were opened up first, and clearance gradually spread throughout most areas of the country; even the upper Pennine slopes and Dartmoor were cleared between 1800 and 1200 BC.

The stamping of territory

Fields were dug with spades and ards, the heavier ones doubtless drawn by oxen; some field boundaries probably date back to the earliest period of farming, suggesting that once land had been cleared, those acquiring it wanted to place their stamp upon it. That is also suggested by the fact that cleared land was used for the erection of the territorial markers of substantial graves and earthwork monuments. Unless more evidence is uncovered in the same vein as the Mesolithic post-holes at Stonehenge, it would seem that this stamping of territory and individuality represented a new departure.

Early dwellings

Earthworks often survive, but evidence for the houses in which these early farming communities actually lived is almost impossible to find. Isolated examples (in Wales, Ireland and Scotland) suggest that the very earliest houses were rectangular halls of some size. Slightly later houses of the period 3500–3000 BC, such as those uncovered at Fengate near Peterborough, in the Essex coastal marshes, in Derbyshire, and above all the Neolithic houses on Orkney (see p. 68), were relatively compact. The Lismore Fields houses in Derbyshire, for example, were each barely 5 x 8 metres/ 16½ x 26 feet. Except for places like Orkney and Dartmoor, where stone was the only available material, these must have been flimsy structures, and the houses of Early Bronze Age peoples can usually have been no

better. Where these houses have been uncovered – like the one fortuitously preserved underneath a Saxon burial mound at Sutton Hoo – they are often irregular in plan, and built of stakes. They may have been fairly temporary structures, and suggest that in the Early Bronze Age at least some of the farming people were heavily engaged in animal husbandry, with cattle herding and migration forming an essential feature of the farming economy. On Dartmoor (see p. 66) the complexity of Bronze Age settlement is clearly visible in the range of stone-built dwellings there, from single units to groups that were almost villages in scale.

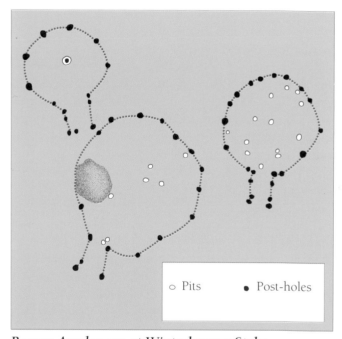

○ Pits	● Post-holes

Bronze Age houses at Winterbourne Stoke
The remains of three wood and thatch houses, the largest 8 metres/26 feet across, include porches and cooking pits.

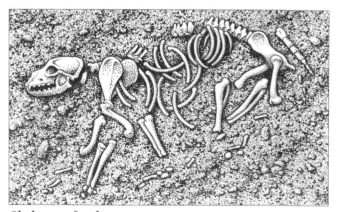

Skeleton of a dog
From an early date dogs were domesticated for hunting, before later herding the increasing numbers of sheep, cattle and goats.

Although the dating of the Dartmoor houses is still controversial – with a tendency to push them further back in time – they are broadly representative of the style of house that can be seen in the Middle to Late Bronze Age. Small groups of these wood and thatch houses, usually circular in plan and reasonably sized, were dotted across the settled farming landscape. The cluster of houses discovered during road building close to the Winterbourne Stoke roundabout, near Stonehenge (see p. 48), was typical in many regards; there are other examples built to a broadly similar plan and size in Sussex and Cornwall. The three houses had entrance porches, and each had clearly demarcated areas within their compact size for cooking and craft working.

A more settled existence

Sheep provided wool, and flax provided the raw material for linen. Evidence for the home-based production of these textiles survives in the form of loom weights and the like from around 2500 BC, suggesting that in the middle part of the Bronze Age the farming economy and domestic economy were closely intertwined. In the environmental data from Stonehenge, the evidence suggests that – just as in the present day – both arable and pastoral types of

Jarsholf Bronze Age village, Shetland

These well-preserved Neolithic houses on Shetland were built of stone, rather than less durable materials prevalent in other parts of the country. They have survived by being covered in sand and earth, which has been left to protect the remains.

agriculture were important, and combined (again like today) with the special responsibility of looking after the complex body of earth, timber and stone monuments there.

In the period of the construction of the stone settings at Stonehenge, crop and animal farming both became more extensive, with field boundaries becoming increasingly permanent. Crops became more important and their cultivation more specialized, while the population was certainly more settled. From the evidence of very large scatters of pottery found on the surface in many parts of the Stonehenge area, for both the Late Neolithic and the Early Bronze Ages, it would seem that farming populations were well established and that there was a considerable local population.

This has implications for the long-running debate over the construction of such an important edifice as Stonehenge, as well as for the many other monuments. If – as now appears likely – farming was firmly and long-established in this area, which was also among the most important concentrations of monuments in southern England, then there was already a substantial local population, which would have been quite capable of organizing the work effort required. Since farming with animals inevitably meant that there were periods in the year when people were little employed, then there was slack labour capacity that could be used in construction. Even the huge amounts of labour required to transport the bluestones and sarsens, and then to erect them, were within the capacity of such a substantial and settled population over the many seasons that these tasks undoubtedly took.

Exchange and Trade

In contrast to the popular view of prehistoric people as grunting savages, the evidence is accumulating for a surprisingly sophisticated system of exchange and knowledge well beyond the local. Artefacts from different places in the country, or from sites throughout the ancient world, turn up in locations far away with surprising frequency: these range from early stone tools made from rock found only on the Isle of Portland or originating in Brittany, both of which are found throughout southern England, to later artefacts that may even have come from Mycenaean Greece, such as a bronze sword discovered in Cornwall. Hengistbury Head on the Dorset coast (identified as the most likely access point to the river system for the Welsh bluestones *en route* to Stonehenge, see p. 82) was undoubtedly the busiest and most important trading port in Neolithic Britain.

From the Neolithic tools of stone, and later metal, were among the most important items in the trading network that linked the various parts of the British Isles and continental Europe (see p. 67). Along with trade and exchange, many of the cultural influences that helped shape the prehistoric world also spread across Europe, while it is entirely likely that the ceremonial centres of the Middle and Late Neolithic world, the causewayed enclosures and the henge monuments were also places where goods were exchanged.

In a materialistic world, trade is seen as an economic fact of life; but trade and exchange among many peoples is just as much a way of establishing and cementing social relations, or expressing political superiority or inferiority. Prehistoric people may have found that, in cementing social relations or conferring status, it was as good to give as to receive. What is abundantly clear is that artefacts and influences travelled far and wide in the prehistoric world.

Primitive tools
Early tools were commonly made of polished flint, like this Palaeolithic hand axe.

Axe hammer
Made of the same Welsh stone as the Stonehenge bluestones, this perforated axe hammer was found in a Wiltshire grave.

Jadeite axe
Jadeite was a precious material that came from the Swiss Alps. This polished example ended up at Breamore, Hampshire.

Axes

It is surely not without significance that most carvings on the sarsens at Stonehenge were of axes. Almost nothing else conveys so perfectly the varieties of trade, farming and prestige of the Neolithic and Bronze Age peoples who built and lived around Stonehenge as axes. They were highly practical objects; but they also appear to have had a much deeper, religious or mystical significance.

In the Mesolithic era, stone tools were characteristically thin with small blades, known to archaeologists as microliths, and were won from stones, especially flints, with particular 'knapping' techniques. The later, Neolithic farming people used tools that were quite different – broader and squatter – employing newer flint-knapping methods. Flints and other hard (usually igneous) stones were made into axes; many were ground and polished to give a smoothed surface. In practical use they were placed into a shaped wooden handle – examples of which have survived – and then particularly used to cut down trees.

Although axes were being made across the British Isles, it appears that many were manufactured in a few, specific locations; but since they are frequently found the other side of the country – Cornish axes turning up in quantity in East Anglia, for instance – there was clearly a fairly sophisticated system of trade and exchange in them, as in other goods. By the Late Neolithic period, axe, and certainly flint, production was being concentrated in a very few places, with a string of mines in Sussex and Grimes Graves in Norfolk being among the most prominent.

Axes were also put to non-practical use. Some, especially the beautiful and highly finished ones made in jadeite, a green stone that came only from the Swiss Alps, could never have had a practical purpose. Axes were deposited – in the same way that cattle jawbones were in the original Stonehenge ditch – in what we can assume was a ritual manner. One of these very superior jadeite axes, for example, was placed beneath a timber trackway in the Somerset Levels that was built in 3806 BC; rather later, a polished greenstone axe (probably from a West Country source) was placed beneath Stonehenge's Altar Stone. The carved images on Brittany's graves and standing stones, much older than their counterparts in the British Isles, frequently incorporated axe symbols alongside, and perhaps protecting, a goddess figure. That is a combination that may recur on the Stonehenge sarsens (see p. 97).

Bronze spearhead
As with most surviving examples of bronze work this was found in a barrow grave, at Winterslow in Wiltshire.

Bronze flanged axe
An axe found in a barrow at Great Durnford, Wiltshire.

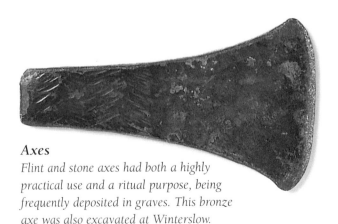

Axes
Flint and stone axes had both a highly practical use and a ritual purpose, being frequently deposited in graves. This bronze axe was also excavated at Winterslow.

Bronze Sword
By 2000 BC bronze was increasingly used to make tools and weapons of all kinds, including swords. Found at Figsbury Rings, this sword may have been ritually broken before deposit as many were in the Bronze Age.

Even the manufacture of the axes may have had a mystical or religious significance that we may now only barely glimpse. Axes made near Carmarthen, for example, used rock from the very same source that supplied the Stonehenge bluestones. Those who quarried stone from Pike o' Stickle in Langdale, in the Lake District, or who mined flints, frequently chose difficult if not dangerous places to work, even when easier sources were available.

The tradition, and sometimes even the form, of stone axes was continued into the age of metal production. Bronze axes and daggers are among the very first metal goods known in Britain, and their manufacture again resulted in considerable and widespread trade. Daggers commonly accompanied burials in the Early and Middle Bronze Age, but axes are usually found singly or in buried hoards. By the

Late Bronze Age – when axes were usually made of inferior metal – they may even have lost their practical function and been designed primarily for exchange and ritual, rather than for cutting down trees.

Tribal Society

Within early Wessex, and indeed in many parts of southern and midland England, there are clear geographical divisions in the distribution of the monuments of the Neolithic and Bronze Ages. Long barrows were built in clusters on the chalk uplands, around the main causewayed enclosures running from Windmill Hill to Maumbury Rings. Broadly, these same divisions formed the basis of the later groupings centred upon the henges from Avebury to Mount Pleasant, frequently with cursuses close by and subsequently clusters of round barrows. It is a straight-forward step to infer that they also represented territorial groupings, political divisions between the tribes that emerged in the Middle and Late Neolithic Ages as society became settled and wealthier.

Grimes Graves

In Norfolk, Grimes Graves became one of the primary sources of flint production during the Late Neolithic period. The many shafts sunk in the area produced this 'lunar' landscape.

The Stonehenge area was significantly represented even in the earlier period, but its importance was evidently far greater by the Late Neolithic era and the Bronze Age. The monuments appear to have been not only the focus for communal activity, but also to have been as important for whom they excluded as for whom they included. Each of the ditch sections of the causewayed enclosures, and even of the henges, may have been the responsibility of particular families or territorial groups.

Professor Geoffrey Wainwright has long argued that the central enclosures in henges may have had the same sort of communal council function as ethnographers have observed among many Native North American tribes, such as the Creek and the Cherokee. The cursuses, on the other hand, were great and physical barriers across a swathe of countryside, and may only have been able to contain a privileged few, in spite of their enormous length. The direct sight of the rising midsummer sun at Stonehenge (or indeed, at an earlier date, the rising midwinter sun at Newgrange) would again have been afforded only to a few, by the sheer physical constraints.

There are indeed many indicators that the societies that built these monuments were tribal and territorial, socially stratified, and powerful.

Kingship and power

Wealth commonly brings power. The coming of settled agriculture, and especially crop cultivation, has always had enormous consequences for society. All the great ancient civilizations were built upon the firm foundations of an agrarian economy, in which eventually surpluses were made, and stored. The transition from a hand-to-mouth subsistence economy to something more extensive, developed and settled was surely fundamental to the development of the type of society that could have undertaken the great building exercises of which Stonehenge is a supreme example.

By the Late Neolithic period, cereals and crop-growing were an integral part of the farming economy of Wessex. Previously, crop failures would have been quite marginal events, since there were many other opportunities for food, but for a population that had come to rely on cereals, the failure of a crop could be the gateway to disaster. Numbers of people were greater: settled farming made raising children easier, for a start, and more people could be supported within a given area of land. When a tribal or chiefdom structure was in place, there was also the assurance of safeguards for the community: in other ancient societies for which there are records, storage facilities

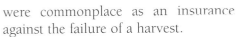

Bush Barrow mace
This stone macehead and intricate bone decorations for a wooden staff, found at Bush Barrow, were important symbols of power.

were commonplace as an insurance against the failure of a harvest.

The surplus from farming was sufficient to release some members of society from the necessity of earning a living from the land. Farmers supported others with more specialist functions: these might be builders, or priests, or kings. Professor Richard Atkinson, the best-known of this century's excavators of Stonehenge, wrote that the structure of Neolithic society 'may have been a great deal less egalitarian than the lack of differentiation in their artefacts might lead us to believe'.

The most commonly held view of Stonehenge in its most developed stage almost always involves some kind of priestly function. This is partly a reference to the Druids, who have been erroneously associated with the stone circle since the seventeenth century, but also derives from the seemingly inescapable conclusion that Stonehenge was some sort of temple. The building and design skills evident in its construction are in themselves likely evidence of a stratified society, with some people being afforded the opportunity to plan and others the opportunity to work. The great monuments were built at a time when the economy was sufficiently developed to support the immense time and effort required.

The evidence for a stratified society is not only to be found in the stone circles at Stonehenge. The monument was the focus of a huge cemetery, and the population had a tradition of barrow building that stretched back into the Middle Neolithic and was to extend into the Middle Bronze Age. The numbers of barrows, and the skeletons and cremations found within them, can only have represented a fraction of the people who lived in the area over many centuries. In at least some periods, the range and occasionally the wealth of the goods that were buried alongside the dead suggest that these were probably not typical inhabitants but members of an élite. The sumptuous burial beneath Bush Barrow (see p. 52), probably the finest Bronze Age assemblage of grave goods ever found in England, seems to have been that of a very significant person indeed, who in death still looked down towards Stonehenge, symbol of his people.

The Dead and the Living

Poking through the side of an excavation trench at Stonehenge that had collapsed during investigations in 1978 was something quite unexpected: the foot and leg bones belonging to the full skeleton of a young man. His remains were excellently preserved, and he lay in a foetal position with his legs flexed. When the skeleton was examined, it turned out that he had died from arrow wounds and had been shot at close range: his ribs were cracked and the points of arrowheads were found in four places within his body. Three broken-tipped arrowheads, of the type known as barbed-and-tanged, were buried alongside him, together with the wristguard that archers wore and three pieces of bluestone. The archer's skeleton had been placed in the filled-in ditch, and radiocarbon

The Stonehenge archer
Three broken-tipped, barbed-and-tanged arrowheads and the stone wristguard (above) found alongside the Stonehenge skeleton (below) indicated that he was an archer.

Execution, murder or sacrifice?
Arrowheads embedded in the archer's bones proved that he had been shot at close range – whether it was an execution, a murder or a ritual sacrifice remains open to speculation.

dating pointed to a date of around 1800 BC. Why was he killed, and why was his the only complete skeleton that has been found within Stonehenge itself? There are many possibilities. Perhaps he was a hero who had died in battle, or more probably (given the close range at which he was killed) he had been executed, either as punishment or as sacrifice. Single bodies were buried in significant places at a number of henge monuments: for example, a little girl's skeleton was found at the centre of Woodhenge (see p. 54). The report that her skull had been deliberately split has recently been disputed, so her manner of death also remains enigmatic. Both burials, however, may well have had a clear dedicatory significance.

Memorials to the dead

For all the wonder of Stonehenge, and indeed of many other prehistoric monuments built on a large scale, it is important to remember that these were – at least for part of their useful lives – intended for the dead as much as for the living. In the timber phase, for example, and indeed long afterwards, Stonehenge was a cemetery. The remains of many burials – of cremations rather more frequently than the burial of bodies – have been found there in the ditch, placed in the bank, and inside the Aubrey Holes. Over the years, bone fragments have been found for fifty-two cremation deposits (some clearly for more than one individual). There were children's bones along with adults' bones, and occasionally goods accompanying the cremations, such as a polished macehead placed with bone fragments in a dug-out recess.

Not only was Stonehenge itself a burial ground, but it stands within a landscape filled with memorials to the dead, principally the mounds of long and round barrows. Buried with the dead were aspects of their lives, and of life itself; carved phalluses, which are found in many prehistoric contexts, including the Stonehenge region, were emblems of human fertility, and perhaps also fertility of the soil in which they were placed. Only in the Late Bronze Age did the living's seeming preoccupation with the dead finally ebb away.

Crisis and Population Pressure

Despite the increased stability that came with settled agriculture, the difficulties must at times have been great. We know of environmental and ecological change at various junctures and from a variety of evidence; sometimes there is clear evidence of disaster.

Some archaeologists, for example, have suggested that the abandonment of marginal uplands, such as Dartmoor, during the Bronze Age was a direct result of the massive eruption of the volcano of Hekla in Iceland in 1159 BC. The ash fall-out was tremendous, while the sulphur in the atmosphere caused acid rain. Whatever the reasons for change, the warming effects that had followed the last Ice Age were certainly reversed in the Middle to Late Bronze Age, with heavier rainfall and a general decline in temperatures.

Before this – which would in itself have had a marked effect upon the quality of harvests – the vagaries of the weather and the low yields must have produced years of severe dearth, as well as occasional bumper crops. In the Iron Age, on the evidence from hill-forts, people knew how to store grain, and this knowledge was almost certainly not new. Part of the function of a chief or tribal leader was to help organize systems to tide a population over the bad years; but no amount of organization could aid in some aspects, notably the constant erosion of soils once the

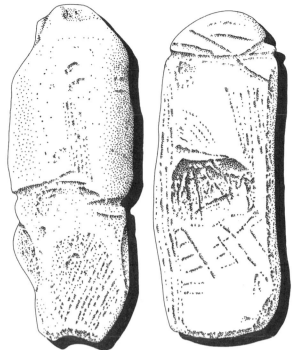

Chalk phalluses
Among the most common crafted artefacts to be found are carved chalk phalluses, clear symbols of fertility.

woodland cover had been cleared. The considerable loss of soil in the Stonehenge area is itself sufficient evidence of that; many more marginal areas were abandoned in the face of environmental degradation.

This high level of knowledge also extended during the Bronze Age to medicine. Surgical operations on the skull and brain were not uncommon, and may have been performed to relieve the pressure caused by wounds to the head. That the patients lived afterwards is evident from the regrowth of bone tissue seen on some of the skeletal remains which have survived.

Most evidence suggests that population numbers grew steadily during the prehistoric era. Any estimate of overall numbers in Britain can only be a wild guess, but figures of upwards of half a million people in the Early to Middle Bronze Age are often quoted. The pressure of numbers, and the establishment of territories within even a relatively compact area, may well have had a social impact in the form of conflict, if not war. We shall never know, for example, why the man fleeing with a child at the Hambledon Hill causewayed enclosure was shot in the back, but the circumstances seem to imply conflict rather than ritual.

Early brain surgery
Trepanning was the removal of a piece of skull to operate on the brain; here the removed piece became a lucky charm and years later was buried alongside the deceased at Crichel Down, Dorset.

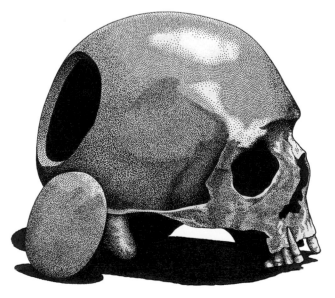

Pots

If prehistoric people are known from their mortal remains, they are also known from their pottery. Broken shards fill the shelves and cases of museums; the study of their distribution, design, size, and of course age, is one of the principal aspects of prehistory.

Making pots required planning – the digging, curing, storing and tempering of the clay – and a firing technology using a kiln, however primitive; trading and exchanging pots required a mechanism of contact and a degree of sophistication. The earliest date from the Early Neolithic: round-bottomed and with little surface decoration, they could be used for cooking by sitting them in the bed of warm ashes. The principal types of Late Neolithic pot are known as Grooved Ware and Peterborough Ware. Grooved Ware was flat-bottomed, decorated with patterns of grooves, and seems to have originated in Orkney. By 2800 BC this pottery was to be found throughout eastern Britain, but rarely in the west and in Ireland. However, examples of Grooved Ware are found in the henge monuments of the southwest, as at Durrington Walls (see p. 56). Peterborough Ware was of the older, round-bottomed type and was decorated with impressions, made in wet clay, of corded rope and bird bones.

These two types very rarely occur together, even when used in the same areas. Peterborough pots were

Grooved Ware pot from Durrington Walls (right)
Grooved Ware pottery dating from the Late Neolithic had flat bottoms and elaborate patterns on the sides.

Early, round-based pot (above)
Primitive pots, dating from the Early Neolithic, had round bases and little decoration. They were generally placed in warm ashes to cook food.

Peterborough Ware pot (left)
Peterborough Ware developed from early round-based pots during the Late Neolithic, with surface impressions of corded rope and bird bones.

Beakers (right)
Tall, slim-waisted beakers, decorated with tooth-combed and cord impressions, characteristic of the Bronze Age.

placed as offerings in rivers, or were used in different contexts: Grooved Ware was found in the henge enclosure at Mount Pleasant; Peterborough Ware in the neighbouring ditched enclosure at Flagstones (near modern Dorchester). Probably the two types were associated with different functions or different times in the ritual calendar. The evidence from both Woodhenge and Durrington Walls suggests that pieces of pottery – whether broken deliberately or not cannot be determined – were deposited on and in the ground in particular places and in a significant sequence, just as bones, antlers and tools were.

The use of metal with the advent of the Bronze Age was accompanied by the best-known type of prehistoric pottery: elaborately decorated beakers. The people who made these beakers, who were buried with them in their graves or whose cremated remains were placed into them, are often known as the Beaker Folk. Beaker pots are commonly tall with open mouths, their fine surface covered with intricate decoration achieved by impressed cord and incised lines. They are found throughout Europe, and a great range of beakers has survived in Britain – usually from burial contexts – for the period between 2700 and 1700 BC.

Their ubiquity, and yet their fineness, suggests a specific purpose in which many people shared; the contents that had spilled from some buried beakers indicate that they contained an alcoholic drink like

Incense pots (right)
Small and intricately decorated, so-called incense pots were introduced in the Early Bronze Age.

Collared urn (left)
Collared urns, featuring a band around the top of the vessel, first appeared in around 2000 BC, usually for cremations.

Food vessels (left)
These vessels developed from the beaker style, sometimes supplanting the beakers, at other times being used alongside them. These too frequently contained cremated remains.

115

mead, while some archaeologists have advanced the idea that the cord used to decorate the beakers' surface was cannabis hemp.

As the beakers became fully established, new pottery styles emerged, notably the collared urns and so-called food vessels, which first made an appearance around 2000 BC, together with smaller vessels known as incense pots. These were regularly used as grave goods, accompanying a burial or holding cremated ashes, before passing into wider and more general use. In some areas the traditions of beakers and urns continued side by side; in others the new pots supplanted the old.

Pots do not provide the same evidence as people, but, in the absence of other indicators, the interpretation of them seems to have a great deal to tell about the people who made and used them.

One People or Many?

It is often tempting to ascribe novelty to the deliberate imposition of a new culture from above, and British history is littered with myths that a native culture was swamped by newcomers. This is typified by the popular belief that in 1066 the Normans (they) conquered the plucky, but ultimately unsuccessful, Anglo-Saxons (us) – despite the likelihood that as much Norman blood as any other kind flows in the veins of English men and women. Daniel Defoe memorably described the true-born Englishman as

A thousand years
From the arrival of the bluestones to its abandonment after 1600 BC, Stonehenge was a symbol of the people who built it.

'your Roman-Saxon-Danish-Norman English'. Britain has continually been open to newcomers, invaders and traders; prehistoric people began that tradition, and each novelty was absorbed to make a new whole.

Invasion
It used to be supposed, for example, that the Beaker Folk were a people who had invaded and overrun the native culture of the British Isles and, indeed, had swept across Europe from the east, as many later waves of invaders were to do. Certainly bronze metal and entirely new shapes and types of pottery were introduced at much the same time, and even gave a new name to the era.

The evidence of different skull shapes in long and round barrows seemed to confirm that invasion theory: the older long barrows held skeletons with narrow skulls, whereas broader skulls were found in the new round barrows. This was perhaps the Victorian legacy of examining head bumps and interpreting intelligence and race from skull shape and size, for it now appears that both of these were much more varied in the Neolithic and Bronze Ages than earlier authorities had supposed. Genetic change was perhaps as powerful a force as invasion in explaining the observable differences in the shapes of people's heads.

Assimilation
Just as the Norman conquerors swiftly became Anglo-Normans, intermarrying with the local population in the late eleventh and twelfth centuries AD, so it may have been that successive newcomers to British shores thousands of years before them were gradually

assimilated and absorbed. The evidence for the advent of farming and of megalith-building suggest that two lifestyles – hunter-gathering and more settled cultivation – coexisted for a considerable period, rather than one forcibly supplanting the other.

With the Beaker culture, there is also evidence that the newer and older styles ran alongside each other; the early Beaker burials occurred well away from the traditional henge centres, and may have been set apart from the rest of society. Yet they sometimes used ritual sites that were older still: the final stages of use at West Kennet Long Barrow (see p. 65) show beakers as well as other forms of pottery being used and discarded in the stone chambers.

There may be a sense in which the old, Neolithic culture and the new, Bronze and Beaker culture underwent some sort of power struggle, which the latter won. Or perhaps the older culture adapted to meet the challenges of the new and was transformed in the process, but with only a limited injection of new blood and new people.

Adaptation

Stonehenge was itself a monumental site that lasted in use for well over a thousand years and the surrounding area was a monumental landscape for longer still. Succeeding generations built and renewed the monuments, adapting them to their new, perhaps changed, needs. The models of invasion and conflict that earlier generations of archaeologists tended to adopt have been replaced by explanations that emphasize continuity. There is little in the archaeological record to suggest that one people was supplanted by another, or that new ways were the result of deliberate imposition, rather than organic change and the blending of novelty with older forms of behaviour. The time periods involved are immense, and there was huge scope for slow adaptation, rather than swift.

Yet the emphasis on consensus and evolutionary change would certainly not fit the whole of British, let alone human, history. There is some evidence to suggest that new ways did arrive with conflict and force, as well as the evidence that shows the old ways adapting. More research will provide a clearer picture of the changing composition of the people of Stonehenge – essentially one people, or many?

The peoples of Stonehenge

In the modern world we have a firm belief in the doctrine of progress. Clearly we are considerably more advanced in our attainments than our predecessor generations; by linear extrapolation, the inhabitants of Stone and Bronze Age Britain must have been so little advanced that they are quite off the scale of achievement. Yet the undertakings of early man at and around Stonehenge on Salisbury Plain are remarkable and include one of the greatest monumental structures of any age. There are clearly limits to the usefulness of ideas of progress that simply place ourselves at the pinnacle of human development and endeavour.

When we look at prehistoric societies, we can no longer treat them as savage and unsophisticated, but see in them rather a different kind of sophistication. Every society has to be regarded on its own merits, and within its own limitations, just as much as it should be judged with the hindsight of history.

RITUAL AND
THE HEAVENS

An eighteenth-century engraving of a druid
collecting mistletoe in the shadow of a stone circle.

W E KNOW THAT the earth moves round the
sun, and not vice versa, but that knowledge barely diminishes the awe with
which even today we regard celestial phenomena – an
eclipse, the midsummer sunrise, the spectacle of a
sunset or harvest moon, even the sheer brightness of
the stars in the night sky. Throughout human history,
men and women have gazed at the heavens and
observed the ways in which they seem to change at
varying scales of regularity. Although we may look at
the skies in a detached way, for many early and non-
Western societies celestial and terrestrial often were,
and are, not separate categories at all. In order to
comprehend other aspects of Stonehenge, we must
examine the sacred alongside the profane.

Archaeoastronomy
The one thing that people know, or think they know,
about Stonehenge is that it is something to do with
astronomy. 'Books on astronomy usually begin with
Stonehenge,' says one expert in the field, 'while books
on archaeology and Stonehenge usually ignore the
subject of astronomy.' The discipline of archaeoastronomy has grown up in order to investigate the
relationship between archaeological remains and
celestial observation, testing popular understanding
and mathematical probabilities, as well as some pretty
wild theories and beliefs. The question of how far the
monuments in the Stonehenge area are related to the
heavens is still very much under active scrutiny.

It is now apparent that Stonehenge, like many other
– but certainly far from all – prehistoric earth and
stone monuments, was indeed aligned to take regard
of celestial phenomena. Its principal entrance faces
northeast – the direction of the rising of the sun at

midsummer – a feature that Stonehenge shares with
other henge monuments, not least its near neighbour
Woodhenge (see p. 54). Indeed, the majority of the
barrows, henges and cursuses within the Stonehenge
region face to the east or northeast and hence towards
the rising sun. Directly opposite, to the southwest, is
the direction of the setting sun at midwinter, and its
dying rays shine between the two huge uprights of the
great trilithon in the inner horseshoe of Stonehenge.

A host of features connected with the sun, the moon
and the stars are claimed for Stonehenge and other
monuments; even if these particular alignments are
recognized, how many others can there be?

Solstice and equinox
The quarter-days – Christmas, Lady Day, St John the
Baptist's (or Midsummer) Day and Michaelmas – are
still occasions on which rents are paid or contracts are
dated, as well as being important religious festivals in
the Christian calendar. They are also dates connected
to the skies, since they are almost identical to the four
principal solar events in the year, the midwinter and
midsummer solstices (the shortest and longest days)
and the spring and autumn equinoxes (when day and
night are of equal length). In many societies, past and
present, the sun's annual round is of crucial significance, guiding the seasonal changes and sometimes
accompanied by the fear that, without appropriate
action, the sun will not repeat its life-giving journey
through the heavens.

The midsummer solstice
*Modern Druids could until recent years watch the sun
rise directly along the Avenue on midsummer morning
from within the sanctity of the stone circle.*

Earth and sky

People around the world believe themselves to be the product of a union between earth and sky. 'Our Father, who art in Heaven...' is the Christian version of this belief (which is perhaps less literal than many others). The ceremonial that links earth and sky in many cultures is both elaborate and evocative:

> *In front of the chief stand his assistants, then the row of the other men present, and then the row of women present. All turn to face the east, singing to call the sun. This is repeated in the anti-sunwise circuit, before each song sprinkling meal from their meal basket or pollen received from the chief assistant... [The chief] points upward with his stone knife. All sing the song of pulling down the sun while the chief makes the motions of drawing something toward himself...*

This description of a sun ceremonial was written early in the twentieth century by the ethnographer Elsie Clews Parsons, who was accorded the rare privilege of watching the midwinter solstice ceremonies among the Hopi people of the southwestern United States. The creation myths and the beliefs of the Hopi, and of many other Native American and Central American peoples, are intimately bound up with the sun and its apparent movements. They believe, for example, that if the sun fails to turn in its annual course, then the future of the community will be jeopardized because their crops will fail. The Pueblo Indians of New Mexico run relay races at the midsummer solstice to help give the sun strength for the start of its journey towards its winter home; the Zuñi, like other Pueblo tribes of the southwestern states, have men who carefully watch the skies to establish the date for the solstice festival.

The possible parallels between such native societies and the people who built Stonehenge are both interesting and plausible.

The Movement of the Spheres

Every morning the sun rises (or, rather, appears to rise) in the east, bringing the dawn, and passes through the sky to sink in the west. During the intervening nights, the moon waxes and wanes through a 29.5-day cycle of birth, death and rebirth. The sun's apparent position both on the horizon and in the sky changes on an annual cycle; the moon has a cycle of 18.6 years in its position in the sky.

The variation in the position of the rising and setting of the sun and the moon is similar: rising and setting range on the east and west (as shown in the diagram), with about 100 degrees between the northernmost and southernmost limits of moonrise and moonset, and 80 degrees between the outermost limits of the positions of sunrise and sunset at Stonehenge's latitude. Repeated, long-term observation has established this set pattern. Such observation is not simply a product

The paths of the sun at the solstices

The chart shows the points at which the sun rises and sets at the solstices, the longest and shortest days of the year. At midwinter (outer yellow arc) the sun sets directly opposite the midsummer sunrise, which occurs beside the Heel Stone (inner yellow arc).

The phases of the moon

In its 18.6-year cycle, the moon rises and sets at different points along its 'minor standstill' (inner arcs) and 'major standstill' (outer arcs). Some archaeologists believe Stonehenge to have had a strong lunar connection, especially during its early phases.

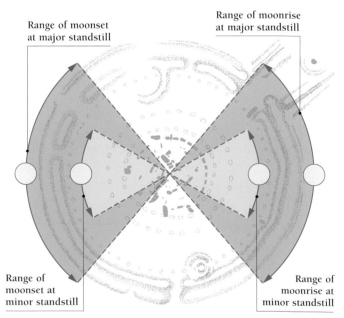

Sun path on midsummer's day

Sun path on midwinter's day

Range of moonset at major standstill

Range of moonrise at major standstill

Range of moonset at minor standstill

Range of moonrise at minor standstill

of a modern Western and scientific culture. Celestial observation and reckoning were an integral part of Inca and Aztec culture in Central America before the advent of white men, and prehistoric buildings throughout the Americas incorporate features that allow the light of the sun to shine directly through particular apertures on solstice or equinoctial days. Even today priests of the Pueblo Indian cultures of Arizona and New Mexico regard skywatching as one of their most solemn religious duties.

Solar observation

Observation and calculation of the heavens may be undertaken with only very limited resources. The (relative) time of day can be told without the benefit of a clock by looking at the sun's position in the sky, while the sun's point in the seasonal cycle may be determined by watching the horizon. Markers – say, stones set or occurring naturally on the horizon, or notches in a line of hills – are frequently employed among pre-literate societies in solar observation, and many examples of these are to be found in the British Isles and elsewhere.

Only on two days of the year does the sun rise directly in the east and set directly in the west, at the equinoxes of spring and autumn, approximately 21 March and 21 September. At the solstices, the days of maximum and minimum length (21 June and 21 December or thereabouts), the sun appears to rest for a few days before resuming its travels. That sequence and its timing do not vary, and that invariability is crucial to any society dependent on cold and warmth, sunshine and rain, for the growing of crops or seasonal migration, and needing a fair degree of accuracy to know when to plant and when to harvest, or the best time to move on to new territories.

When a whole belief system is bound up with the interplay of sun, sky and earth, then the movements of the sun, the moon and the stars take on an even greater significance.

The Stonehenge experience

What this means in practice at Stonehenge is that, famously, at the midsummer solstice the sun rises beside the Heel Stone, when viewed from the centre of the stone circle, because of its very particular alignment. In the past, when the Heel Stone's partner was

The Devil's Arrows

Although most marker monuments seem to have either solar or lunar aspect, some archaeologists have interpreted the grooves down the sides of this Yorkshire megalith as sightlines to the stars.

North American petroglyph, Montana
As the last rays of the midsummer's day sun shine on the rock face, two points of the jagged shadow, cast by the broken edge, just touch the lefthand side of the spiral.

121

still in situ, the sun's first appearance would have been framed by this pair of standing stones and it would have shone down a stone corridor into the heart of the monument. (The many photographs showing the sun appearing 'out of' the Heel Stone are in fact a fraud, taken when the solstice sun has already begun to travel through the sky.) Less famously, but – at least in clear weather, just as effectively – the midwinter sunset is framed between the uprights of the great trilithon.

The axes of the monument, if drawn through the positions of the four Station Stones, also appear to indicate the direction of midsummer sunrise and midwinter sunset. The Station Stones may have a lunar aspect as well; their positions form a rectangle, the longer sides of which seem to indicate the direction of moonrise and moonset at their furthest points, the so-called 'major standstill' at either end of the 18.6-year cycle. The exact position of Stonehenge has also been hailed as significant in itself, since only at this particular latitude do the solar and lunar alignments, possibly marked here by the Station Stones, meet at right angles. (As with so many other astronomical features, there is a need for circumspection, since this remains controversial; some experts are sceptical of these findings, pointing to difficulties of measurement.)

Was this intersecting alignment the reason why Stonehenge was built at this particular spot, or is that pure coincidence? The likelihood that *all* these alignments arise from chance appears remote. Yet if that was the reason, and if this celestial aspect was so important to the builders of the Neolithic age, why do no other major monuments with these special features seem to have been built at this latitude? Perhaps only in certain localities did these possibilities present themselves. At the latitude at which Stonehenge stands, there is a range of 80 degrees between the points of the sunrises and sunsets at the solstices, midsummer and midwinter. On the more northern latitude of Orkney (see p. 68), however, these four directions intersect at exactly 90 degrees; this is a feature that the early inhabitants clearly recognized and exploited, since the Neolithic houses uncovered at Barnhouse were built with hearths aligned on these four solar positions.

Lunar hypotheses

There can be no doubt that Stonehenge, like many other prehistoric monuments, incorporated certain features that exploit known regularities in the sun's observed movements. Some scholars maintain that it

Alignments through the Station Stones

The lines indicate the midsummer sunrise, midwinter sunset and the furthest points of moonrise and moonset. Only at Stonehenge's latitude do these alignments meet at right angles.

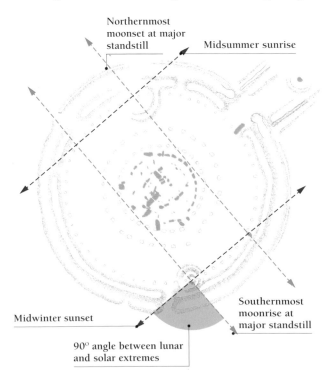

Northernmost moonset at major standstill

Midsummer sunrise

Midwinter sunset

Southernmost moonrise at major standstill

90° angle between lunar and solar extremes

Heel Stone (right)

This substantial sarsen was part of the complex of stones along the Avenue, most of which are now long gone, that framed the sun as it appeared on midsummer's morning.

Variations in the solar cycle

At Stonehenge's latitude in southern England there is a range of 80 degrees between the sunrises and sunsets of the summer and winter solstices. At the more northerly latitude of Barnhouse in Orkney, the same four extremes of the solar cycle intersect at exact right angles, a phenomenon marked by the design of the hearths in the centre of each house.

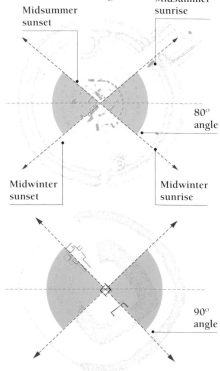

Midsummer sunset

Midsummer sunrise

80° angle

Midwinter sunset

Midwinter sunrise

90° angle

was also dedicated to using the regularity of the moon's cycle. Aubrey Burl, for example, who is one of the foremost authorities on stone circles and alignments, has long held the opinion that Stonehenge, at least in its early phases, was more concentrated on the moon than on the sun. The vast majority of pre-Stonehenge long barrows were, according to his calculations, orientated within the range of the moon's movements, while he and others have also advanced the notion that the post-hole settings in Phase 2 at the northeastern entrance were placed on the lines of the moon's risings (rather then being, as is generally assumed, simply a screen or a narrow point of access). Since the southeast represents the moon's limit, and it appears from the excavation evidence that cremations and human remains were buried in that portion of the monument more often than in any other, scholars have proposed a link between the sector 'governed' by the moon, representing night and hence death, and burial places. The more accurately realigned central axis in Phase 3, meanwhile, suggests to some authors that there was a new, or more exact, interest in the sun at that time, which eclipsed the earlier concentration on the moon.

Yet so much of this remains pure conjecture: the lunar connections are weak by comparison with the strong solar alignment, and the confused nature of the evidence of both post-holes and cremations opens up these conclusions to serious doubt. It would be surprising if, as the weight of evidence suggests, there was considerable interest in the daily and seasonal movements of one celestial body, the sun, and little or no interest in the other celestial body, the moon, with its own pattern of regularity; but by the same token, there is little to suggest that the moon, or indeed the stars, played a great part in the cosmology of those who built and used Stonehenge.

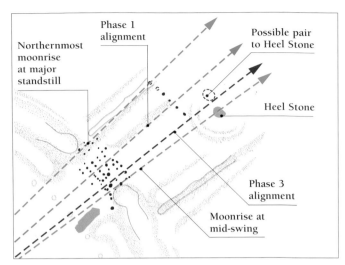

Possible lunar alignments
Aubrey Burl, an authority on stone-circle alignments, maintains that initially Stonehenge may have been most closely linked with lunar phenomena. The post-holes outside the northeastern entrance in Phase 2 may have been aligned with the moon's risings. This focus was then replaced by a greater interest in the sun with the realigned central axis in Phase 3.

Alignments

Between Phases 2 and 3 of Stonehenge's construction, the main axis on which the monument is aligned was shifted slightly, to place it more squarely in the direction of the rising midsummer sun, which suggests that its northeastern aspect was considered even more crucial at that time. The Avenue, Stonehenge's grand approach route built as part of the stone monument, also approaches on this northeastern line, having turned in a great loop from the River Avon.

It is now abundantly clear that astronomy does have some considerable part to play in the way we interpret the monument. At the very least its solar alignment

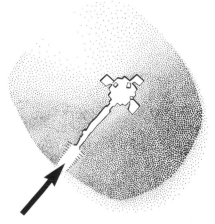

Maes Howe – midwinter sunset

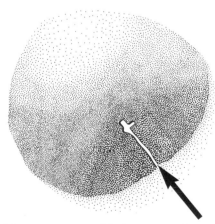

Newgrange – midwinter sunrise

Coneybury – midsummer sunrise

had some ritual significance at midsummer, and possibly also at midwinter. The example of the penetrating shaft of light at Newgrange (see p. 70), in itself older than Stonehenge, shows how meticulously the midwinter sunrise alignment was achieved there. The tomb at Maes Howe on Orkney similarly exploits the midwinter sun – the sunset that signifies the end of one year and the imminent birth of the next. The stone alignments in Argyll have been shown – by statistical analysis as well as by gut feeling – to have had an order and likely lunar alignment that was considerably greater than would have been achieved by chance.

Among cursuses in England, the example at Godmanchester in Cambridgeshire incorporated the intersections between the large posts from an older enclosure to line up with both solstice and equinox positions of the sun and the moon. The Dorset Cursus was aligned on the setting of the midwinter sun, that at Dorchester-on-Thames on the midsummer sunset. In many cases, the monuments were lengthened to take greater advantage of these solar features. Near Stonehenge, Durrington Walls, Woodhenge (see p. 54) and the Stonehenge Cursus (see p. 46) had alignments on the midsummer and equinox sunrises respectively.

Whether there was a specific lunar significance to Stonehenge remains, as we have seen, open to greater doubt, although given the sophistication of so many other features of this and other monuments, recognition of the 18.6-year moon cycle can surely not have been beyond the builders' capabilities. The meanings of the orientation of Stonehenge and elsewhere, and the rituals associated with it, may become more apparent when we have considered other aspects of its design. People have been drawing lines on the plan of Stonehenge to try to interpret it for decades. Perhaps they have been doing so for millennia. The question remains, what does it all mean?

Stonehenge as Observatory and Calendar

If we are ready to accept that Stonehenge has some astronomical aspects, and was built and adapted to take advantage of alignments with the skies, that still does not go as far as some would like. There was a time in the 1960s when people began to ask if Stonehenge was some sort of astronomical observatory, a giant stone computer, designed to predict the passage of the moon and its eclipses.

More detailed examination of alignments and celestial observation began with the pamphlets published by C.A. Newham. He was following in part a lead taken by Professor Alexander Thom, who had investigated many monuments in Scotland, Brittany and elsewhere to discover and identify possible astronomical features; he was later to apply his knowledge and methods to Stonehenge. Newham's lead was followed by Gerald Hawkins, who famously used an IBM computer to help prove his hypotheses, and subsequently by Fred Hoyle.

A Neolithic computer?

Most of the new findings about astronomy employed the Station Stones and the Aubrey Holes – elements in Stonehenge's construction history that are perhaps as much as a thousand years apart. Newham identified a sightline for equinoxes from Station Stone 94 to a hole near the Heel Stone, and a lunar alignment in the long sides of the rectangle formed by the four Station Stones. Hawkins, with the aid of his IBM, dubbed Stonehenge a Neolithic computer, so accurate were (some of) the alignments between fixed points at Stonehenge and the risings and settings of the sun and moon. These alignments were, he thought, more accurate in the first phase of Stonehenge than in the

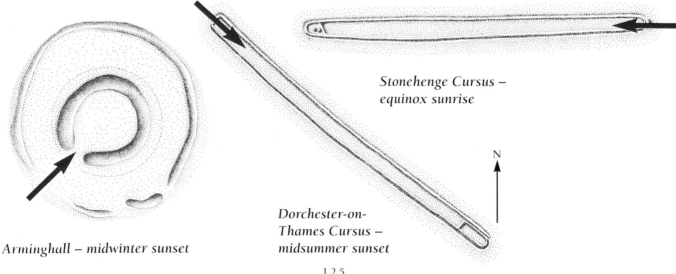

Arminghall – midwinter sunset

Stonehenge Cursus – equinox sunrise

Dorchester-on-Thames Cursus – midsummer sunset

N

later stone structure (even though the monument had been realigned on a better solar solstice axis in Phase 3). The Aubrey Holes, he decided, were dug to act as a predictor of lunar eclipses, relating to a cycle of one-third of the fifty-six holes and measured by moving marker stakes around their circle.

Hawkins's calculations were scrutinized and found to be wanting in many areas, not least in his contention that the alignments he found could not have occurred by chance. In any event, the Aubrey Holes had been filled in and used as cremation pits within a short space of time, the later Station Stones being built on top of some of them. His lead was, however, followed by Fred Hoyle, the Cambridge-based astronomer, who again found, by different means, a way of predicting eclipses by counting using the Aubrey Holes. He thought these were "an inviolate reference standard" since less permanent markers were easily displaced. He believed that the astronomer priests moved large stones from hole to hole, at rates varying from twice a day to three times a year. Yet again, his evidence was assailed by a barrage of criticism, notably that the notion of a 56-year cycle was in error: similar 'predictors' may be devised using varying numbers of holes, and 56 does not, in itself, have very special qualities. Although now generally discounted, its legacy remains in the popular imagination.

Gerald Hawkins's 'neolithic computer'
Gerald Hawkins devised a method for predicting eclipses that involved six markers (moved one Aubrey Hole a year), three fixed positions in the north, and a moon marker moving by one stone of the sarsen circle each day.

'Megalithic science' and the skies
Professor Alexander Thom, an engineer by training, became the foremost authority on what he termed 'megalithic science'. In the years after 1954 he published many studies on early monuments, pointing to astronomical alignments and developing the idea of the so-called megalithic yard, a regular length of measurement in the design of such monuments.

In the end, after the flurry of activity during the 1960s, it was clear that Stonehenge *could* have been used as some sort of astronomical observatory and calendar device, but there was no clear evidence that it *had been* so used. Many of these authors' conclusions have since been discredited, or at the very least severely questioned. Newham, for example, incorporated both the car-park post-holes and the Station Stones – features separated in time and use by many thousands of years – in his analysis of markers, to identify and predict sun and moon settings, while many of Thom's detractors pointed out that his megalithic yard was the same as a human pace. Academic opinion began to swing decisively away from the astronomical theories, although by then they had become clearly fixed in the public consciousness.

In the twentieth century, and indeed for many preceding centuries, industrial and urban life, inventions and gadgets, and the quest for precision

Fred Hoyle's eclipse predictor
Fred Hoyle's simpler method of eclipse prediction used three markers – Moon (M), Sun (S) and Node (N) – moving at different rates around the Aubrey Holes following the celestial bodies. Both these methods have been found wanting by later work.

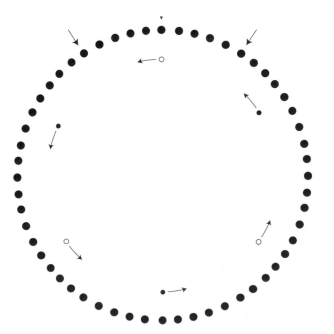

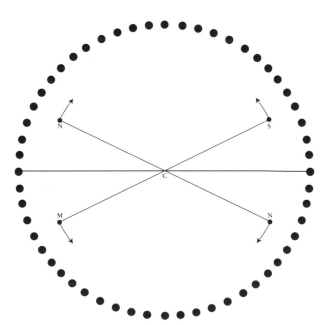

have removed the need to know what happens in the sky. It is simply there. But for people who tell the time by the sky, ascertain from the position of sun and moon or even from the movement of the stars when the year's seasonal changes are under way observation is the key. Early man would have been far more conscious of the night sky than we are, and farming communities traditionally use the sun as a clock and as a seasonal guide. So it would be very surprising indeed if prehistoric people paid no heed to the skies, the sun, the moon and the stars, and indeed there is every indication that they used their knowledge in laying out some – but surely far from all – their monuments in the British Isles.

Some authorities have argued that alignments on the stars were an integral feature of many great prehistoric monuments. This view is widely challenged – the argument for solar (and lunar) alignments is far more compelling – but the brightness of the stars, especially at the times of the solstices, may

have given an added dimension to the religious experiences that Stonehenge embodied. It is but a short step from necessity and regard for the seasons to inquisitiveness and enquiry. That may readily be admitted, but so may scepticism about a class of wise astronomer-priests designing monuments and dispensing knowledge from their inner fastnesses in the henge circles. Although there have been many fanciful suggestions and extravagant claims, the evidence clearly suggests that it had an astronomical, and calendrical, component. Certainly, when the archaeologist John Barber surveyed the recumbent stone circles of County Kerry in Ireland in the early 1970s, he was struck by what farmers knew:

Many could indicate fairly accurately the setting-points of the sun at its limiting positions. Several were conscious of the moon's cycle, and... the farmers living in the mountains know of a period... when the moon is so low in the sky that it does not rise above the surrounding mountains for a period of several weeks.

The summer night sky
As the constellation of Cygnus moves within the triangle of bright stars – Deneb, Vega and Altair – it creates one of the most prominent features of the early summer night sky. These stars may have guided participants in Stonehenge's rituals along the Avenue approach.

The winter night sky
The Greek playwright Aeschylus described these constellations, the 'bringers of winter and summer', as stars that 'burn with power and rule their empty spaces like kings.' The stones and lintels of Stonehenge will also have framed the stars rising in the dark skies.

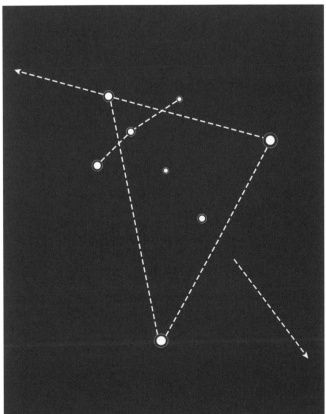

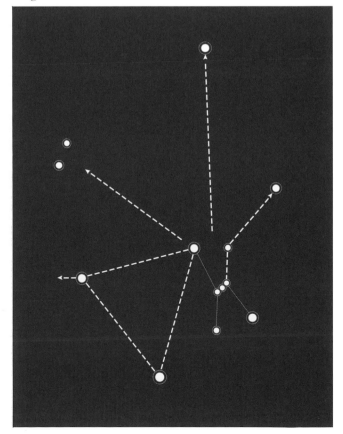

Interpreting Circles

Even the most cursory examination of Stonehenge and its attendant monuments discloses one of the most important things about them: the regularity of their shape, and the way in which they exploit some basic geometry to achieve their effect. The cursuses and the Avenue are lines inscribed on the ground; the henges are composed of concentric circles; long barrows are trapeziums or rectangles; round barrows are as circular as their name implies. Some of these structures are now barely two-dimensional, marks in the grass or even now in the imagination, but all once were – and some still are – three-dimensional objects. Understanding the geometry and the spaces that these monuments occupy are a further key to this landscape.

A perfect circle is relatively easy to draw in the ground, using just a peg and a line. A circular building is also fairly straightforward to construct, since it lacks awkward angles. So we should not be surprised that so many early monumental structures, and indeed houses, were circular in plan. Circles, however, have many other properties and associations, both sacred and profane. The causewayed enclosures and their successors, the henges, were usually circular, although often imperfect circles. That the Stonehenge monuments in the different phases are almost exactly circular shows not only that prehistoric people were capable of constructing them, but also perhaps that it did not always matter if the circles were not perfect.

Circles are full of meaning. First, a circle is a reference on earth to the heavens. The sun is always a circular object in the sky, except on those rare occasions when it is eclipsed. The full moon is a disc from which portions are 'removed' as it wanes and 'added' as it waxes. Gold 'sun discs' were included among the grave goods of Wessex and Ireland in the Early Bronze Age, just as they were part of the culture of the Aztecs.

One of the oldest and most basic forms of dance is in a circle. In ancient Sumer, some 4,000 years ago (and thus at much the same time as Stonehenge's Phase 3), priests incanted the prescribed prayers for the Circle of Protection, just as a medieval magician would withdraw into the safety of his circle inscribed in the ground; even today, conjurors are elected members of the Magic Circle. Labyrinths and turf mazes, a few of which still survive in the English countryside, were usually circular in form, and the pathways were – at

Gold sun disc

'Sun discs' were a common feature of the Aztec culture as well as both megalithic and Celtic Europe.

Gorsedd stone circle: Wales

Stone circles, such as this one in Wales, have many levels of symbolism, both sacred and secular.

least in the recorded past – deemed to be routes of prayer, long lines up, down and around to be trodden by the penitent.

Symbol of eternity

Within the Christian tradition, the circle is a potent symbol of the oneness of God, without beginning or end. 'God is a circle whose centre is everywhere and the circumference nowhere,' wrote St Bonaventura, one of the earliest Christian authors, while the image of the serpent biting its tail was an enduring motif of the Church. We wear wedding or engagement rings not just because they fit conveniently onto a finger, but because they also symbolize unbrokenness, faithfulness:

Love is a circle that doth restless move
In the same sweet eternity of love

in the Stuart poet Robert Herrick's words. As with love, so with life: a circle is also an expression of renewal and rebirth. If – as seems entirely plausible, given the importance of the dead in these circular monuments – one purpose was to honour the ancestors, the circle embodies the idea of return.

It is not necessary to know that the earth is a globe to realize that the physical environment is round, 'ringed by the flat horizon'; within a landscape, the

Circle dance
In the 1580s, John White, an English explorer in Virginia, drew the circle dances of the Native Americans celebrating celestial events and harvests.

horizon creates a circle within which a person is set. In a woodland – and the early Stonehenge landscape was heavily wooded – glades that occur naturally are round, while the spaces cleared by early farmers are likely also to have been circular. A monument that forms a circle is therefore a microcosm; it embodies memories of a landscape that may have gone. And even when, as in the case of Stonehenge, a high bank obscures the view of the world beyond, the monument may represent a mental map of that world.

Interpreting Lines

A line has a purpose. To walk in a straight line is to take the most direct route, 'the line of least resistance'. The contemporary artist Richard Long, whose work has been essentially concerned with making marks in the landscape and re-creating aspects of the landscape in a gallery space, believes that the most significant of man's actions is to walk in a line with purpose, which is 'a statement fundamental to any place commemorative of ritual'.

Throughout the prehistoric past, lines and linear structures have been as predominant as circles in monument building, and at times considerably more so. In the Neolithic period, before the first steps in building Stonehenge were taken, the southwest of England had a tradition of earthen long barrows, while

Pueblo Indian medicine wheel
The sun's rays hit this inscribed circle in Arizona in a ritual which reinforces the power of the priests of the Pueblo Indians.

further west in Wales, the Borders and Ireland, as well as in Orkney, there were chambered and passage graves that exploited linear features. Contemporary with the earliest phases of Stonehenge were the cursuses, immense lines constricted by earth banks, which provided some sort of ceremonial routeway as well as an alignment on some celestial feature.

The barrow cemeteries, with Bronze Age round barrows built in line, also exploited the idea of linearity. This is very clearly seen at Winterbourne Stoke (see p. 48), but it also occurs elsewhere in Stonehenge's landscape – on the King Barrow Ridge (see p. 51), the Cursus barrow, and in front of Woodhenge (see p. 54). For a line is a link: and perhaps a link between the generations, a 'blood line' even, in a row of barrows. It is certainly a link between places. The best example is the Avenue, from the River Avon via Stonehenge Bottom to the circle itself, while there are avenues to be found at other major sites too, above all at Avebury and West Kennet (see p. 64). The latter avenue was marked by rows of stones – the evidence for stone settings along the Stonehenge Avenue is at best ambiguous – and stone lines occur in many prehistoric settings. The stone rows on

William Stukeley's view of the Cursus

The linear nature of the Stonehenge Cursus acted as a boundary as well as having a ritual purpose.

Dartmoor (see p. 66) are the most complete English example, but the alignments at Carnac in Brittany are by far the most spectacular.

Lines as boundaries

As the example of the Stonehenge Cursus (as well as that of other cursuses) shows, a line is also a boundary. Features such as these cursuses, which seem to have divided one area (one type of settlement perhaps) from another, or the palisades that are being discovered at many sites (including Stonehenge, see p. 30), were effective barriers as well as having a ceremonial aspect of their own. It is readily assumed that a cursus or an avenue was designed specifically for walking along, possibly in approaching a vantage point at an auspicious occasion such as a solstice sunrise. Even in looking at the sky, it is important to be able to stand in a particular place in order to view the constellations or the position of the moon. By walking along a line, the appearance of the night sky changes. Perhaps that was indeed one of the uses to which the Stonehenge Avenue and other linear structures were put – as a line upon which to walk at night, 'guided' by the moon or the stars towards an event.

Stonehenge Cursus Barrows

The bowl and bell barrows of the Cursus barrow group lie parallel to the Cursus itself and are likewise aligned with the equinoctial sunrise.

West Kennet Avenue

The double line of standing stones that make up the Avebury Avenue echo the stone alignments on Dartmoor and at Carnac in Brittany.

At the top of the page, a diagram labelled with sites along a ley line: Tumulus, Stonehenge, Old Sarum, Salisbury Cathedral, Clearbury Ring, Frankenbury Camp.

Old Sarum Ley

One of two ley lines drawn through Stonehenge runs southwards through Old Sarum, Salisbury Cathedral and two Iron Age forts.

Ley lines

One of the commonly held beliefs about the landscape is that there are ancient lines that underpin it, connecting significant and ancient sites, and which may act as conduits for special forces and mystical powers. Belief in the existence of these lines – ley lines – is not simply the province of a New Age sensibility. The pursuit of ley lines was first advocated by Alfred Watkins, who claimed to have discovered an underlying geometry in the landscape in his native Herefordshire, and whose book *The Old Straight Track* remains in print after seventy years. In his 1922 book, *Early British Trackways*, he wrote:

> A visit to Blackwardine led me to note on the map a straight line starting from Croft Ambury, lying on parts of Croft Lane past the Broad, over hill points, through Blackwardine, over Risbury Camp, and through the high ground at Stretton Grandison, where I surmise a Roman station. I followed up the clue of sighting from hilltop to hilltop, the straight lines to my amazement passing over and over again through the same class of objects.

Basically, leys are held to criss-cross the countryside, with remarkably straight lines (some over 150 km/ 93 miles in length) running through prehistoric features, ancient churches, old lanes and trackways, and natural eminences. There are two supposed ley lines drawn through Stonehenge, which connect it in the first instance with Castle Ditches and Grovely Castle to the southwest, via the Avenue, to Sidbury Camp and a string of barrow mounds; and, in the second instance, in a more or less southerly direction through Old Sarum, Salisbury Cathedral and the Iron Age forts at Clearbury Ring and Frankenbury Camp.

Geometry in the landscape

Where Stonehenge is, Glastonbury Tor cannot be far behind; the hamlet of Whiteleaved Oak near Midsummer Hill camp in the Malvern Hills is equidistant from Glastonbury and Stonehenge, for example, and the triangle between the three is in the ratio 5:3:3. On this basis, an ancient and significant relationship has been claimed, although the significance – let alone the contemporaneity – of the three sites is presumed, rather than ever proved. The whole notion of ley lines is surprisingly tenacious, despite the efforts of authors such as Tom Williamson and Liz Bellamy to debunk it. Critics point out, for example, that these features are often of wildly differing dates, as in the Stonehenge–Salisbury ley, and that attempts to explain, say, the inclusion of a parish church by insisting that the church stood on an already ancient and sacred site are commonly disprovable.

West Kennet Long Barrow

One of the largest in Britain, this long barrow stretches for 100 m/110 yards. The burials inside may all have been members of the same family.

Connecting places by straight lines in an undulating landscape and without sophisticated surveying equipment is a difficult task, while even a multiplicity of points in the landscape may be 'connected' by straight lines through sheer chance. If dead-straight lines were the object, as transmitters perhaps of some unseen psychic energy, why are the monuments in even such an important landscape as Stonehenge not absolutely in straight alignment? The most cursory glance at the map will show that some, but not all, of the monuments are in roughly straight lines, and may meet at approximate right-angles, but it is all far from being a geometric grid. The conclusion seems inevitable that the workings of chance and an active imagination are more important explanations of ley lines than deep and mysterious underground forces.

Vertical and Horizontal

Stonehenge is, in Lord Renfrew's words, 'miraculous for its verticality'. Although the initial reaction to many prehistoric structures is to remark on their extensiveness and spread – especially in those cases, like a cursus, where the monument has been largely destroyed and is now only a pale mark in the ground – many were clearly designed to be tall. With the exception of the lintels on the sarsen circle and the

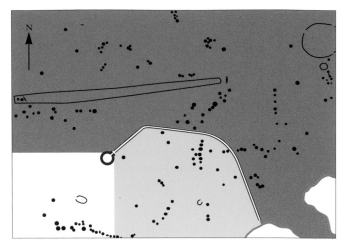

The dead and the living
The curving approach of the Avenue (outlined in red) separated the older monuments on the right, representing the dead (shown in brown), from the world of the living on the left (shown in green).

trilithons, all Stonehenge's standing stones originally stood upright, and all are of a very considerable height. Four adult men standing on each other's shoulders would still not reach to the top of one of the stones from the great trilithon. The smaller bluestones are slim and vertical. All the stones reach for the skies.

Many of the monuments of this era with a circular setting, in the West Country and elsewhere, incorporate uprights that must have had a powerful effect. Given the girth of the timbers used, monuments such as Durrington Walls (see p. 56) would also have had a distinctive sense of verticality when the participant was among them. Likewise, the timber palisades that have been identified at Stonehenge, Mount Pleasant in Dorset and at West Kennet near Avebury (see p. 64) were composed of tall uprights set very close together. Not only did they form a wide barrier, but a tall one as well. The banks (and accompanying ditches) of the earth structures, the henges and cursuses, also combined height with breadth to form an effective barrier, with occasional access points.

The largest monuments were also three-dimensional objects, stepping up (like the very early pyramids in Egypt) from their outermost limits to the inner space. Stonehenge and Durrington Walls both had a slightly lower innermost space, accentuating the feeling of isolation and exclusion that all these structures were undoubtedly intended to create.

Male and female stones at Avebury
The consistent differences in the paired stones at Avebury may have identified them as 'male' and 'female'.

Up and down, left and right

The theme of verticality and height among these monuments is continued by examining Stonehenge in its physical and topographical setting. People often remark on the position in which Stonehenge stands; it is not on the crest of a ridge or the top of a hill, but can be looked down upon. It is placed on a spur of land, a slight eminence, and some have described the bowl of the dry valley as rather like a set of nesting bowls. This was a landscape through which people moved: the use of the cursuses, the bringing of stones, the ceremonials in the henges were all based upon the fact of motion.

The formal approach to Stonehenge, the Avenue which makes its way through a landscape that was already filled with monumental graves and other structures when it was built (and was to be enriched by still more), exploits the contours of the land for its route and its visual effects. It also describes a path that keeps the older monuments, and hence the dead, always on the right-hand side in its approach. The new world, the living, were on the left.

Within Stonehenge there are similar differences between right and left. Looking at each pair of stones in the trilithon horseshoe, as Alasdair Whittle has recently remarked, it is noticeable that the left-hand stone of each pair is smoother than its counterpart on the right. Some of these left-hand stones also carry the carvings of axeheads and the like, which are one of Stonehenge's special features. Avebury, and particularly the West Kennet avenue, share some of these pairing features, and it has long been suggested that the different stone shapes there – uprights and squatter lozenges – in some way represent a male/female difference. Certainly, the much-disputed 'goddess' figure at Stonehenge is carved on a left-hand stone.

Careful analysis of all the material deposited on the floor and placed in pits and ditches at Woodhenge and at Durrington Walls similarly suggests a difference between right and left, with most deposited material at Woodhenge being on the right of the entrance axis. Given that one would usually walk around inside a circular monument, and that the solar component of Stonehenge would suggest the likelihood of walking in the direction of the sun's movement – left from the principal entrance – these directions may have had very particular resonances that we may now only guess at.

Water and land

A noticeable aspect of the Stonehenge landscape is that it is remarkably dry. The modern definitions of the landscape as a study area are bounded by the valleys of the River Till on the west and the more substantial

Rough and smooth
The stones of the trilithon horseshoe show remarkable contrasts between left and right: the uprights on the left being smoother than the ones on the right (and also carrying carvings).

River Avon on the east. These valleys are fairly steep-sided; dry valleys where water had once flowed, such as Stonehenge Bottom and that in which Durrington Walls was built, are a feature of the higher chalk ground, but there is little else in the way of running or standing water. This may seem surprising, given the need for water for living and the sheer numbers of people to be catered for in a construction phase or a ceremonial occasion.

Originally the river valleys would have been substantially wooded, and it has often been assumed that the upper ground of Salisbury Plain was easier to clear and live on, in addition to the narrow footing for habitation that the river itself offered. Today, by contrast, settlement is almost wholly concentrated in these valleys. Yet the rivers, and especially the Avon, were intimately connected to the Stonehenge landscape. Since it is most likely that the bluestones, and probably other materials, were transported up the Avon from the sea, its importance was obvious. The Avenue connects the river with Stonehenge, passing through some of the most important areas of this ritual landscape; some writers have advanced the notion that

the Avenue was built to commemorate the route along which the bluestones were carried in the final stage of their journey from Wales. Even if there was not such a direct and literal link, the Stonehenge Avenue was a connection between sacred water and sacred stones, across sacred earth.

Religion, Ritual and Power

It has always been tempting to imagine the sort of religious ceremonials that were conducted in and around Stonehenge in the Neolithic and Bronze Ages. Many flights of fancy have been devoted to that imagining. In the end, however, we are left with many clues but no real overall picture.

One clue is the importance of burial rituals, which have been so prominent in the archaeological record: from the exposure of corpses and then the scattering or interment of disarticulated bones in the causewayed enclosures, through the burial of a significant few in long barrows to the cremation and interment rites associated with the Bronze Age burials in round barrows, with attendant beakers and grave goods. Another clue may be the contents of one particular barrow grave excavated at Upton Lovell, only 14 km/ 9 miles west of Stonehenge (where some of the most beautiful gold objects from Wessex culture graves have been found). This contained the material effects of a man who is assumed to have been a shaman – a wise man or priest – from the Early Bronze Age. The artefacts from his grave, which are today displayed in Devizes Museum, include the bone points from a necklace and from the fringe edging of a coat, together with a hammer stone, a stone axe and cups made from flint. This, and the sumptuous burial in Bush Barrow of what was probably a chiefly personage (see pp. 50 and 52), point to a developed religious and ritual culture.

Shaman's grave goods
A stone axe, hammer stone and bone points from a necklace, found in a barrow grave at Upton Lovell in Wiltshire, probably belonged to a shaman or wise man.

The principal clue, though, must be the surviving monuments in their landscape. A succession of earth, stone and timber structures – some with alignments on celestial phenomena, and most incorporating deliberate references to the past, as well as a record of deposits and ritualized meetings and feasts – stand as testimony to the power of the territorial groups who had these monuments as their focal points. The celestial phenomena, the solstices (and perhaps the equinoxes), doubtless reflect above all the importance of the annual seasonal round, the life-giving properties of the sun, and the ideas of renewal, birth and death, which the changes in the cycles of both the sun and moon evoke.

Survivals

The first direct literary evidence for religious observance in early England is the description by Roman authors of the practices of the Celts, the Ancient Britons who were conquered by the invading Romans. If there was a substantial degree of continuity between the peoples of Neolithic and Bronze Age Britain, rather than an invasion and subjugation of one people by another (see p. 116), then there may also have been considerable continuity throughout the Bronze Age and into the Iron Age.

Features such as woodland and water, which played a significant part in Celtic religion, were almost certainly present in earlier rites. Although there was less emphasis on grandiloquent and labour-intensive monuments, and Celtic ceremonies were often conducted in woodland groves and clearings, there was always a sense in which many earlier monuments had grown out of, and memorialized the woods.

Gold from Upton Lovell

Gold artefacts also found at Upton Lovell are among the most beautiful objects from Wessex culture to have been discovered.

Shafts, such as that at Wilsford (see p. 58), were an element in Celtic religious observance across Europe, providing closer access to the gods and the elements. Weapons that possessed magical qualities fill the pages of Celtic mythology, and metal objects (including weapons that were ritually deposited in graves, streams and ponds) were a feature of religious observance in the Bronze Age and thereafter. The tradition of ritual deposit of 'cult' or venerated objects stretched back to the antlers and cattle jawbones in Stonehenge's first phase, and even earlier to the causewayed enclosures.

The Stonehenge landscape was largely abandoned from the Middle Bronze Age as a site of religious significance – at least as expressed in buildings and artefacts – and to expect any direct survival from that period is probably unwise. The argument of continuity may be taken too far, and we should guard against an over-emphasis on survivals. That Christmas occurs at the winter solstice and embodies some older 'pagan' rituals, for example, does not necessarily mean that there was a continuous tradition of solstice observation and knowledge – as some claim – from the era of Stonehenge right through to the modern era. In fact, the reinvention and revival of ancient ways is often a more potent argument than one of continuity. Similarly, it is often said that the legend of Merlin bringing the stones of Stonehenge from Ireland by

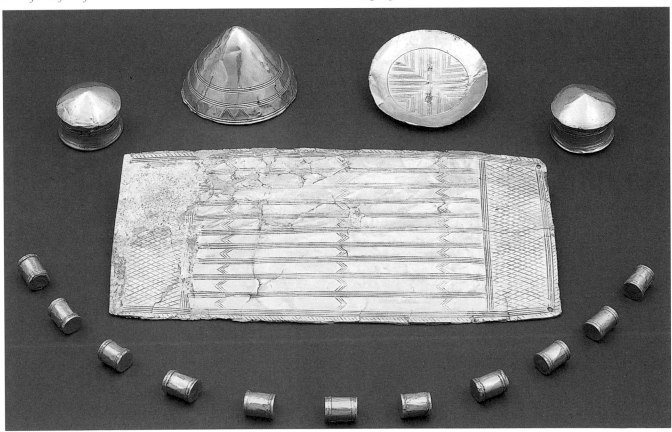

magic, which is recorded in the eleventh century, embodies a folk memory of the real stones being brought from afar, especially the bluestones coming from Wales. At first sight that may appear persuasive, but the evidence is thin, and may instead simply be an attempt to explain the otherwise inexplicable in terms of a known figure and an appropriate source.

A Ritual Landscape

We know more and more about these great structures, but still relatively little about how and where people lived their ordinary lives. The previous chapter focused on the people of Stonehenge – how they farmed, how they were buried, where they lived, indeed who they were. In this chapter, the monuments and the physical landscape are once again prominent, as are the ideas that may have animated them.

Many authors have defined Stonehenge as a set of exclusion zones, a phrase that may evoke the Falklands spirit as much as prehistoric

Stukeley as Chyndonax
In his antiquarian pursuits, William Stukeley imagined himself as the Arch-Druid.

belief: rituals being confined to one area, and living to another. Such elements as the Avenue, the palisade, the Cursus and the barrow cemeteries all divided up the landscape, often with barely penetrable barriers.

Yet the weight of evidence points to the whole Stonehenge area as having been one of intensive cultivation, as well as one of intensive religious and ritual observance. There was a metre depth of soil in the Mesolithic period at Stonehenge, which disappeared – washed into the streams – because the farming was so intensive for so long. The extensive and considerable scatters of flint and pottery, especially of the Beaker and Early Bronze Age periods, around Robin Hood's Ball in the first instance, and subsequently on Stonehenge Down and the nearby ridges, suggest that this was very much an inhabited area. This amount of material, had it been found other than at Stonehenge, would probably have been acclaimed as denoting a densely settled site, but is seen as somehow inappropriate or anomalous in an area that was clearly so very special.

The people who built the monuments almost certainly lived close at hand. Although the first direct evidence of habitation comes from Winterbourne Stoke in the Middle Bronze Age, like the Pueblo tribespeople

Celtic spring
Woodland and water played a prominent role in Celtic rites – ceremonies often taking place in woodland clearings, and springs being seen as having healing properties.

whose stories opened this chapter, there may have been particular individuals who were involved in regular skywatching and guardianship of sacred sites, and particular times of the year when many more people were closely integrated in ritual observance. Both aspects were woven into the general fabric of life. The people who lived close at hand also farmed nearby, and the surplus from their agriculture provided the means and the labour to build ever-greater monuments.

Druids

If there is one particular group associated in the popular mind with Stonehenge, it is the Druids – the priests of the Celtic religion of the Iron Age, which preceded the Roman conquest. Since the early years of the twentieth century, the 'revived' Druids (with a largely invented ritual and history) have celebrated the midsummer solstice at Stonehenge, as it is erroneously presumed their predecessors did.

Much of the blame, if it can be called that, is placed on the shoulders of William Stukeley. Although his archaeology was path-breaking, his historical analysis was flawed. Investigators had long searched for the kind of people who could have built such a prodigious wonder. Inigo Jones was convinced it was Roman; other authors thought it Anglo-Saxon or Dark Age. Stukeley's distinguished predecessor John Aubrey, a century beforehand, had first identified Stonehenge with the Druids, and Stukeley vigorously promoted the idea that the monument was a cult centre for a religious group that in reality had flourished something approaching 1,000 years after Stonehenge had been abandoned.

Perhaps that association with Druidism would by now have been forgotten, had it not been for the self-conscious revival – some would say invention – of a Druidic tradition in the latter part of the nineteenth century. Ancient Celtic culture, which was most prominently displayed in saving the Welsh and Gaelic languages from extinction, a poetic renaissance and the crowning of bards at eisteddfods, became intertwined with Druidism. The Ancient Order of Druids was a Freemasonry-like society formed in 1781; by 1905, when it first visited Stonehenge, it was a byword for respectability. It was confronted in succeeding years by the Celtic Revival form of Druidism, the Church of the Universal Bond, which became the better-known face of Druidism and conducted a running battle with the authorities over use of and access to Stonehenge (prefiguring the problems of the 1980s and 1990s), until an accommodation was reached in the mid-1920s.

A Stukeley Druid
Stukeley was largely responsible for our identification of Stonehenge as a place of Druid worship.

Why was Stonehenge so Special?

Although its origins may have been relatively insignificant, Stonehenge, built on an unprecedented scale, came to acquire a very great importance indeed.

A place of memories...

Stonehenge incorporated many memories within its form. There were both wooden and stone circles, as well as other shapes and forms using these materials, throughout the British Isles and the Atlantic fringe. A regularly spaced arrangement of timber uprights recalls a wood: in many instances, the woodland setting had been eradicated within recent memory, or was still present nearby. Pits recall the positions where trees once stood. Coneybury Henge (see p. 45), which is now within sight of Stonehenge itself, had almost certainly been constructed in a woodland clearing; when it was abandoned the woodland may have taken over the site once more. And it has been suggested that the localized clearing of the forest and the erection of substantial timbers in the Mesolithic post-holes discovered in the car park would have had a lasting effect on the local vegetation, so that Stonehenge's site in later millennia already had some discernible difference – and hence significance – attached to it.

There was indeed a timber setting at Stonehenge in its second construction phase; the various stone settings employed techniques that are more common in woodworking than in masonry to fix the elements together. Possibly these features recalled what was previously there, rather than being the result of ignorance of stone techniques on the part of the builders. Even the massive stone uprights display a vestigial sense of woodland. Since all the stones were transported with considerable labour many miles, they too embodied communal memories: of places or episodes of conquest and power, or of the particular qualities that the areas from which the stones came may have possessed, and thereby conferred on their new home.

The very fact that three successive types of monument were built one upon the other is itself evidence of Stonehenge being a place of continuity and memory. Although some of the other monuments, especially barrows, were reused or partly built upon by later generations, no other place had such a lengthy history of use, adaptation and reuse by different peoples separated by vast periods of time.

In many of those phases, Stonehenge was a burial ground, principally for cremation burials, and the remains of hundreds of individuals were interred within its circle. It also stood at the centre of an extensive barrow cemetery, comprising both long barrows and later varieties of round barrow. It embodied a communal memory, both of the recently dead and buried, and of long-vanished ancestors and predecessors.

The solar orientation carried with it a memory of the seemingly eternal annual round, the rising of the sun on the longest day and its setting on the shortest day, the transition of the seasons. Deliberate depositing of objects into the structure of Stonehenge was another way of recalling the past to mind. Recent re-evaluation of Durrington Walls and Woodhenge has shown how the non-random way in which apparently mundane items – animal bones, flint tools, broken pottery and partial human remains – were scattered over the floor contains hidden meanings, concealed memories of past ceremonies and activities. Features at Stonehenge, such as the already centuries-old cattle jawbones placed in the terminals of the original ditch, likewise carry a significant emphasis on the past and the power that it undoubtedly conferred.

... and a place of futures

Even if one does not necessarily subscribe to the notion that Stonehenge was a predictor of eclipses, or even the likely apparent movements of the moon and the sun, this great monument was nevertheless a place for looking forward. Its construction is intimately bound up with ideas of renewal and rebirth, the cycle of annual change, if not longer periodicities.

Sheer size and monumentality, moreover, helped ensure the survival of Stonehenge into the modern age. Other important sites from the Neolithic and Bronze Ages may have fallen prey to later development and the pressure of greater numbers of people; there may be other important places still to be found. The fact that the future held stagnation and agricultural marginalization for the higher chalkland of Salisbury Plain also helped ensure Stonehenge's survival, as well as that of many of its surrounding features. For, from the later part of the Bronze Age, interest in building and maintaining these monumental – even megalomaniac – structures waned.

In the centuries that followed Stonehenge was largely forgotten, only to be revived and to become again the symbol of the archaeology and the achievement of the people of early Britain.

Midsummer's morning
Whatever the meaning of Stonehenge, the midsummer sun shining down the Avenue was the climax of the ritual year.

THE LEGACY OF STONEHENGE

The power of Stonehenge has continued to fire the
imagination of artists through the twentieth century.

'THERE WAS NOT one Stonehenge but many. The place was always there, but the sense of place and space changed radically.' Professor Timothy Darvill's summing-up of this great monument in its prehistoric phases can also stand for the way in which Stonehenge has been treated and regarded in the centuries AD; it has borne heavy responsibilities, of myth and conjecture, inspired artists, withstood the development of archaeology as a discipline, the demands of mysticism and the expectations of visitors. The great trilithons have come to symbolize the prehistoric past. Now, finally, the enduring problem of how to fulfil the needs of the many visitors is approaching a solution. The legacy of Stonehenge is also a pointer to the future.

An icon through the ages

That Stonehenge had many visitors in the centuries of Roman rule and the so-called Dark Ages is evident from the archaeological record of dropped and lost items or of occasional burials. Such a substantial and enigmatic structure must surely have occasioned some of the wonder and admiration with which it has since been regarded. Yet no documentary references survive, except ambiguous and unspecific comments by a Roman historian, until after the Norman Conquest.

Henry of Huntingdon's history of England, written in *c.* 1130, described 'Stanenges, where stones of wonderful size have been erected after the manner of doorways, so that doorway appears to have been raised upon doorway; and no one can conceive how such great stones have been raised aloft, or why they were built there.' This was one of the wonders of Britain. Geoffrey of Monmouth's *History of the Kings of Britain*, which was written in 1136, also addressed the question of Stonehenge.

Merlin's magic

Geoffrey's history attempted to explain 'how such great stones have been raised aloft', invoking the magician Merlin: Stonehenge was a memorial to Aurelius Ambrosius's battle victory at Amesbury, and was brought from Ireland by Merlin's magic. The Irish stones had in turn been erected by giants. Through this legend Stonehenge is linked to the story of Arthur, nephew of Aurelius and Merlin's protégé. Geoffrey's history survived – much embellished and illustrated – for centuries, and Merlin's intervention was still being celebrated in the sixteenth century. By that time, more sceptical counsels had begun to prevail, and the twin processes of more rational investigation and tourist visiting began.

Yet Merlin has been revived in recent years, not simply with the interest in mysticism and the New Age, but also by the late Stuart Piggott, who suggested that the story embodied a residual folk memory of the bluestones' transportation from the far west – albeit from Wales rather than Ireland. This may, however, be pressing the point too far. Geoffrey of Monmouth's stories contained many personal embellishments, bringing in ancient figures, wonders and events.

Many of the increasing number of visitors from the sixteenth century onwards wrote about their experiences and tried to make sense of what they saw. Some of the most important of them we have already met: John Aubrey, William Stukeley, Sir Richard Colt Hoare. In their case wonderment was inextricably linked to a developing method of archaeology.

Turner's watercolour

Like many artists, Turner was drawn to paint Stonehenge. His Romantic portrayal of the stone circle throws the stones into relief against a characteristically turbulent sky.

Tess of the d'Urbervilles

Perhaps it is surprising that Stonehenge has inspired so little in the way of imaginative literature. There have been Victorian melodramatic potboilers, a crucial scene in Peter Ackroyd's *Hawksmoor* (1987) and modern science fiction – while many attempts to explain Stonehenge over the years have been as good as any fiction – but only one major literary landmark. The dénouement of Thomas Hardy's *Tess of the d'Urbervilles* (1891) takes place at Stonehenge, memorably expressing the power of the ages, weighing down upon the tortured heroine. Exhausted, Tess lies down to sleep on the Altar Stone, and at daybreak the circle is surrounded by men come to arrest her.

'Let her finish her sleep!' Clare implored in a whisper of the men as they gathered round. When they saw where she lay, which they had not done till then, they showed no objection, and stood watching her, as still as the pillars around. He went to the stone and bent over her, holding one poor little hand; her breathing now was quick and small, like that of a lesser creature than a woman. All waited in the growing light, their faces and hands as if they were silvered, the remainder of their figures dark, the stones glistening green-grey, the Plain still a mass of shade. Soon the light was strong, and a ray shone upon her unconscious form, peering under her eyelids and waking her.

'What is it, Angel?' she said, starting up. 'Have they come for me?'

'Yes, dearest,' he said. 'They have come.'·

'It is as it should be,' she murmured.

Sir John Soane

Soane used painted perspectives and plans of Stonehenge to illustrate his lectures to the Royal Academy and helped to bring about a revival of interest in its architecture.

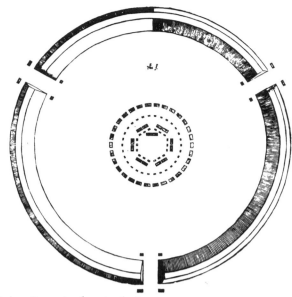

Inigo Jones's classical view

Jones viewed Stonehenge as a Roman monument comprising a geometrically precise circle in which all the elements were regularly spaced and exactly positioned.

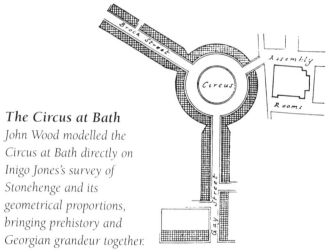

The Circus at Bath

John Wood modelled the Circus at Bath directly on Inigo Jones's survey of Stonehenge and its geometrical proportions, bringing prehistory and Georgian grandeur together.

Art and Architecture

If Stonehenge has had relatively little place in imaginative literature, it has certainly been of major importance in the visual arts and in architecture. Prose can rarely convey the power of the place in the way that an image does, and has. The first pictorial representations of Stonehenge date from the fourteenth century, embellishing manuscript histories and the story of Merlin's wizardry. Since then, Stonehenge's image has been used and distorted to carry a wealth of meaning.

The first person to survey Stonehenge on a systematic basis was Inigo Jones, architect and masque designer to the court of Charles I. He believed that Stonehenge was a much-dilapidated Roman monument. Jones, whose greatest importance as an architect lay in his introduction to England of the designs of Andrea Palladio from Italy, based upon antique precedents, turned Stonehenge into a geometrical temple that closely followed classical ideals: a circle containing an exact hexagonal central enclosure of the trilithons, and three regularly spaced entrances through the surrounding bank. Although Jones's conclusions were a dead-end as far as archaeology was concerned, they have survived in the form of the Circus, one of the grand set-pieces of Georgian Bath, which the developer John Wood consciously modelled on Jones's survey of Stonehenge.

The engravings of the monument published in the 1740s by William Stukeley, who brought both Stonehenge and Avebury to the attention of a wider reading and antiquarian public, are among the achievements of an age that seems

Early interpretations of Stonehenge

Sir Richard Colt Hoare compared his predecessors' interpretations of Stonehenge's architecture with the results of his own archaeological inquiry.

to have become besotted with topography. Stonehenge entered the architectural mainstream once more through the investigations and scholarship of Sir John Soane. His lectures to the Royal Academy in the early nineteenth century, which rank among the most important architectural pronouncements of any age, included dissertations on the form of Stonehenge (and a few other 'Druidical antiquities'). His museum in Lincoln's Inn Field, London still houses the painted perspectives and plans, forerunners of the lecture-room slide show, that he used to illustrate his

INIGO JONES.

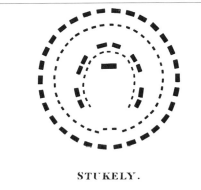

STUKELY.

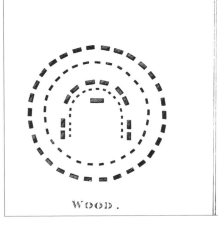

WOOD.

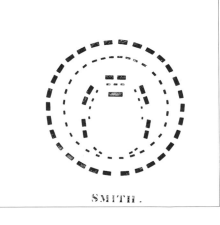

SMITH.

discourse, as well as a cork model of Stonehenge, which stands alongside other models of important buildings from classical Greece and Rome.

Romantic and mystical interpretations

Apart from inspiring the neo-classicists, Stonehenge became an object of importance in both the Romantic and the mystical traditions of the late eighteenth and nineteenth centuries. William Blake's work, which he himself described as 'Visionary or Imaginative; it is an endeavour to Restore what the Ancients called the Golden Age', incorporated Stonehenge and Druidical fancies that derived from Stukeley. In *Jerusalem* (1804),

John Constable

Constable's Stonehenge, *painted in 1835, was starker and more dramatic than Turner's image, focusing more closely on the fallen stones, but with the sky again assuming a prominent role.*

the children of Albion walk beneath a vast trilithon framing the new moon, and heroic muscular figures measure out a lintelled stone circle from which serpentine avenues extend.

The shepherd of Salisbury Plain, a repository of wisdom in his solitary occupation that allowed ample time for reflection, was a figure in many pictorial representations of Stonehenge, as well as the subject in 1802 of one of the most treacly moralizing tracts by Hannah Moore. Above all, Stonehenge was the sublime and often highly dramatic subject for some of the great painters of the early nineteenth century (as well as for some of the less accomplished). Turner and Constable both painted views of Stonehenge that survived long in the popular mind, not least because they were frequently reproduced as engravings. J.M.W. Turner painted Stonehenge in 1811–13, depicting the stones in all their Romantic magnificence both at sunset and

at daybreak. His sky is the Sublime writ large, a precursor of his later expressive style, while the everyday protagonists of farm life – carts, labourers and naturally a shepherd with his flock of sheep – play just as important a role as the stones. Lightning, shafts of light and swirling cloud heighten the dramatic effect. The shepherd also made his appearance in John Constable's equally celebrated view (painted in 1835 from sketches he had made in 1820). More accurate in its depiction of the stones than Turner's portrayal, Constable's picture again gave the sky, being 'the keynote and chief organ of sentiment', an important place in the scheme.

The monolithic character of the hewn stones has appealed to contemporary artists in the same way that their setting did to the Romantics. Photography has been the principal medium – Bill Brandt produced some of the most enduring images of Stonehenge in 1947, captured in his characteristic, brooding monochrome – but not the sole form. Henry Moore's lithographs of 1974, showing the stones at close quarters and thus emphasizing their monumentality, derived from his first sight of the stones at night. 'I was alone and tremendously impressed,' he wrote to Sir Stephen Spender. '(Moonlight as you know enlarges everything, and the mysterious depths and distances made it seem enormous.)' Spender's own thoughts on the finished lithographs are a fitting comment on the power of the stones themselves: 'Such works have not been made into art objects. The hand of man has only assisted to make them look more overpowering.'

Henry Moore
Moore's lithographs of Stonehenge were influenced by a visit that the sculptor made at night, when moonlight seemed to magnify the proportions of the stones.

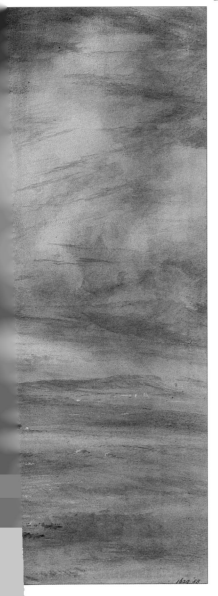

New Age

If ours is an age that seems to have lost much of its religious faith, Stonehenge is one place that has become invested with an ever-greater mystical power. For some, within the broad group that is given the shorthand title 'New Age', the mystery of Stonehenge has become even more powerful than the actual monument itself.

The monument has long been the focus of an alternative vision of religion and supernatural power. It was part of the heady mystical brew in the writings and illustrations of William Blake, and became one of the focuses of the revival (or creation) of a nature-worshipping Druid religion in the nineteenth century. In the twentieth century, with the development of the idea of ley lines – 'archaic whispers from the landscape', linking significant places across the landscape, and increasingly thought of as energy lines – and with the supposed discovery of astronomical features in Stonehenge and other prehistoric monuments, these alternative visions have been further developed. The rise of anthropology has opened our eyes to other societies, which observe the heavens and worship the heavenly bodies, or which believe that spirit forces run in straight lines across the earth, making these beliefs less alien than they might otherwise appear.

Earth and sky mysteries

There are many aspects to Stonehenge and similar sites that are being investigated by 'alternative' researchers. The Dragon Project, for example, instituted in 1977, has been but one attempt (albeit with ambiguous results) to assess the beliefs that anomalous electromagnetic energies are to be found at the major megalithic sites. Light effects have been observed at this and other megalithic locations, which has underwritten the notion that Stonehenge is a focus for UFO (unidentified flying object) activity. All the writing about ancient mysteries connected with Stonehenge has fuelled further speculation. John Michell's *A View over Atlantis* in 1969, for example, which became a key text in the early stages of New Age thought, revealed the sacred dimensions of Stonehenge as the new Jerusalem. Almost every year a new publication makes similar claims for Stonehenge as embodying eternal and mystical verities – although Stonehenge still has a long way to go in this regard compared with the body of publications on the meaning of the Pyramids in Egypt. In the 1990s the phenomenon of ever-more elaborate crop

Crop circles
Recent crop circles mysteriously (or perhaps mischievously) appearing within the vicinity of Stonehenge have aroused amazement and scepticism in equal proportions.

circles – the regular, flattened patterns in growing crops, which appear at speed without warning or obvious physical cause – has caught the imagination of press and public alike. Stonehenge specifically and the Wiltshire chalk uplands generally have been among the major centres of crop-circle activity, and in most summers crop circles close to Stonehenge attract both amazed and sceptical visitors.

Druids and festivals

Earth mysteries are one variety of the different views of Stonehenge that exist outside the mainstream; the activities of the Druids, and the Stonehenge festivals of the 1970s and 1980s, are another. Druidic ceremonies, especially at the midsummer solstice, have been a feature of Stonehenge throughout the twentieth century. Usually fewer than a hundred people took part in these ritual observances. In 1974 the modern free festival at Stonehenge began, with its alliance of hippies, travellers, music-lovers and New Age believers, who celebrated paganism and the sacredness of the earth. The annual festival was the occasion for increasing antag-onism between, festival-goers and farmers, the police, and the National Trust on whose land they were squatting. In 1984, 30,000 people attended, bringing disruption, litter and noise, arousing considerable public and official hostility. Matters came to a head the following year, when an 'exclusion zone' around Stonehenge was instituted; the violent Battle of the Beanfield between police and a travellers' convoy ensued on 1 June. In subsequent years the festivals have been stopped, and all have been refused access to the stones at

midsummer – a move described by the Arch-Druid of the Glastonbury order in 1989 as 'like closing Westminster Abbey at Christmas'. An uneasy peace has since ensued, and alternative venues have been found.

Stonehenge and its surroundings are as much sacred territory to some people today as they were to the prehistoric peoples who built them. In some aspects – notably astronomy and the study of alignments in monuments – the archaeological world is coming towards an intellectual accommodation with New Age thinking. In other aspects – whether it concerns Atlantis or geomagnetic force fields – the two are as far apart as ever. Continuing and avid interest in the para-normal, and a growing sense of respect for the earth, account for a considerable part of general interest in Stonehenge. It is as much a part of the late twentieth century as is respect for the scientific basis of modern archaeological investigation.

Modern Druids
From their nineteenth-century revival the Druids followed the lead of William Stukeley and adopted Stonehenge and the celebration of the midsummer solstice.

Stonehenge's Future

If people in the Middle Ages associated Stonehenge with Arthur, there are those today who have hoped that the once and future king would come again to the rescue in Stonehenge's hour of greatest need. The story of Stonehenge in the twentieth century is not simply that of the development of archaeology as a discipline, but also of the growing interest in the mysteries of the earth and of the rising tide of popular interest in survivals from the past and the desire to visit them. Tourism and the visiting of historic sites is nothing new. What has changed beyond all measure is the sheer volume of visitors. For Stonehenge to survive intact into the centuries to come, the pressures of the present age need urgently to be addressed.

This great monument is being besieged in ways that it has never been before; having stood for millennia, the fear remains that without appropriate policies it may be ravaged by a few decades of concentrated, mass tourism and by new road networks that will speed traffic to and across its landscape.

Past, present and future

Three views of the monument and its setting (opposite) express the history, the fears and the hopes for the future of the site. In John Constable's vision of more than a century and a half ago, Stonehenge stood alone in a downland grass landscape. A pair of lonely tracks connected this upland spectacle to the outside world. By the late twentieth century, the tracks have become major highways which cross the World Heritage Site passing either side of the stone circle from east to west, threatening its long-term existence, severing the site into three pieces, endangering and restricting the public's access and enjoyment. The southern road, the A303, provides one of the principal access routes to the holiday destinations of the south-west. It is the car, the bus and the lorry that have been the bane of twentieth-century Stonehenge. Since the 1930s the volume of motor traffic has increased inexorably, and is expected to double in the next ten years. Off the northern road, now the A344, lies the official car-park for visitors to Stonehenge. The cafeteria there may sell rock cakes, but the lack of appropriate facilities for such an important site have become the despair of English Heritage, parliamentary committees, and the visiting general public.

The paradox of Stonehenge is that, although it is generally revered as being among the largest and most awe-inspiring of prehistoric monuments anywhere in the world, the central circle of stones is too small to meet all the demands that are placed upon it. Three-quarters of a million people come to Stonehenge every year (half as many again as came in the late 1960s), while very many more see it as they pass along the neighbouring highways. The great stones, which would have seemed huge to an eighteenth-century visitor on horseback, are dwarfed by the coaches that bring their twentieth-century successors. The central stone circle has been closed to visitors since the late 1970s, because it became frequently grossly overcrowded, the land surface was being rapidly eroded, and even the stones were in danger of sustaining serious damage. Those who come now, although they have to view the stones from 10 metres/33 feet or more away, are at least given a more total picture than they might otherwise get. They would have an even more complete picture if they were to explore the wealth and variety of the 451 other monuments and features in the vicinity.

Meanwhile, although it is dual carriageway for most of its length, the A303 is reduced to a single carriageway and is a notorious traffic bottleneck as it passes by Stonehenge and through the neighbouring village of Winterbourne Stoke. Official plans to more than double the width of the A303 in this incredibly sensitive area have provided a focus for anger and dissent; finally, after a definitive planning conference late in 1995, the British government accepted in 1996 that if the landscape was to be respected any upgraded road must be underground.

This is a vision for Stonehenge's future that in some ways brings it all full circle once more, and the prospect of the millennium has galvanized action. The vision is for a landscape without the sound and sight of the roads: in which the land is returned to grazed downland pasture, in which visitors will be free to wander throughout this broad, sacred sweep of ground and have access to the stones themselves which has been denied for so long. A 'virtual reality' version of Stonehenge has already been developed, which allows spectators to 'wander' at will among electronic versions of the standing stones. There may yet be an 'actual reality' version of the same.

Such plans have been in the making and remaking for some time, but the impetus created by the Millennium Commission's search for popular projects which will be welcomed worldwide has become the catalyst for bringing English Heritage, who are responsible for the stone circle, and the National Trust, who own the land in the immediate vicinity, into joint partnership. As the means are found, so the plans for change are in place.

Engraving after Constable

In the early nineteenth century Stonehenge could easily be approached and must have appeared massive in the landscape.

Stonehenge today

With more than three-quarters of a million visitors, Stonehenge is enclosed by fences, entrance to the inner circle is prohibited and traffic roars past on the nearby trunk roads.

The 21st century?

If the A344 is closed and the A303 tunneled, Stonehenge will once again become part of the sacred landscape in which visitors can absorb the unique atmosphere of the stone circle.

A Millennium Park

The visual motif of the trilithons has been a gift to advertisers and international image-makers for well over a century. From pub-signs to bank commercials, telephone cards to petrol posters. These images are perhaps the most obvious and everyday instance of the power of Stonehenge in the popular imagination. Yet, as has been the consistent theme of this book and the thrust of archaeological opinion, there is a great deal more to Stonehenge than the massive central stones, however important they may be. A proper understanding of the ritualistic landscape, and a better comprehension of sacred geometries and ritual space, would add immeasurably to the power of Stonehenge.

Stonehenge's supreme importance was recognised by its inscription by UNESCO in 1986 as a World Heritage Site because of its outstanding universal appeal. Its place in the development of British and world archaeology is assured. The plans for the future are designed to enhance and to conserve that privileged position.

The scheme for the future

The primary objective of the plans is to create a setting and environment for Stonehenge that is appropriate to its status as a World Heritage Site, and with minimal disruption to the landscape and the archaeology. This involves the removal of the existing car parking and visitor facilities, roads, fences and all the other accumulated twentieth-century clutter, the closure of the A344 and the restoration of the natural landscape. This is a landscape in which some 80 per cent of the land is currently in arable production. The scheme provides for the National Trust to extend its already not inconsiderable landholding of 587 hectares, so as to encompass the core area of the World Heritage Site (1,064 hectares of the total 2,665 hectares), and to promote grassland rather than crop-growing agriculture. Management of the whole park would then be undertaken by a specially-constituted Trust. These proposals are expected to take some twenty years to come to full fruition.

Additionally, in order to manage public access and enjoyment, new facilities providing for the physical needs of the visitors (parking, catering and retailing) will be built outside the World Heritage Site, 4 km/2½ miles from the central stones, close to the Countess Roundabout near Amesbury where the present stretch of the dual carriageway A303 ends. A low emission, low impact transport link, travelling along existing tracks, one that is therefore environmentally acceptable, would provide a connection for those visitors who are unable or unwilling to walk the few kilometres over the grass to Larkhill whence all those except the unable would walk to the stones.

Grassland and woodland

Undisturbed chalk downland is usually very rich in species of plants. An unexpected benefit of the presence of the armed forces on Salisbury Plain throughout this century has been the preservation of many such areas of chalk land, together with rare butterflies and other insects that feed there and the birds that nest on the ground. By creating a grassed landscape once again, sowing a permanent mix of typical unimproved grassland species, encouraging herbaceous species to spread into the surrounding turf, and controlled grazing with sheep, the whole Stonehenge area will become the largest and most important natural and archaeological park in Europe.

Meanwhile, many of the plantations of trees within the area are inappropriate (in scale, position and species). They damage archaeological remains (especially on Normanton and Wilsford Downs), and are already in many instances at the end of their natural span. The aim is therefore to provide appropriate new woodland, remove or thin woods in offending positions, and manage both new and existing woodland to encourage diversity of age and species.

Deepening understanding

Above all, the objective is to create a park with free access for all those who choose to walk and transport for those who are disabled or willing to pay, a prehistoric park where there is no sign of modern intrusion, a natural landscape where visitors will be encouraged to roam in safety and to walk among the stones as our ancestors did for thousands of years. This will enhance the experience of Stonehenge, and deepen understanding of it. The plans for the new visitor facilities, the result of a Private Finance Initiative, at Larkhill from which the circle of stones will be visible will provide for the spiritual needs of the visitors and will incorporate a number of architectural and interpretative features to aid the understanding of Stonehenge and its setting. The scheme includes such elements as a woodland setting (sheltering buildings from view) and state-of-the-art display technology.

The landscape without the roads will be more readily interpreted and understood than is ever possible at present. There is the visual bowl within which Stonehenge is set, the natural spur above Stonehenge Bottom on which it stands, and the relationship with

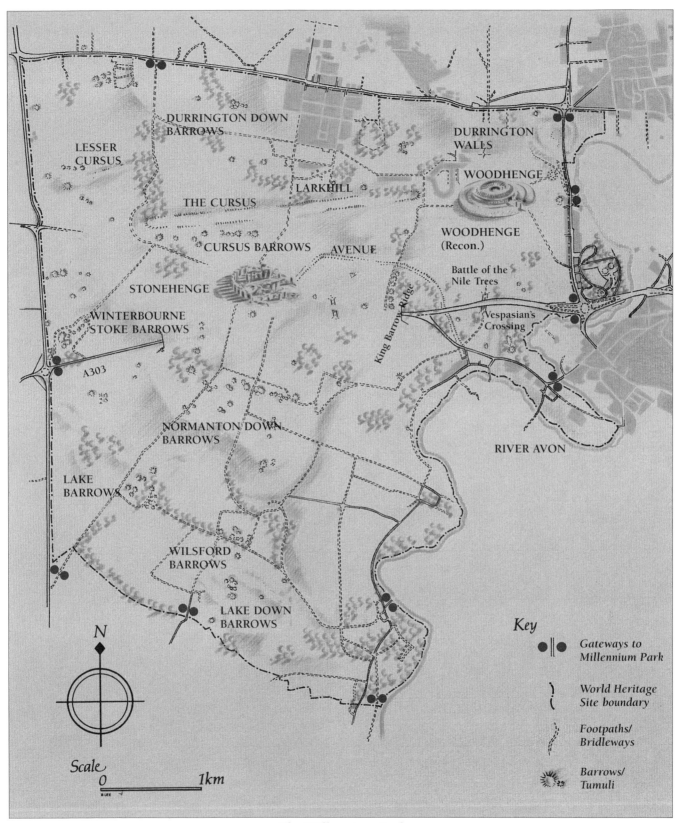

Key

● ‖ ● Gateways to Millennium Park

) World Heritage Site boundary

) Footpaths/ Bridleways

Barrows/ Tumuli

The Millennium Park

The Millennium Park will contain all the principal monuments within the sacred landscape and cover most of the World Heritage Site. Land purchase and management agreements, together with the removal of the roads, will preserve Stonehenge and its environs for posterity.

the other monuments such as the Cursus and the Avenue. The experience will be enhanced by improved information about these other features. A number of areas within the World Heritage Site have been designated as the focus of the likely next stages of archaeological investigation, whether in the form of excavation or less intrusive but highly revealing geophysical techniques, building on the initiatives of the previous twenty years. These plans include not only Stonehenge itself, the Avenue and the Palisade, but also many of the barrows which have remained undisturbed since Colt Hoare's day. That so many fortuitous discoveries were made alongside the A344 and in the car park bodes well for the prospect of what is yet to be revealed as Stonehenge enters its fifth millennium.

By understanding Stonehenge, we will also come to have a better comprehension of other prehistoric areas, even of other cultures. One leading archaeologist, fearing that over-concentration on this tiny enclave constricts the intellect, exhorts colleagues to go and sit in front of the Taj Mahal and return both reinvigorated and with new insight. For Stonehenge, the Taj Mahal, the Pyramids, or Chichen Itza are all marvels: of architecture, of construction, of civilization, of power.

Stonehenge for all

Stonehenge is a monument that has been invented and reinvented over the centuries. It has been variously a Roman temple, a Druidic enclosure, the monument to King Arthur's family's exploits in war, the world's first computer. Stonehenge has been seen as exemplifying eternal truths in architecture, as a testbed for astronomical observation, and as a vehicle for space and time travel. A symbol of the New Age, an episode in the development and containment of civil rights, and an object lesson in archaeological enquiry, it has been the proving ground for public policies that seek to match the demands of visitors with the need to protect the built heritage for future generations. Jacquetta Hawkes's dictum, that every generation gets the Stonehenge it desires, or deserves, remains as true as it ever was. The late twentieth century both desires and deserves to preserve and revitalize. We might also remember Sir Richard Colt Hoare's words when he stepped within the framework of the stones. *How grand! How wonderful! How incomprehensible!*

Hale Bopp over Stonehenge
The Hale Bopp comet travels across the night sky above Stonehenge personifying the power and mystery of the Heavens which prehistoric man tried so hard to understand.

Bibliography

The literature on Stonehenge and its surroundings has been transformed in recent years by a wealth of specialist studies, culminating in:
R.M.J. Cleal, K. Walker and R. Montague with others, *Stonehenge in its landscape*, English Heritage Archaeological Report 10 (1995).

Reactions to and developments from that volume are published in:
Proceedings of the British Academy, 92 (1997), the proceedings of the 1996 Royal Society/British Academy/English Heritage conference on Stonehenge.

Before that, there were two outstanding studies of the region:
Julian Richards, *The Stonehenge Environs Project*, English Heritage Archaeological Report, 16 (1990), and
Royal Commission on Historical Monuments (England), *Stonehenge and its environs* (Edinburgh University Press, 1979).

These provided the backbone for
Julian Richards, *Stonehenge* (English Heritage/Batsford, 1991).

Most successful of the previous generation of more general books on Stonehenge is:
Richard Atkinson, *Stonehenge*, 3rd ed. (Penguin, 1979).

A wholly different tack, looking at Stonehenge through the eyes of succeeding ages, was taken by:
Christopher Chippindale, *Stonehenge complete*, 2nd ed. (Thames & Hudson, 1994).

Among other studies and works consulted for this book are:

Albert J. Ammerman and L.L. Cavalli-Sforza, *The Neolithic transition and the genetics of populations in Europe* (Princeton University Press, 1986)

Paul Ashbee, *The earthen long barrow in Britain*, 2nd ed. (Geo Books, 1984)

Paul Ashbee, Martin Bell and Edwina Proudfoot, *Wilsford Shaft: excavations 1960-2*, English Heritage Archaeological Report, 11 (1989)

R.J.C. Atkinson, *Stonehenge and neighbouring monuments*, 5th impression (English Heritage, 1993)

A.F. Aveni, *Skywatchers of Ancient Mexico*, (University of Texas Press, 1981)

Paul G. Bahn (ed.), *The Cambridge illustrated history of archaeology* (Cambridge University Press, 1996)

Paul G. Bahn (ed.), *The story of archaeology* (Weidenfeld and Nicholson, 1996)

M. Balfour, *Megalithic mysteries* (Dragon's World, 1992)

J.W. Barber, 'The orientation of the recumbent stone circles of the south-west of Ireland', *Journal of Kerry Historical and Archaeological Society*, 6 (1973)

Michael Barnes et al., *Secrets of Lost Empires. Reconstructing the glories of ages past* (BBC Books, 1996): Cynthia Page, 'Stonehenge', pp. 8–45

John C. Barrett, *Fragments from antiquity. An archaeology of social life in Britain, 2900–1200 BC* (Blackwell, 1993)

J.C. Barrett, R. Bradley and M. Green, *Landscape, monuments and society. The prehistory of Cranborne Chase* (Cambridge University Press, 1991)

M. Bell, P.J. Fowler and S.W. Hillson (eds), *The Experimental Earthwork Project, 1960–1992*, Council for British Archaeology Research Report (1996)

Barbara Bender, 'Theorising landscapes, and the prehistoric landscapes of Stonehenge', *Man*, 27 (1992)

Robert Bewley, *Prehistoric settlements* (Batsford/English Heritage)

Peter Bogucki, *Forest farmers and stockholders: early agriculture and its consequences in north central Europe* (Cambridge University Press, 1988)

Richard Bradley, *The prehistoric settlement of Britain* (Routledge & Kegan Paul, 1978)

Richard Bradley and Mark Edmonds, *Interpreting the axe trade. Production and exchange in Neolithic Britain* (Cambridge University Press, 1993)

Aubrey Burl, *A guide to the stone circles of Britain, Ireland and Brittany* (Yale University Press, 1995)

Aubrey Burl, *Prehistoric Avebury* (Yale University Press, 1979)

Aubrey Burl, 'Stonehenge: slaughter, sacrifice and sunshine', *Wiltshire Archaeological and Natural History Magazine*, 87 (1994)

Aubrey Burl, 'The Heel Stone, Stonehenge: a study in misfortunes', *Wiltshire Archaeological and Natural History Magazine*, 84 (1991)

Aubrey Burl, *The Stonehenge people* (Dent, 1987)

Humphrey Case, 'Beakers: deconstruction and after', *Proceedings of the Prehistoric Society*, 59 (1993)

Humphrey Case, 'Some Wiltshire beakers and their contexts', *Wiltshire Archaeological and Natural History Magazine*, 88 (1985)

Rodney Castleden, *Neolithic Britain: New Stone Age sites* (Routledge, 1992)

Rodney Castleden, *The making of Stonehenge* (Routledge, 1993)

Rodney Castleden, *The Stonehenge people. An exploration of life in Neolithic Britain 4700–2000 BC* (Routledge, 1987)

Luigi Luca and Francesco Cavalli-Sforza, *The great human diasporas. The history of diversity and evolution* (Addison-Wesley, 1995)

Christopher Chippindale et al., *Who owns Stonehenge?* (Batsford, 1990)

D.V. Clarke, T.G. Cowie and A. Foxon, *Symbols of power at the time of Stonehenge* (National Museum of Antiquities of Scotland, 1985)

Sir Richard Colt Hoare, *The ancient history of Wiltshire*, 2 vols (1812)

Keith Critchlow, *Time stands still: new light on megalithic science* (St Martin's Press, 1982)

Barry Cunliffe (ed.), *The Oxford illustrated prehistory of Europe* (Oxford University Press, 1994)

Timothy Darvill, *Prehistoric Britain from the air* (Cambridge University Press, 1996)

Mark Edmonds, *Stone tools and society: working stone in Neolithic and Bronze Age Britain* (Batsford, 1995)

George Eogan, *Knowth and the passage tombs of Ireland* (Thames & Hudson, 1986)

J.G. Evans, 'Stonehenge: the environment in the late Neolithic and early Bronze Age, and a Beaker Age burial', *Wiltshire Archaeological and Natural History Magazine*, 78 (1984)

Alex Gibson, 'The Sarn-y-Bryn-Caled cursus complex, Welshpool, Powys, and the timber circles of Great Britain and Ireland', *Proceedings of the Prehistoric Society*, 60 (1994)

Alex Gibson, 'The timber circle at Sarn-y-Bryn-Caled, Welshpool, Powys: ritual and sacrifice in Bronze Age mid-Wales', *Antiquity*, 66 (1992)

Alex Gibson and Ann Woods, *Prehistoric pottery for the archaeologist* (Leicester University Press, 1990)

Bo Gräslund, 'Prehistoric soul beliefs in northern Europe', *Proceedings of the Prehistoric Society*, 60 (1994)

Jan Harding, 'Social histories and regional perspectives in the Neolithic of lowland England', *Proceedings of the Prehistoric Society*, 61 (1995)

P. Harding, 'The Chalk Plaque Pit, Amesbury', *Proceedings of the Prehistoric Society*, 54 (1988)

Richard J. Harrison, *The Beaker folk. Copper Age archaeology in western Europe* (Thames & Hudson, 1980)

Jacquetta Hawkes, *A land* (1951; reprinted David & Charles, 1978)

Jacquetta Hawkes, 'God in the machine', *Antiquity*, 41 (1967)

Jacquetta Hawkes, *Man and the sun* (Cresset Press, 1962)

Gerald S. Hawkins with John B. White, *Stonehenge decoded* (Souvenir Press, 1966)

Andrew Hayes, *Archaeology of the British Isles* (Batsford, 1993)

Fred Hoyle, *On Stonehenge* (Heinemann Educational Books, 1977)

Ronald Hutton, *The pagan religions of the ancient British Isles. Their nature and legacy* (Blackwell, 1991)

Ronald Hutton, *The stations of the sun. A history of the ritual year in Britain* (Oxford University Press, 1996)

ICOMOS UK, *Heritage & tourism* (ICOMOS, 1990)

Roger G. Kennedy, *Hidden cities: the discovery and loss of ancient North American civilization* (Penguin, 1994)

E.C. Krupp, *Echoes of the ancient skies*, 2nd ed. (Oxford University Press, 1995)

Rodney Legg (ed.), *Stonehenge antiquaries* (Dorset Publishing Co., 1986)

E.W. Mackie, *Science and society in prehistoric Britain* (1977)

Ron McCoy, 'Archaeoastronomy: skywatching in the Native American southwest', *Plateau*, 63 (1992)

Jean McMann, *Riddles of the Stone Age. Rock carvings of ancient Europe* (Thames & Hudson, 1980)

R.J. Mercer, *Hambledon Hill: a Neolithic landscape* (Edinburgh University Press, 1980)

John Michell, *A little history of astro-archaeology: stages in the transformation of a heresy*, 2nd ed. (Thames & Hudson, 1989)

John Michell, *Megalithomania*, 2nd ed. (Thames & Hudson, 1982)

C.A. Newham, *The astronomical significance of Stonehenge* (Moon Publications, 1972)

John North, *Stonehenge. Neolithic Man and the cosmos* (HarperCollins, 1996)

John North, *The Fontana history of astronomy and cosmology* (Fontana, 1994)

Michael J. O'Kelly, *Newgrange. Archaeology, art and legend* (Thames & Hudson, 1982)

Michael Parker Pearson, *Bronze Age Britain* (Batsford/English Heritage, 1993)

Stuart Piggott, *Ruins in a landscape* (Edinburgh University Press, 1976)

Stuart Piggott, *William Stukeley. An eighteenth-century antiquary*, revised edition (Thames & Hudson, 1985)

M. Pitts and A. Whittle, 'The development and date of Avebury', *Proceedings of the Prehistoric Society*, 58 (1992)

Joshua Pollard, 'Inscribing space: formal deposition at the later Neolithic monument of Woodhenge, Wiltshire', *Proceedings of the Prehistoric Society*, 61 (1995)

Andrew B. Powell, 'Newgrange – science or symbolism', *Proceedings of the Prehistoric Society*, 60 (1994)

R.B. Pugh and Elizabeth Crittall (eds), *Victoria County History of Wiltshire*, volume I, part 1 (Oxford University Press, 1957), part 2 (Oxford University Press, 1973)

Colin Renfrew, *Approaches to social archaeology* (Edinburgh University Press, 1984)

Colin Renfrew, *Before civilization. The radiocarbon revolution and prehistoric Europe* (Penguin, 1973)

Colin Renfrew, *Problems in European prehistory* (Edinburgh University Press, 1979)

Colin Renfrew, 'The archaeology of religion' in C. Renfrew and E.B.W. Zubrow (eds), *The ancient mind. elements of cognitive archaeology* (Cambridge University Press, 1994)

Lawrence H. Robbins, *The archaeologist's eye. Great discoveries, missing links and ancient treasures* (Robert Hale, 1990)

C.L.N. Ruggles (ed.), *Records in stone. Papers in memory of Alexander Thom* (Cambridge University Press, 1988)

C. Ruggles and A. Whittle (eds), *Astronomy and society during the period 4000–1500 BC*, British Archaeological Report 88 (1981)

Andrew Sherratt, 'Instruments of conversion? The role of megaliths in the Mesolithic/Neolithic transition in north-west Europe', *Oxford Journal of Archaeology*, 14 (1995)

George Smith, 'Excavation of the Stonehenge Avenue at West Amesbury, Wiltshire', *Wiltshire Archaeological and Natural History Magazine*, 68 (1973)

William Stukeley, *Stonehenge: a temple restor'd to the Druids* (1740)

Timothy Taylor, *The prehistory of sex* (Fourth Estate, 1996)

Richard S. Thorpe, Olwen Williams-Thorpe, D. Graham Jenkins and J.S. Watson, 'The geological sources and transport of the bluestones of Stonehenge, Wiltshire, UK', *Proceedings of the Prehistoric Society*, 57 (1991)

Geoffrey Wainwright, *The henge monuments. Ceremony and society in prehistoric Britain* (Thames & Hudson, 1990)

G.J. Wainwright, 'Stonehenge saved?', *Antiquity*, 70 (1996)

Christopher Walker (ed.), *Astronomy before the telescope* (British Museum Press, 1996)

Alfred Watkins, *The Old Straight Track* (1925; Garnstone Press, 1970)

Alasdair Whittle, 'A late Neolithic complex at West Kennet, Wiltshire', *Antiquity*, 65 (1991)

Alasdair Whittle, 'Eternal stones: Stonehenge completed', *Antiquity*, 70 (1996)

Alasdair Whittle, *Neolithic Europe*, 2nd ed. (Cambridge University Press, 1995)

A.W.R. Whittle, R.J.C. Atkinson, R. Chambers and N. Thomas, 'Excavations in the neolithic and Bronze Age complex at Dorchester-on-Thames, Oxfordshire, 1947–1952 and 1981', *Proceedings of the Prehistoric Society*, 58 (1992)

Tom Williamson and Liz Bellamy, *Ley lines in question* (World's Work, 1983)

Kenneth Woodbridge, *Landscape and antiquity* (Clarendon Press, 1970)

Index

Acknowledgements

I wish to thank the many people and organizations who have helped me in the writing of this book: individuals who kindly gave their time to meet me or who corresponded with me, and many libraries and museums. Thanks are particularly due to Professor Geoffrey Wainwright, Dave Batchelor and Val Horsler of English Heritage; Andrew Lawson, Dr Julie Gardiner and Dr Mike Allen of Wessex Archaeology; Professor Lord Renfrew; Dr Clive Ruggles; the organizers and participants in the conference on 'Science and Stonehenge' at the Royal Society; Dr Lester Borley; Mark Lintell and Land Use Consultants; Mike Russum; the Salisbury and South Wiltshire Museum; Devizes Museum; Sir John Soane's Museum; the National Monuments Record; Cambridge University Library. I am most grateful for the invitation from Mark Collins to write this book, and for the considerable support I have received from him, Colin Ziegler, Robin Gurdon, and others at Collins & Brown. The assistance and companionship of my wife, Nicola, has been, as ever, invaluable.

Picture Acknowledgements

Photographs:
English Heritage Photographic Library: 1, 6, 11, 21 (left), 27, 35 (top left), 36–7, 41 (both), 65, 85, 88 (right), 94 (Salisbury and South Wiltshire Museum), 110, 131 (below), 132, 147. **Agnew & Sons, London/ Bridgeman Art Library, London**: 141. **AKG Photo, London**: 71, 128 (above). **The Ancient Art and Architecture Collection**: 68, 72 (both), 75 (left). **AP/Alistair Grant**: 152–3. **Mick Aston**: 48. **Mrs Judith Atkinson**: 25 (right). **British Museum, London/ Bridgeman Art Library, London**: 129 (above). **Christopher Chippindale**: 40, 90. **Collections/Fay Godwin**: 23 (right), 105. **Devizes Museum**: 24 (left), 25 (left), 26, 46 (above), 49, 50 (above), 52–3 (all), 59, 98, 108 (right), 111, 114 (below left), 115 (all), 130 (above), 134, 135, 136 (above), 143. **Robert Estall Photo Library**: 21 (right), 23 (left), 61, 64, 66 (both), 67, 69, 73, 89, 97, 107, 121 (below right), 128 (below), 130 (below right). **Fortean Picture Library**: 70, 74, 129 (below), 131 (above), 136 (below). **John Haddington/English Heritage**: Front cover, 7, 8–9, 22 (left), 28–9, 50 (below), 51, 77, 116–17, 119, 123, 130 (below left), 133, 139, 146. **John Hedgecoe**: 2–3, 35 (right), 81 (both), 86–7 (all), 88 (left). **Images Colour Library**: 82. **Sherry G. Mangum**: 75 (right), 121 (above right). **Courtesy Henry Moore Foundation**: 145. **Projection Visual Communications**: 149 (centre and bottom). **RCHME © Crown copyright**: 20 (left), 22 (right), 43, 54, 57 (below). **Salisbury and South Wiltshire Museum**: 45, 99, 108 (left, centre, below), 109 (all), 112 (centre left), 114 (above left, above right, below right). **Science Photo Library**: 16, 17. **Courtesy of the Trustees of Sir John Soane's Museum**: 142 (bottom). **Brian Hope-Taylor, courtesy** *Antiquity*: 140.

By courtesy of the Board of Trustees of the Victoria & Albert Museum: 144, 149 (top). **Richard Waite**: 91. **Werner Forman Archive**: 44, 80. **© Trust for Wessex Archaeology Ltd**: 25 (centre), 35 (below left), 95. **Wessex Archaeology/© John Evans**: 112 (below left). **West Air Photography**: 20 (right), 47.

All artworks are the copyright of English Heritage and were created by:
Arka Cartographics: 12–13 (based on aerial photographs provided by Cambridge University), 100–103 (based on maps produced by Dr Mike Allen at Wessex Archaeology). **David Ashby**: 30 (based on objects at Wessex Archaeology), 31 (above), 38, 39, 48, 55, 58 (both), 70, 78, 79, 89. **Julian Baker**: 46 (below), 62, 124–5 (below). **English Heritage, Archaeometric Branch**: 57. **Andrew Green**: 31 (below), 33, 34, 37, 40, 42, 64, 69, 83, 91, 106 (above), 120 (both), 122 (all), 124 (above). **Debbie Marshall**: 93, 126 (both), 127 (both), 132. **Les Smith**: 60 (based on a photograph provided by Robert Estall Photo Library), 92 (both), 96 (both), 100 (top) and 101 (top, based on photographs provided by Wessex Archaeology), 106 (below, based on an object in The Alexander Keiller Museum, Avebury), 112 (based on a photograph provided by Wessex Archaeology), 113 (below left), 113 (top right, based on objects in The Alexander Keiller Museum, Avebury). **Brian Lee/Visual Connection**: 151

These illustrations came from the following books:
Inigo Jones, *Stone-heng Restored*, 1725 edn.: 76, 142. **F. Grose**, *Antiquities of England and Wales*, 1773–87: 118. **William Stukeley**, *Stonehenge*, 1740: 137.